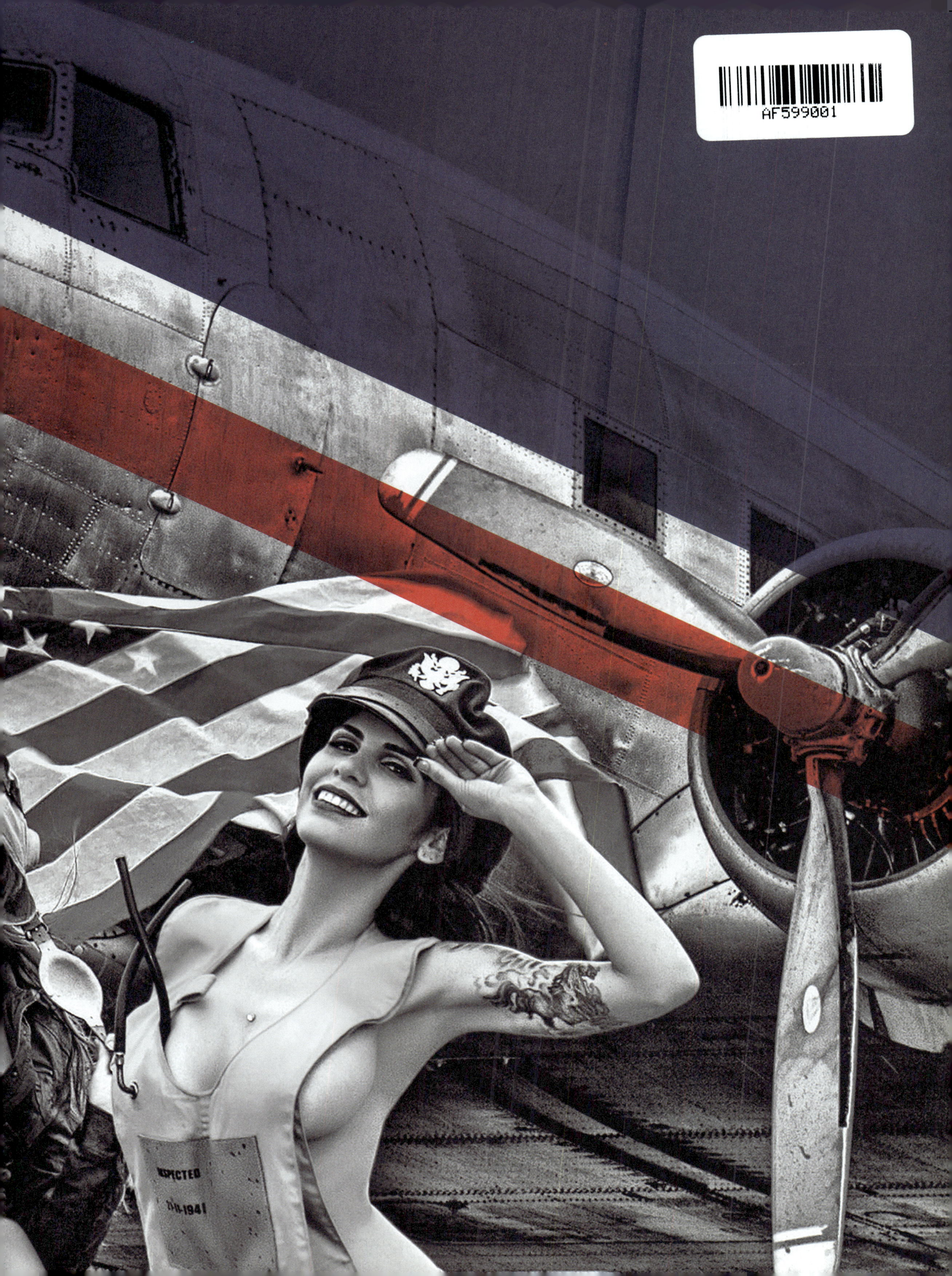

Alvarado's Military Pin-Ups

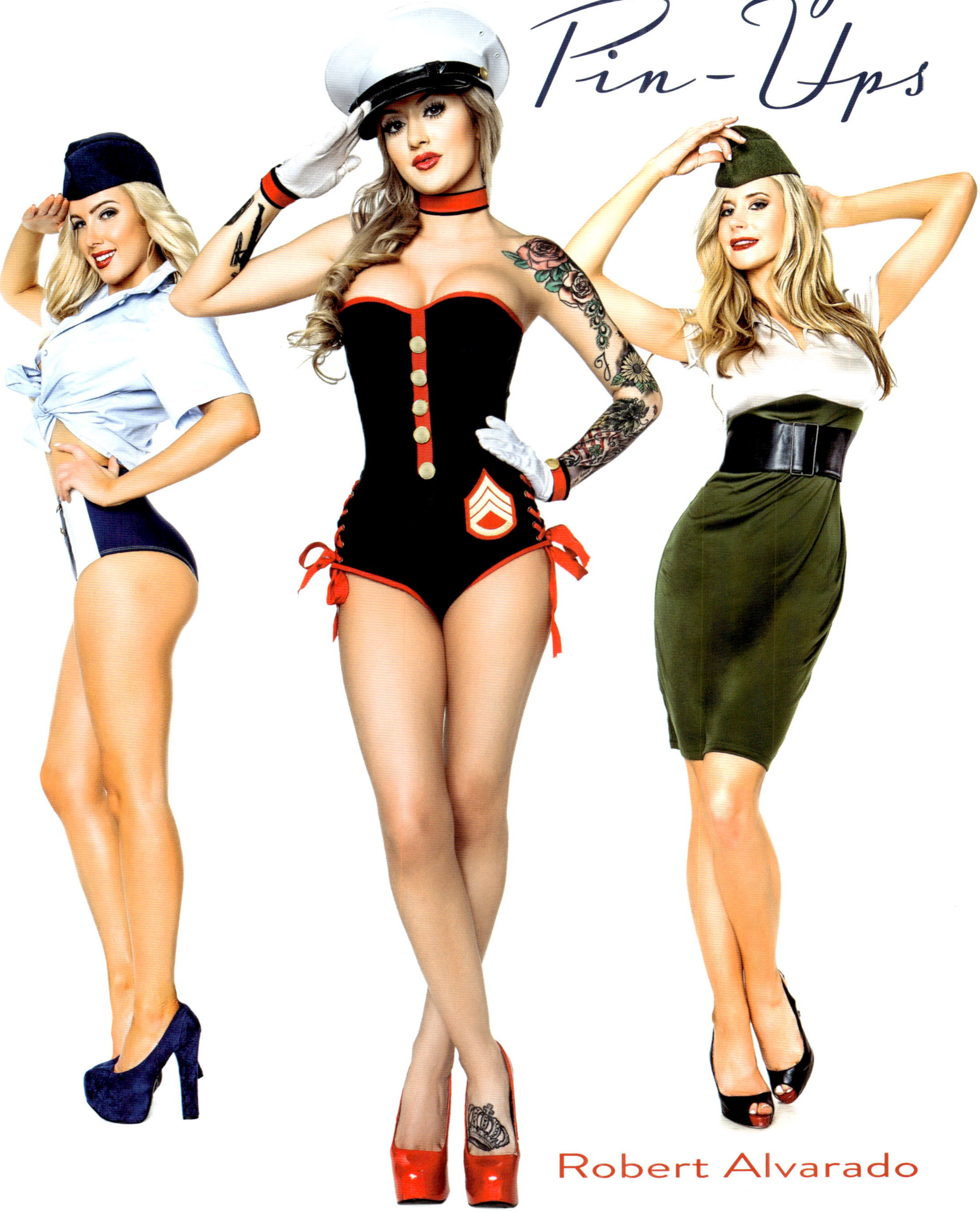

Robert Alvarado

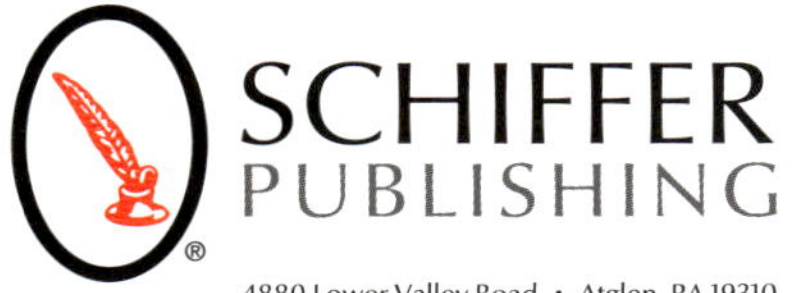

4880 Lower Valley Road • Atglen, PA 19310

Other Schiffer books by the author

Alvarado's Pin-Up Nudes, 2nd Edition
978-0-7643-5807-4

Alvarado's Classic Modern Pin-Ups
978-0-7643-3892-2

Alvarado's Cosplay Pin-Ups
978-0-7643-5514-1

Alvarado's All-American Girls
978-0-7643-5141-9

Library of Congress Control Number: 2023941053

Designed by Christopher Bower
Cover design by Christopher Bower
Type set in Luxus Brut/Brandon Grotesque

ISBN: 978-0-7643-6733-5
Printed in China

Published by Schiffer Publishing, Ltd.
4880 Lower Valley Road
Atglen, PA 19310
Phone: (610) 593-1777; Fax: (610) 593-2002
Email: Info@schifferbooks.com
Web: www.schifferbooks.com

For our complete selection of fine books on this and related subjects, please visit our website at www.schifferbooks.com. You may also write for a free catalog.

Schiffer Publishing's titles are available at special discounts for bulk purchases for sales promotions or premiums. Special editions, including personalized covers, corporate imprints, and excerpts, can be created in large quantities for special needs. For more information, contact the publisher.

We are always looking for people to write books on new and related subjects. If you have an idea for a book, please contact us at proposals@schifferbooks.com.

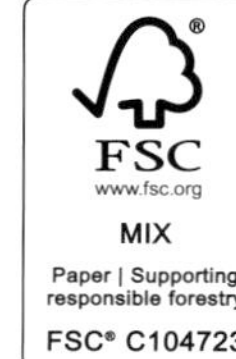

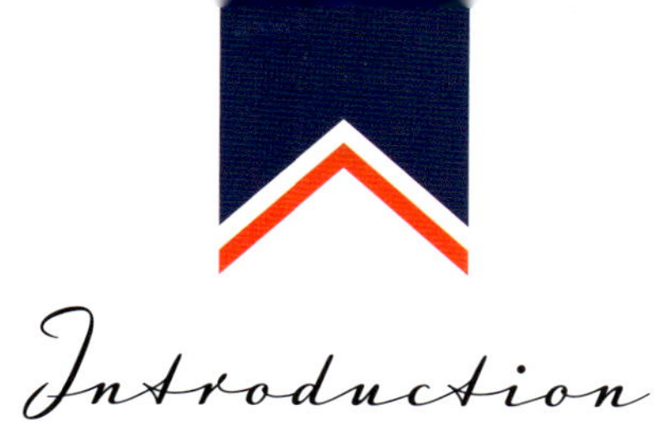

Introduction

I was born and raised in Southern California. My father was a US Navy aircraft mechanic in World War II; hence my affinity for aircraft of that era. I've been taking pictures since my childhood, and around 2005 I started working with studio lighting. My inspiration is Norman Rockwell, and I try to make the images look illustrated or painted. My purpose is to bring that old school pin-up feeling into the twenty-first century.

I just love what I do, and now that I'm getting older, I wanted to make sure and get a book published about all the work I've done dedicated to the armed services of our country. I am deeply indebted for their service, and I hope they appreciate what I've done for them, since I can never hope to repay them for all that they have done for our country.

As you can see, I shoot mainly on white seamless paper (High Key setup) and occasionally shoot on different-colored seamless papers. I always use a three-light setup, main and two sidelights. My outside shots I just use my flash gun (I shoot Canon) with the setting on the flash set to –1 TTL and P mode. I try and use the "Keep It Simple, Stupid" method. I don't always get the lighting correct on the outside shots, but with the help of Lightroom I can usually bring back or add to what I didn't get with the exposure.

As always, my main goal is to try to make the images look painted or illustrated, so if they look "Photoshopped," they are, since that process makes the images look the way they do.

The main reason I wanted to do this book is because my father just recently died. He was 94 and was proud of his service in the Navy during World War II. He told me some great stories about his time stationed on Bougainville in the South Pacific during the war. He also had a small scrapbook of photos of his time in the Solomon Islands. Because of that, I have always had a big soft spot in my heart for the men and women who serve our country.

The images you see with aircraft were shot with vintage planes at local air shows here in Southern California. I would take models with me and add wardrobe and props, and we just walked around shooting with the different aircraft. And the tattoos you see on the models are all real as well!

The other images are all inspired by the different US armed services. I try to make them sexy but always fun. Something that brings a smile to your face and in the spirit of vintage pin-up.

I'm pretty much retired now, since I really can't get around like I used to, and I really miss shooting and creating with different models; a huge thank-you to all the models I have worked with—you were all amazing.

I hope this will bring back some memories of service men and women who served in the military or memories of their mothers, fathers, and grandparents who served our country.

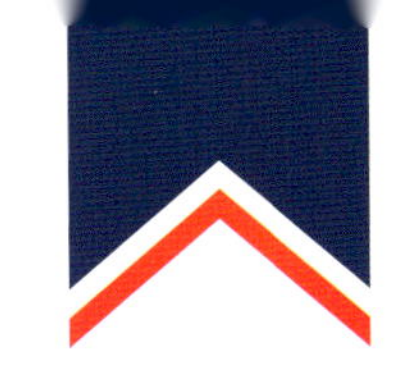

Before & After

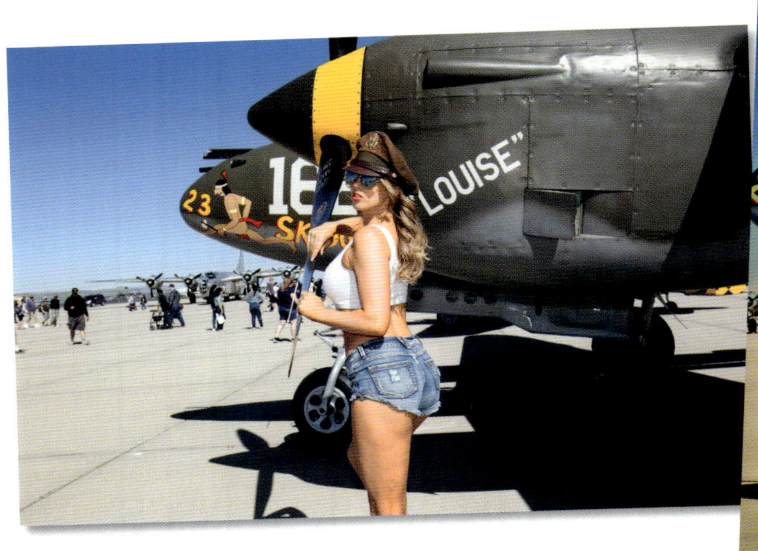

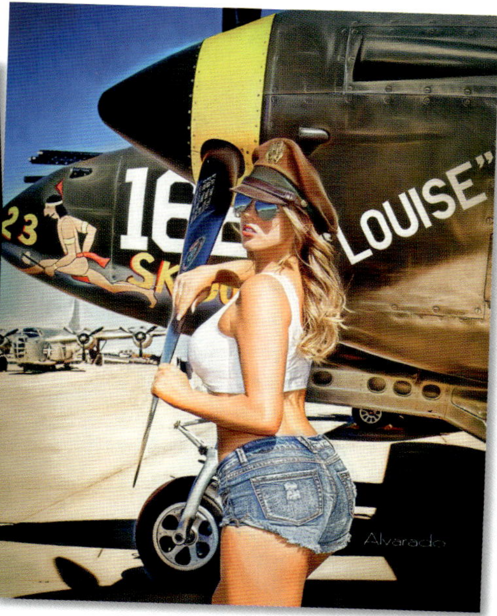

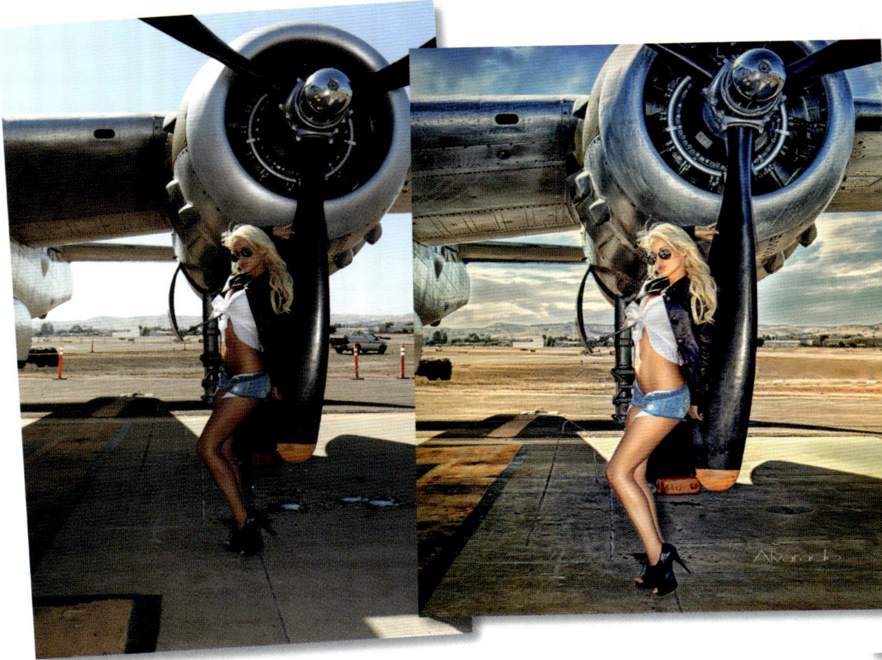

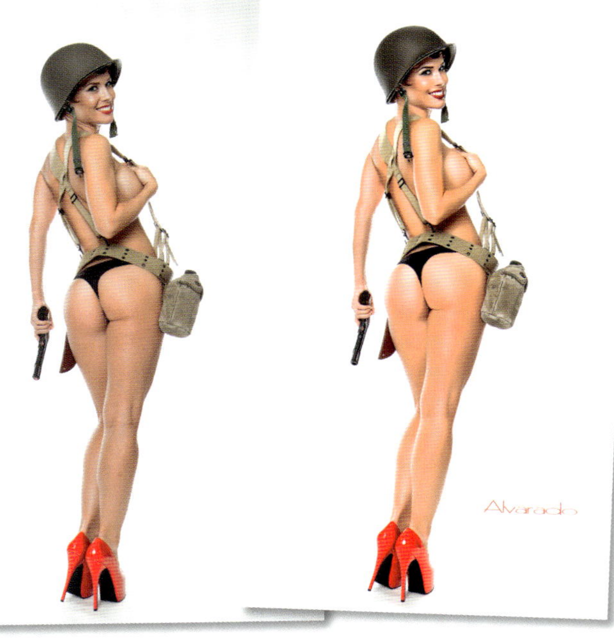

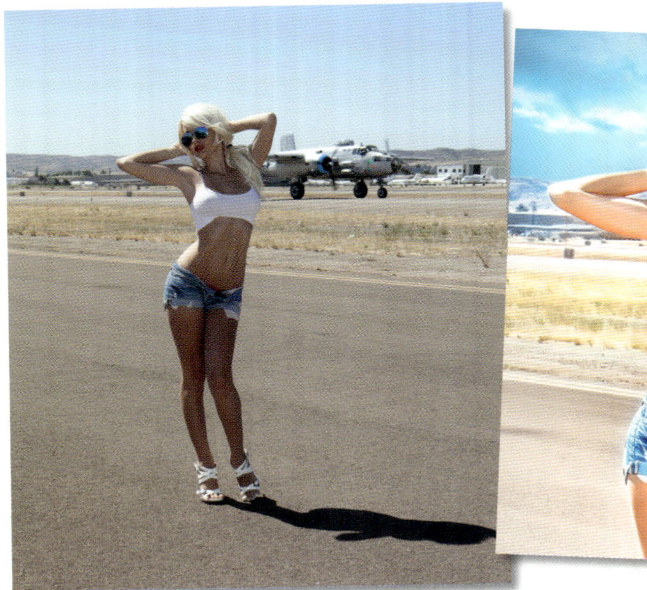

Alvarado

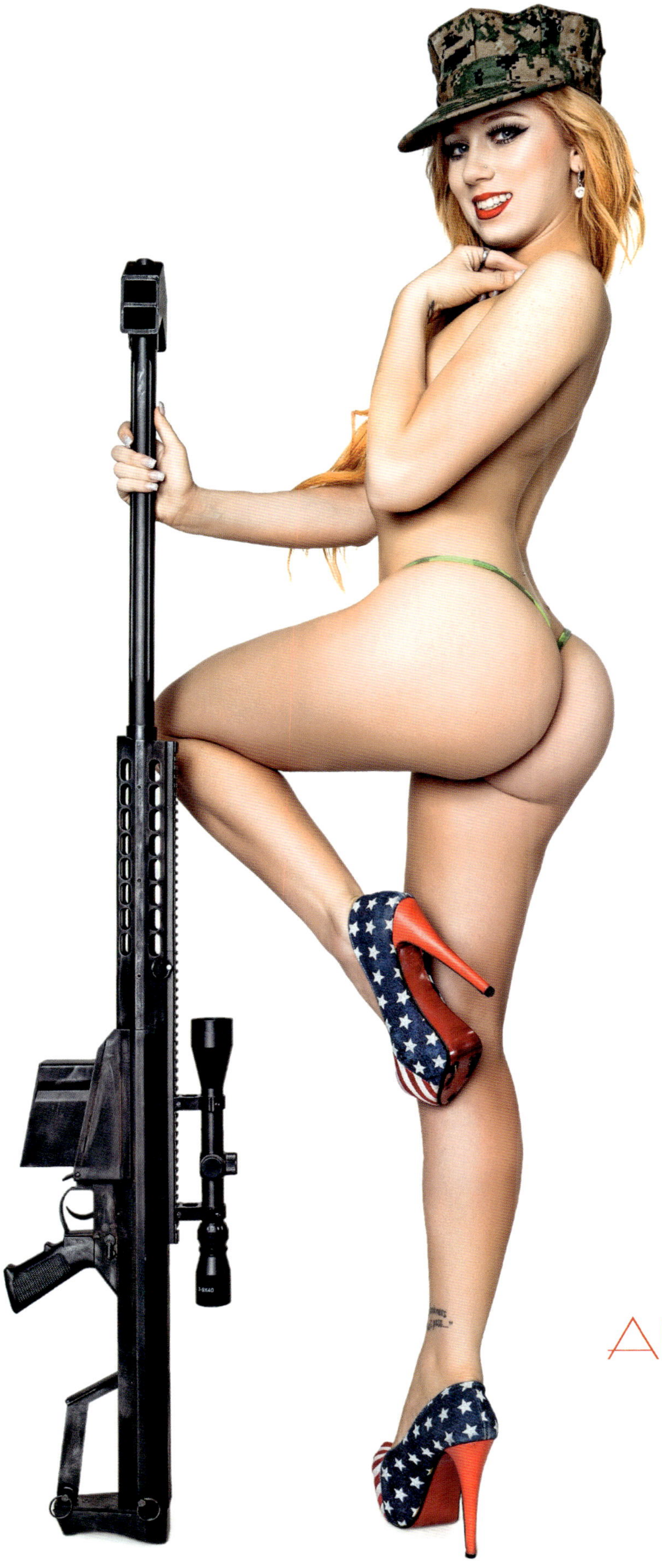

Alvarado

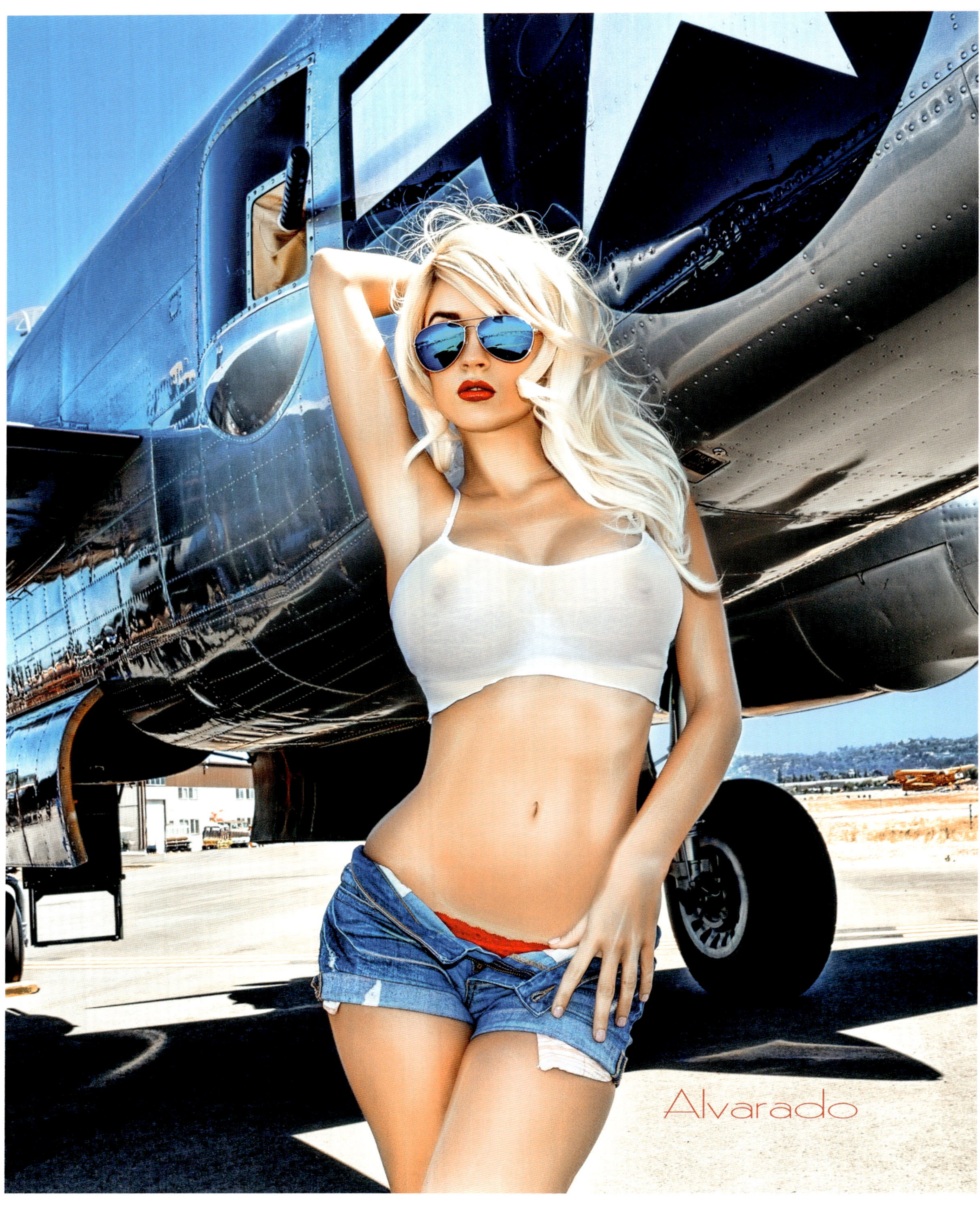
Alvarado

Alvarado

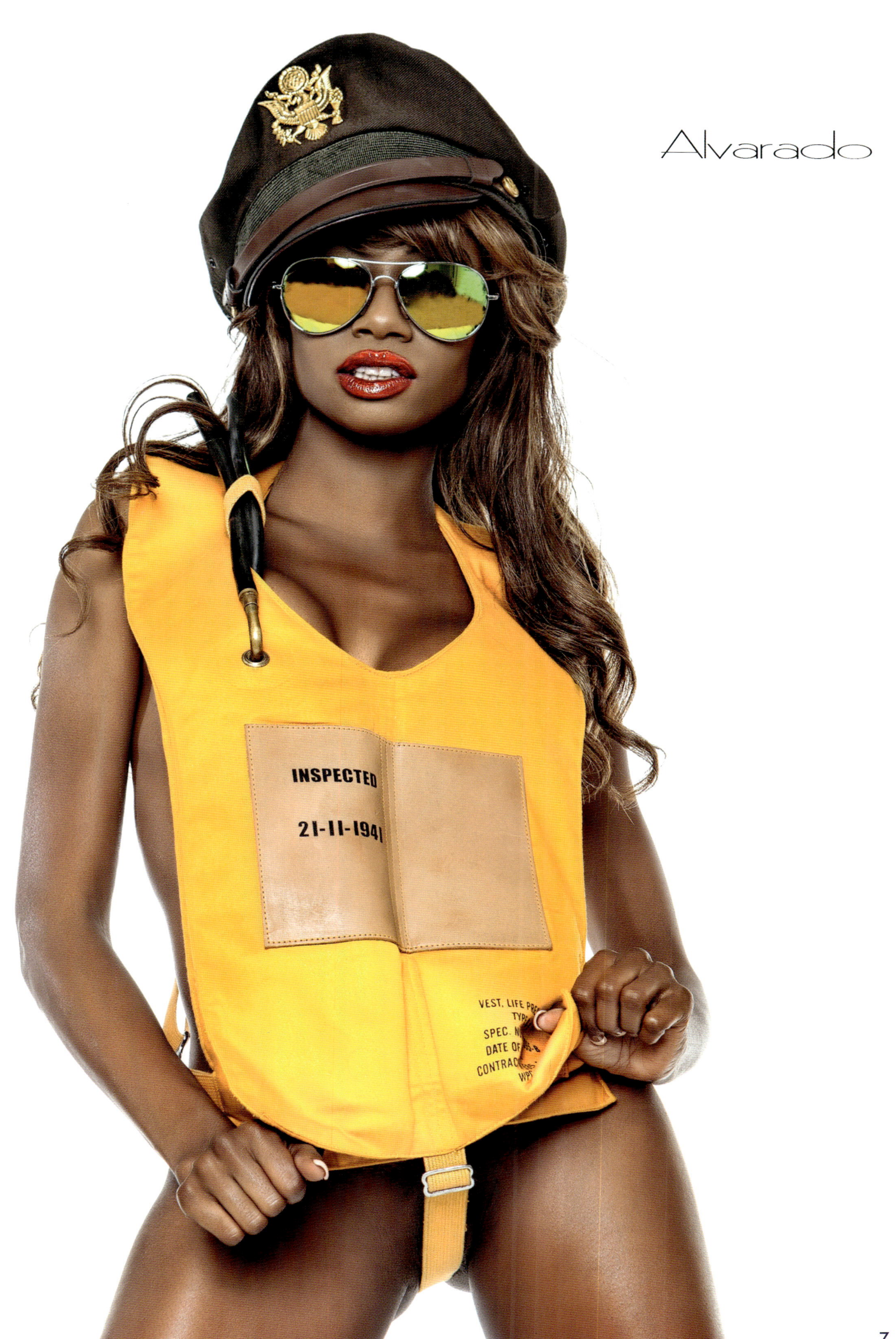

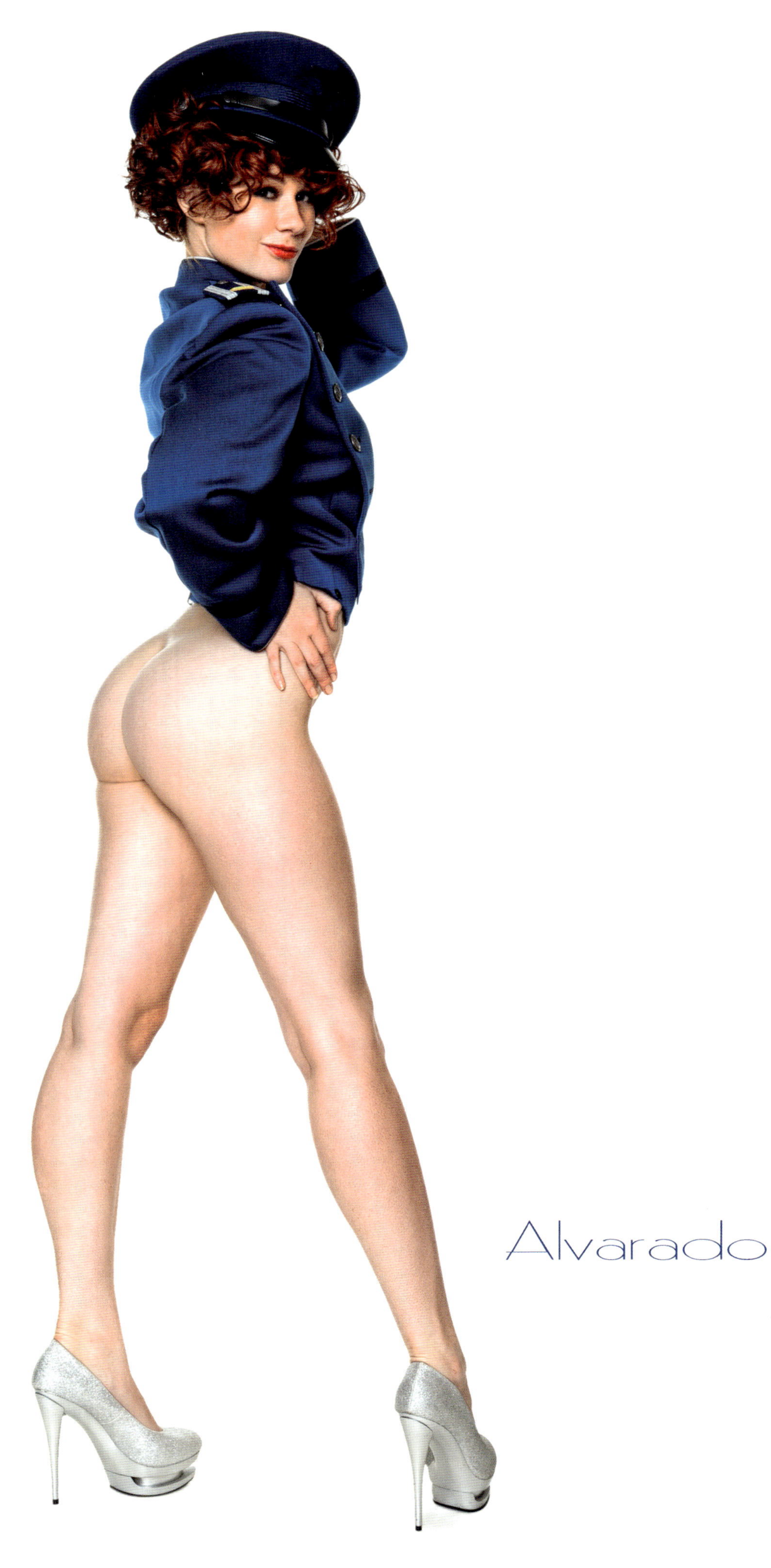

Alvarado

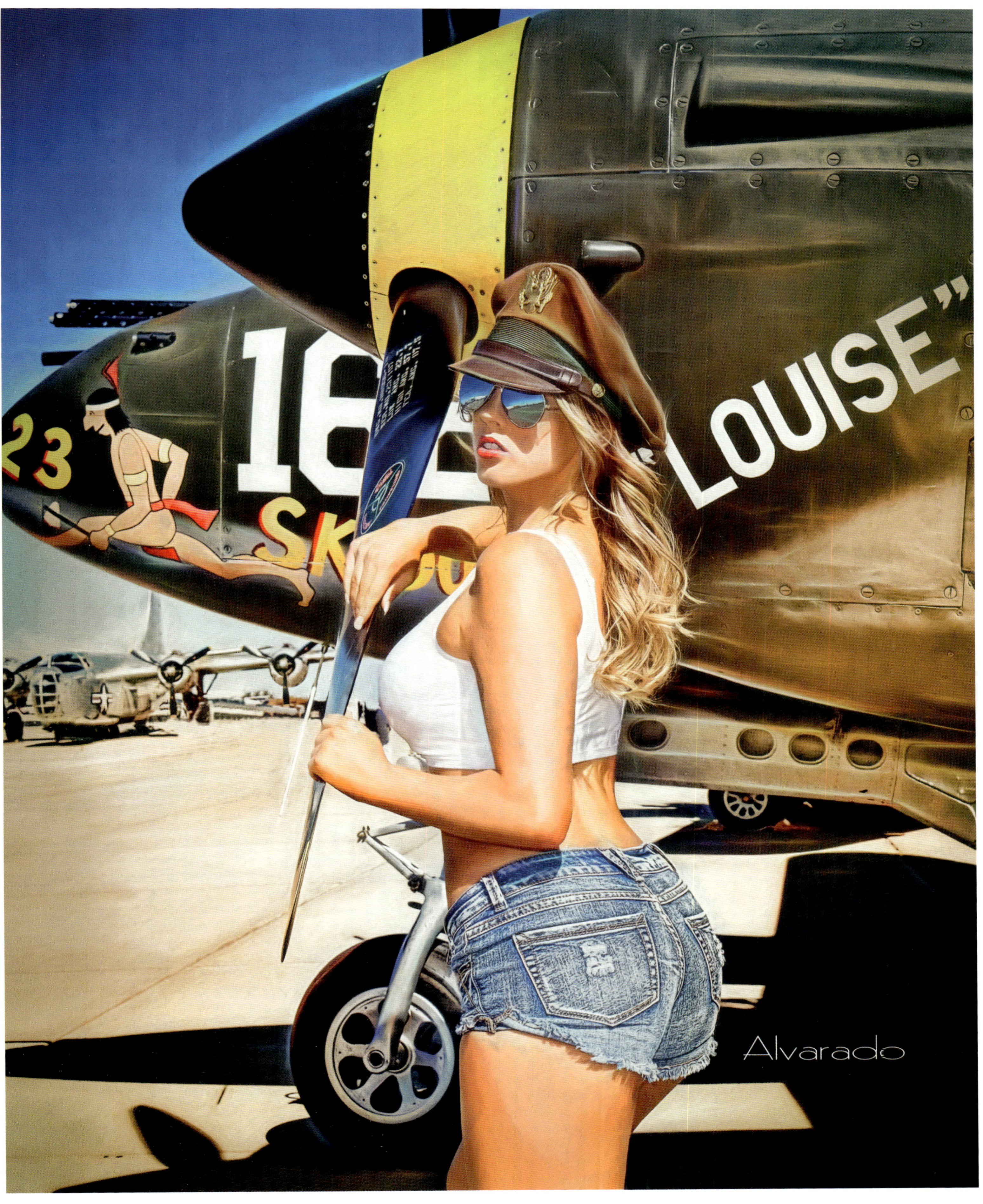
23
LOUISE”
Alvarado

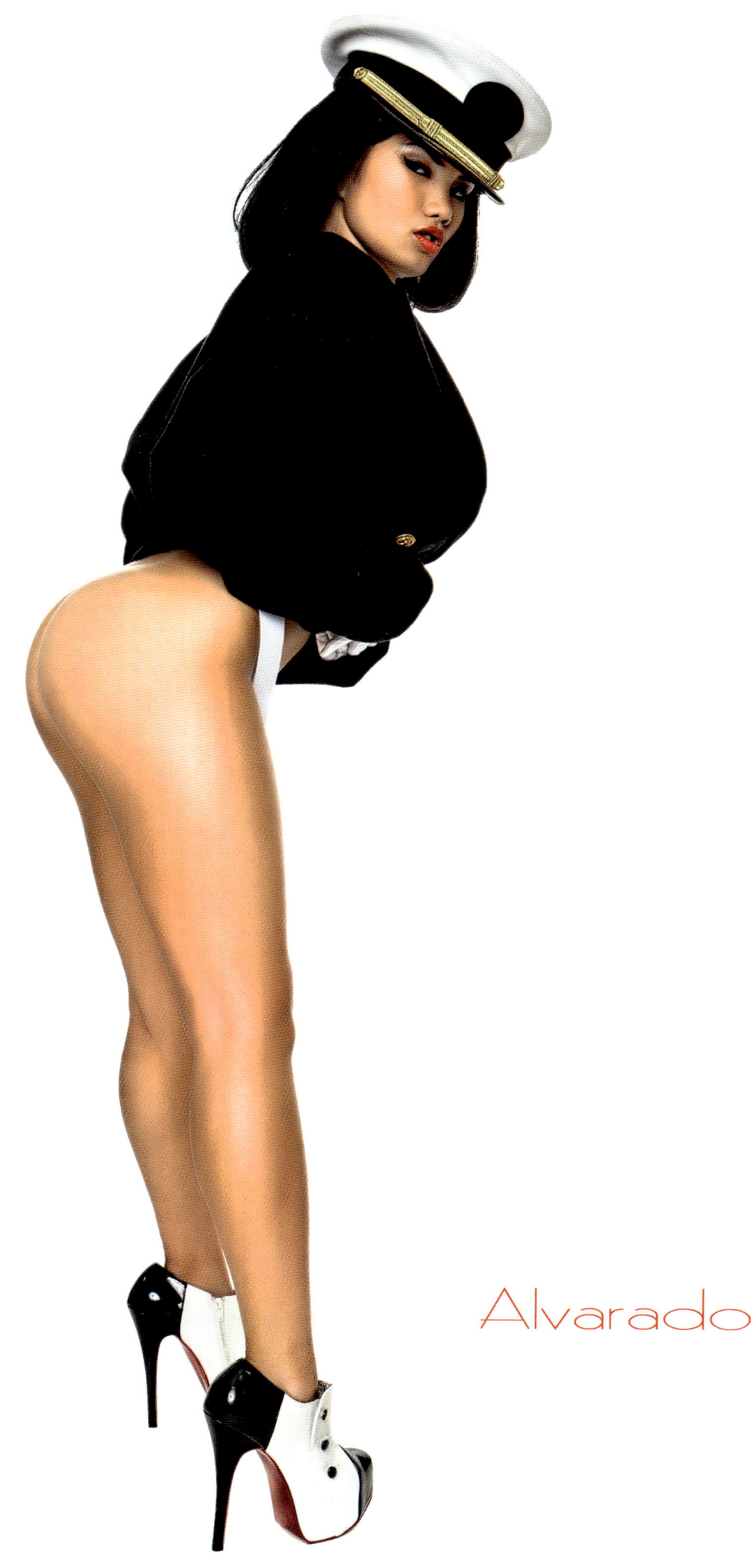

Alvarado

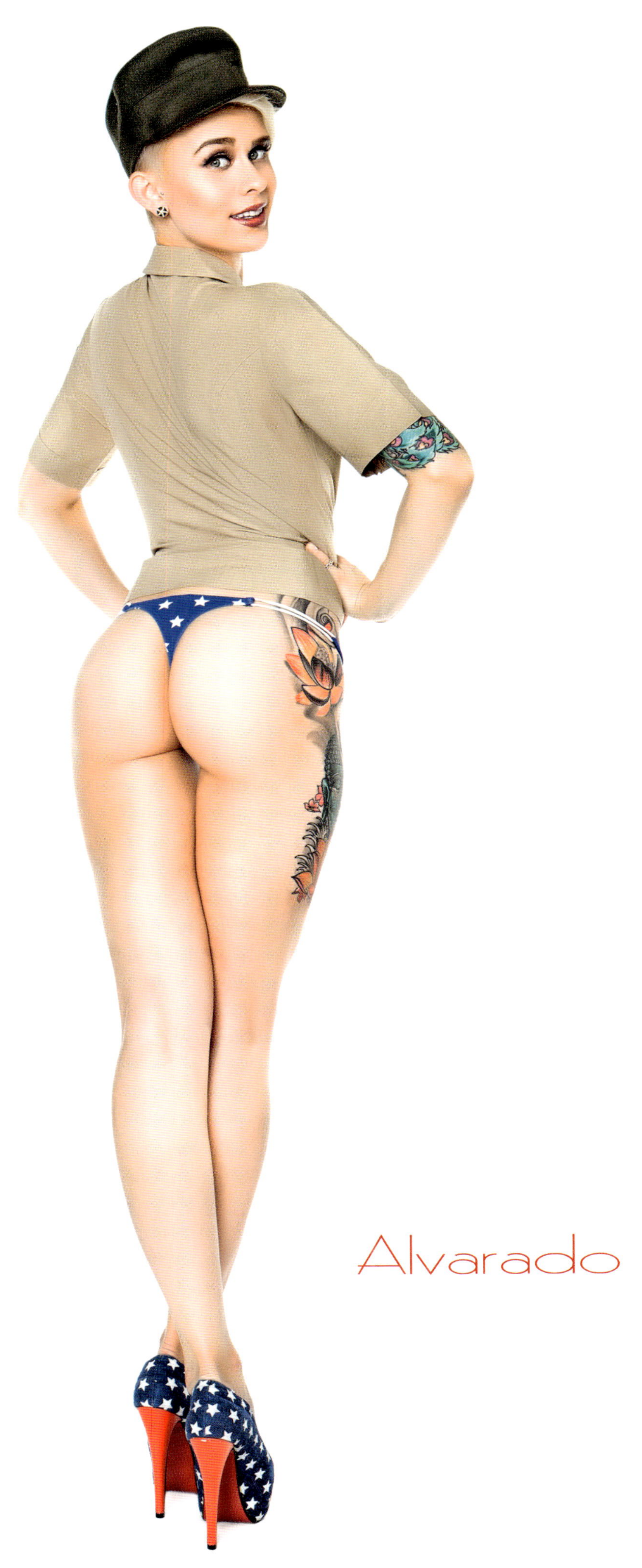

Alvarado

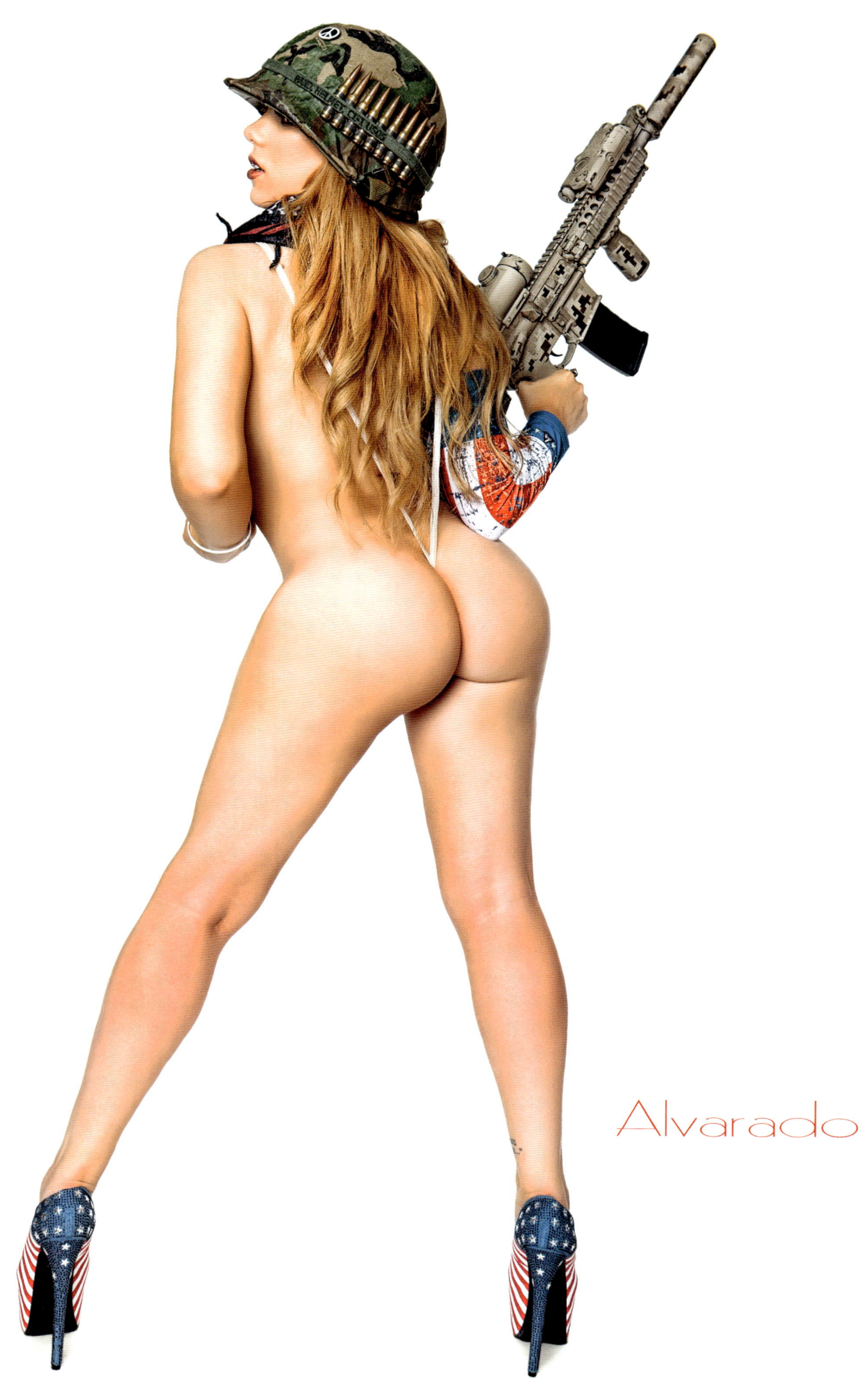
Alvarado

Alvarado

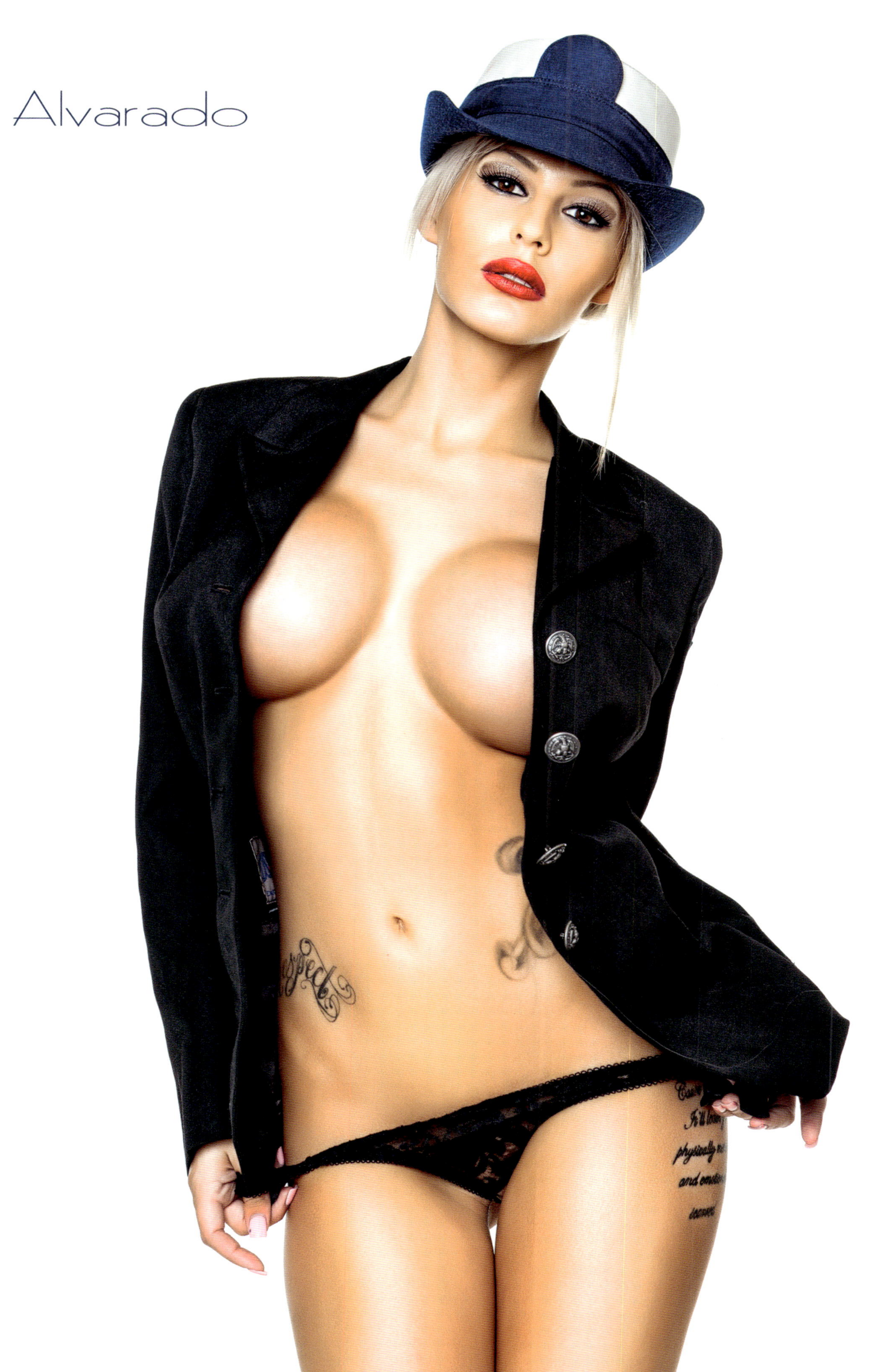

Alvarado

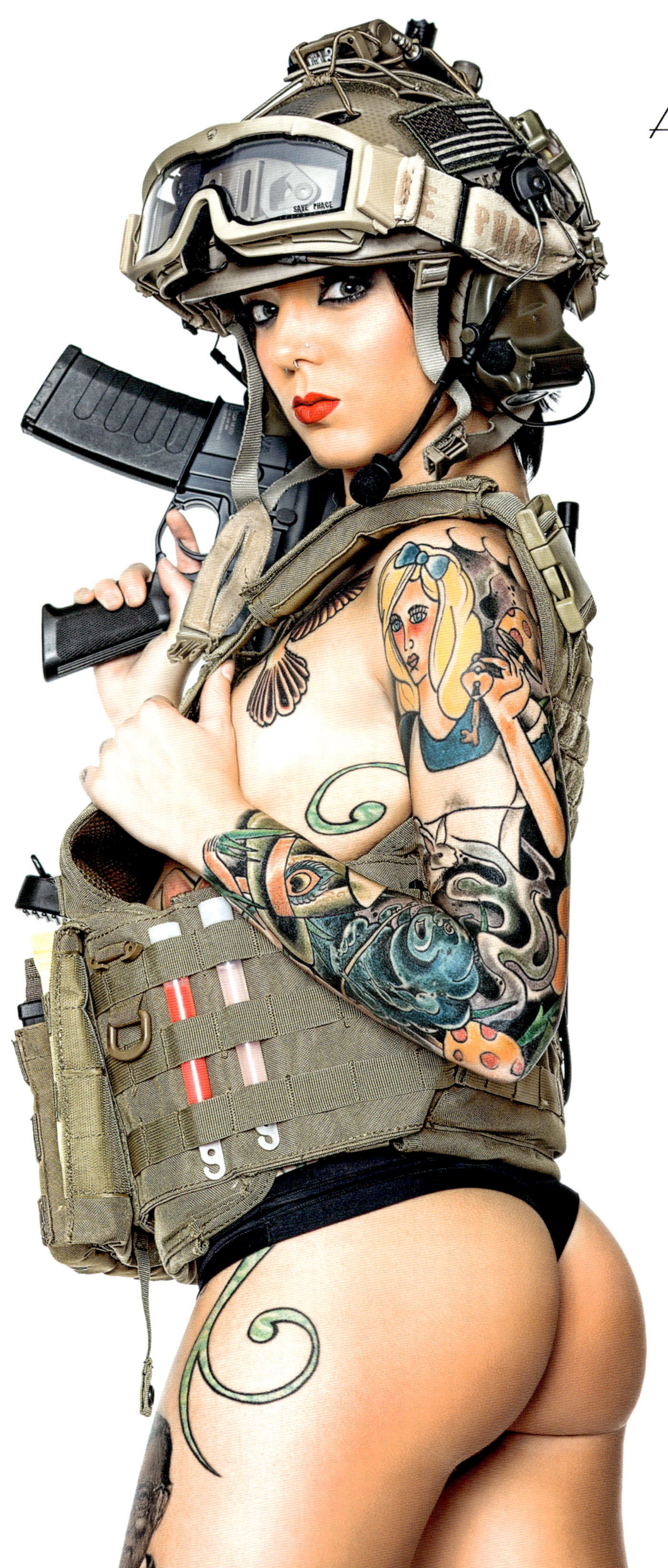

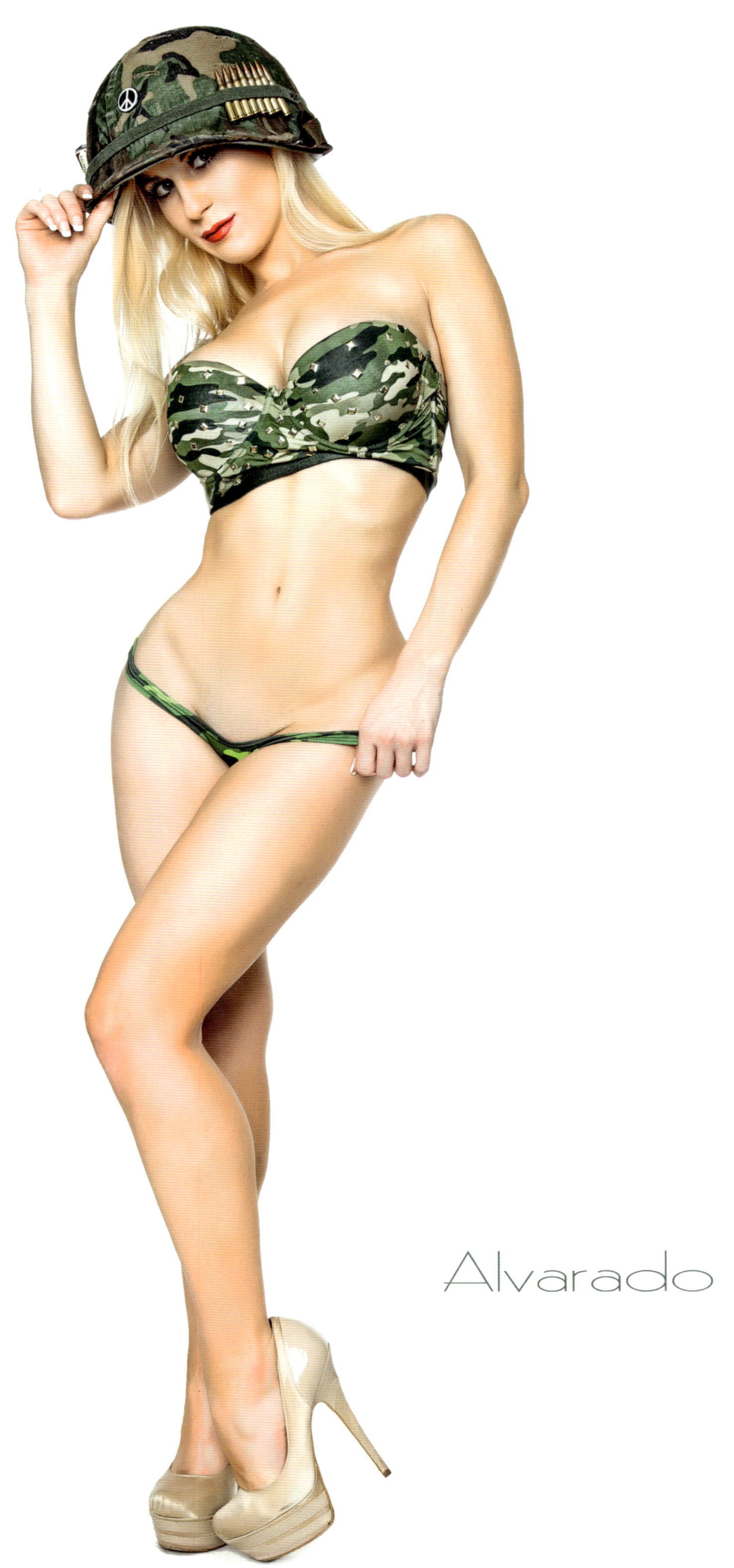

Alvarado

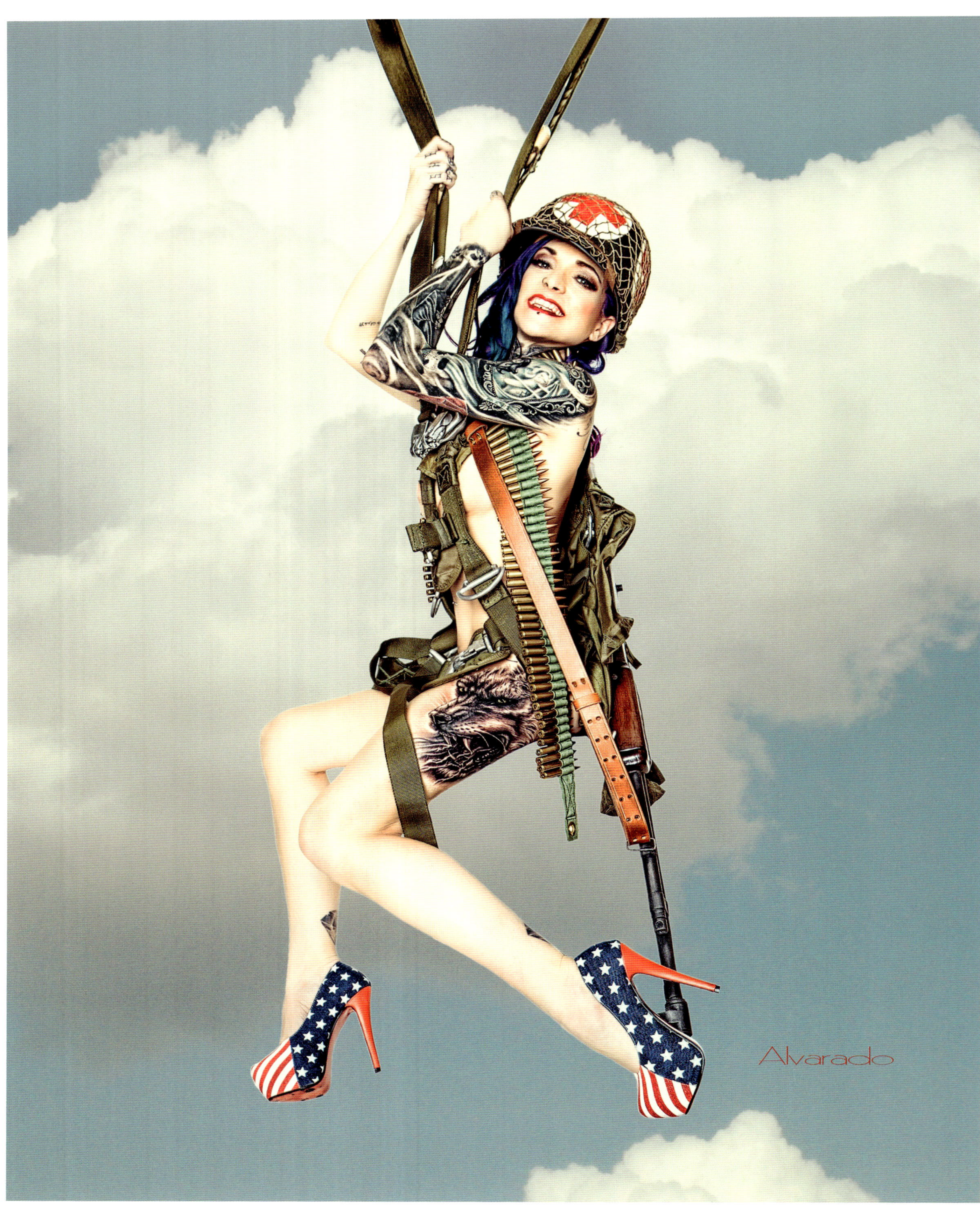
Alvarado

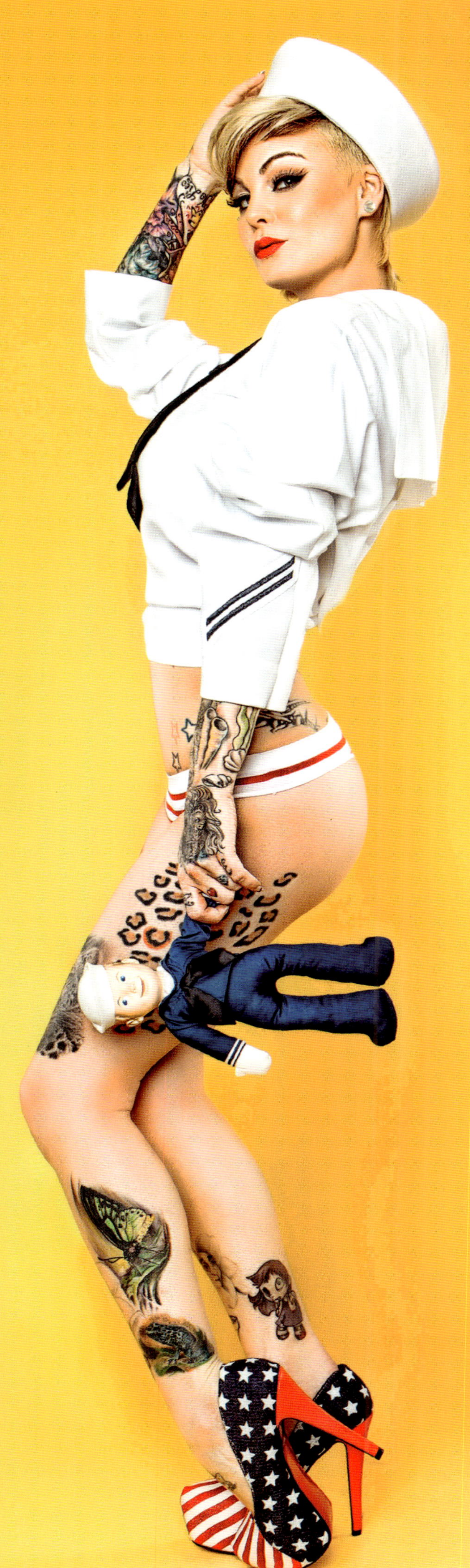

Alvarado

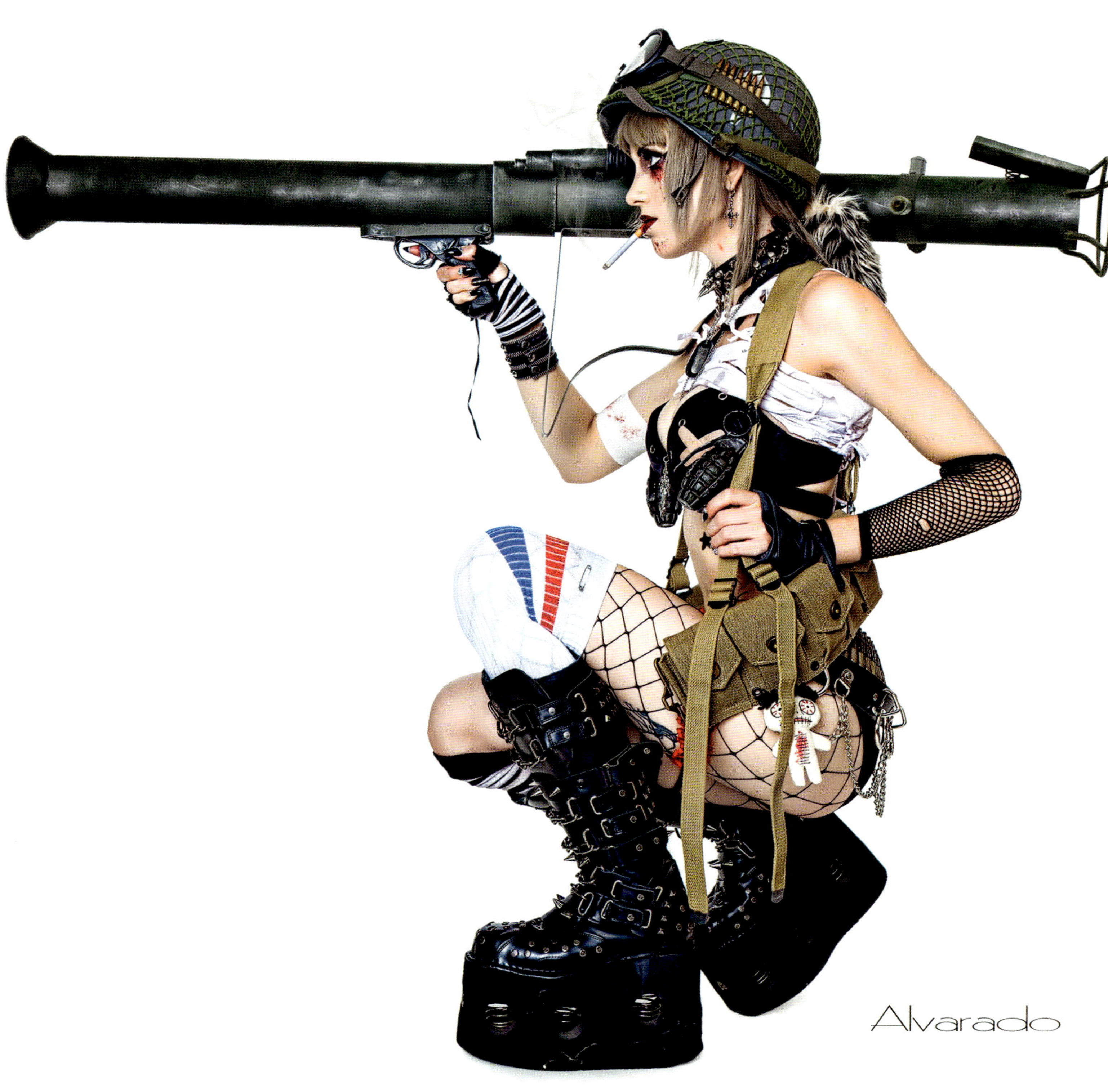
Alvarado

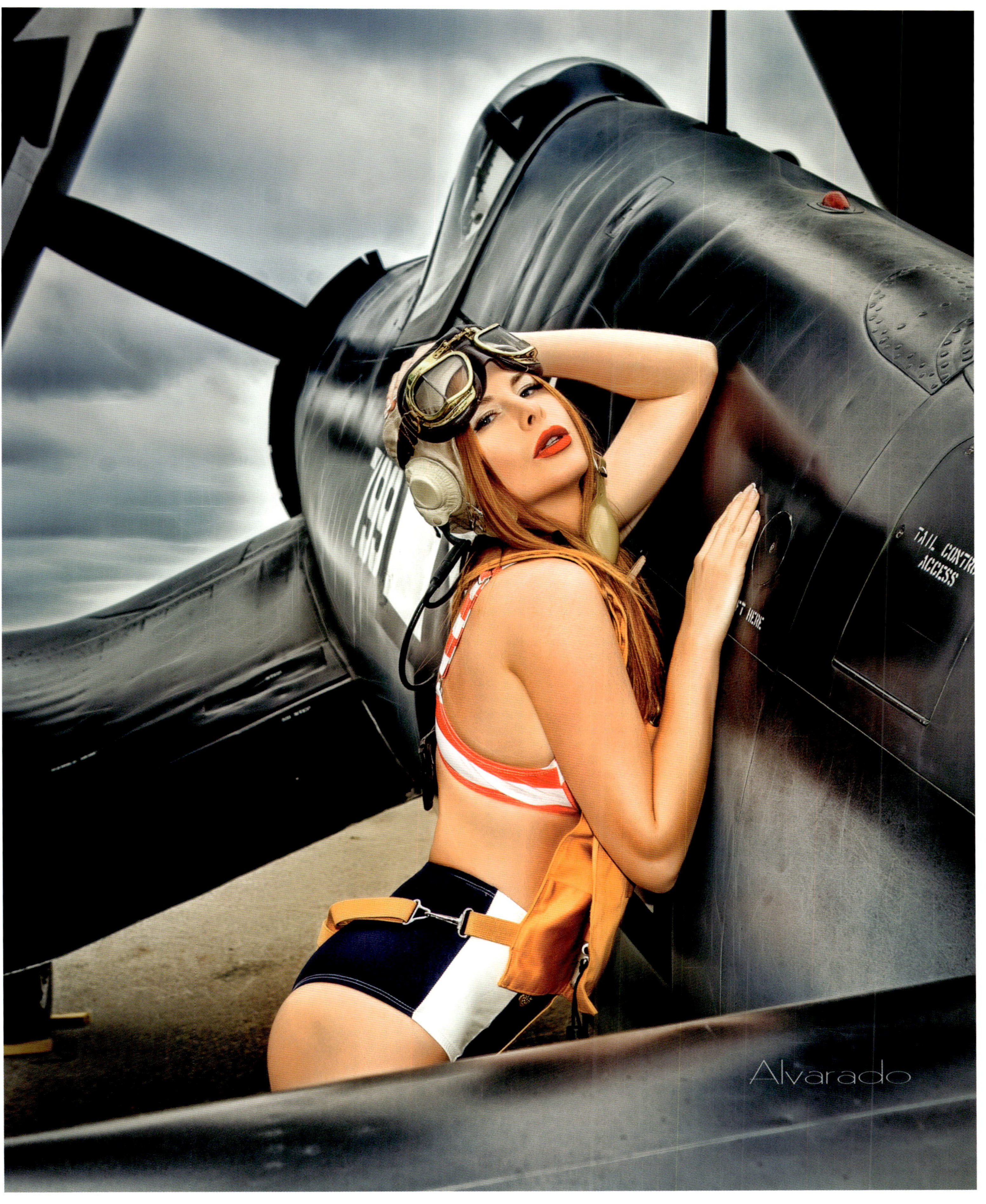
ACCESS
Alvarado

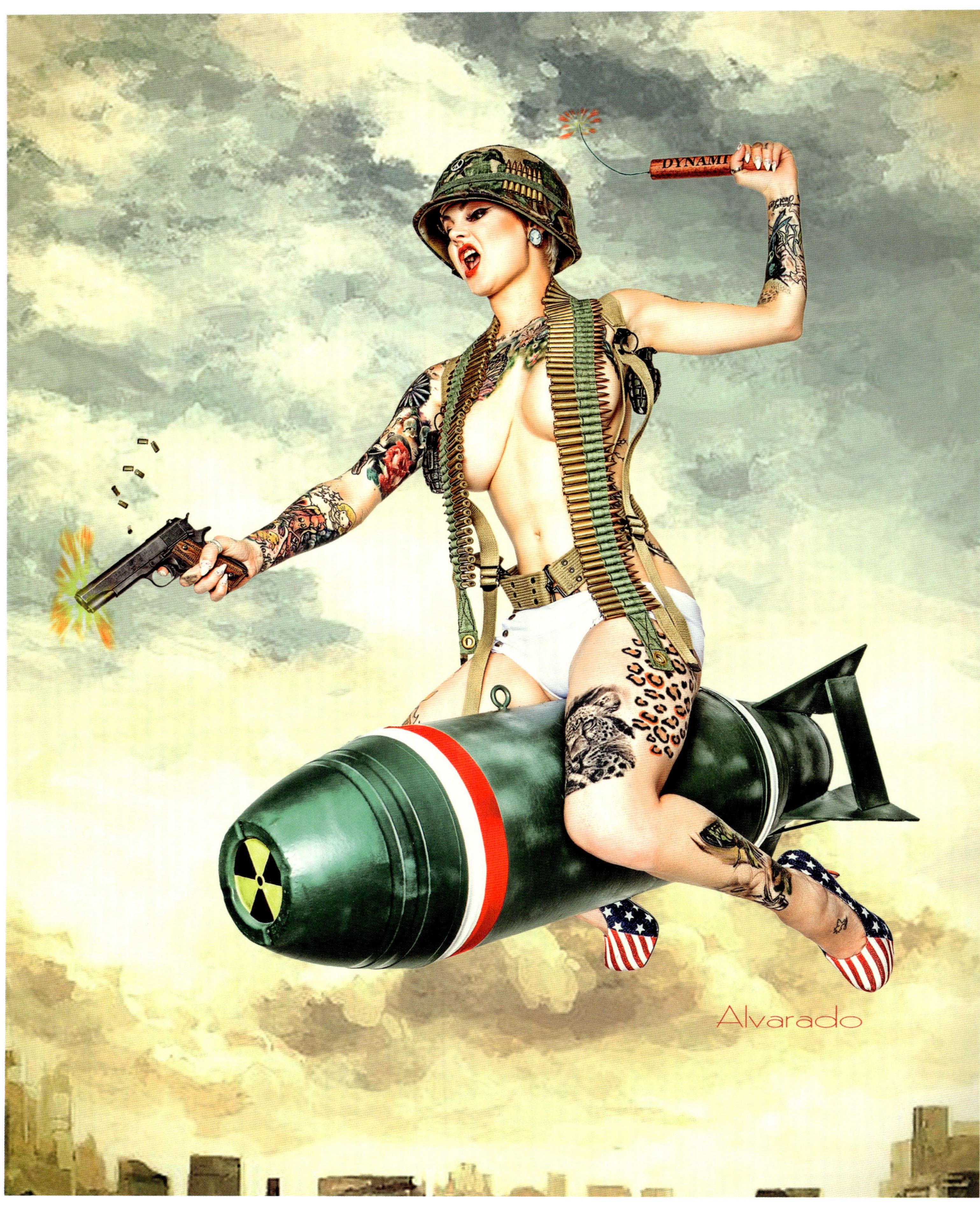
DYNAMI
Alvarado

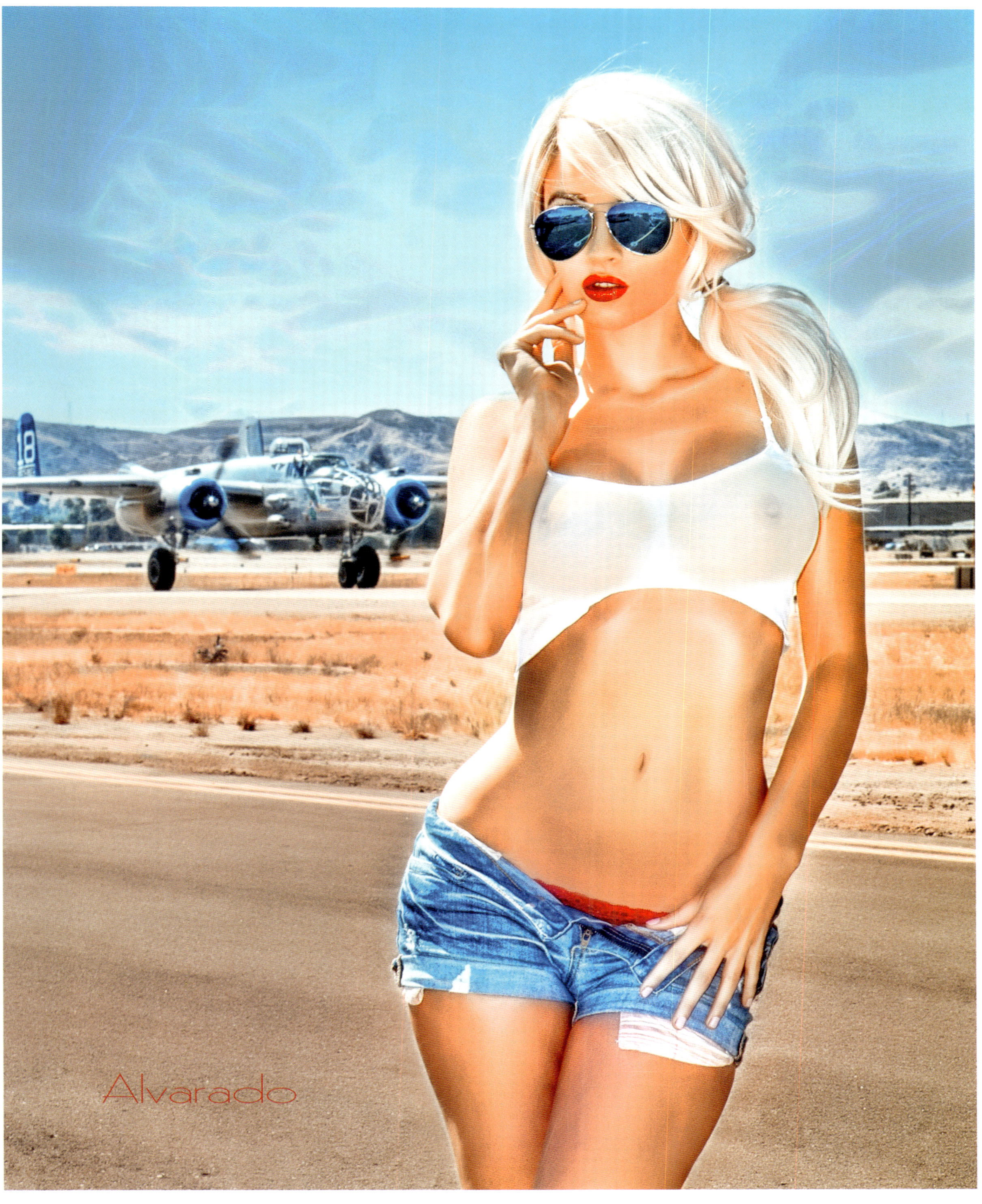
18
Alvarado

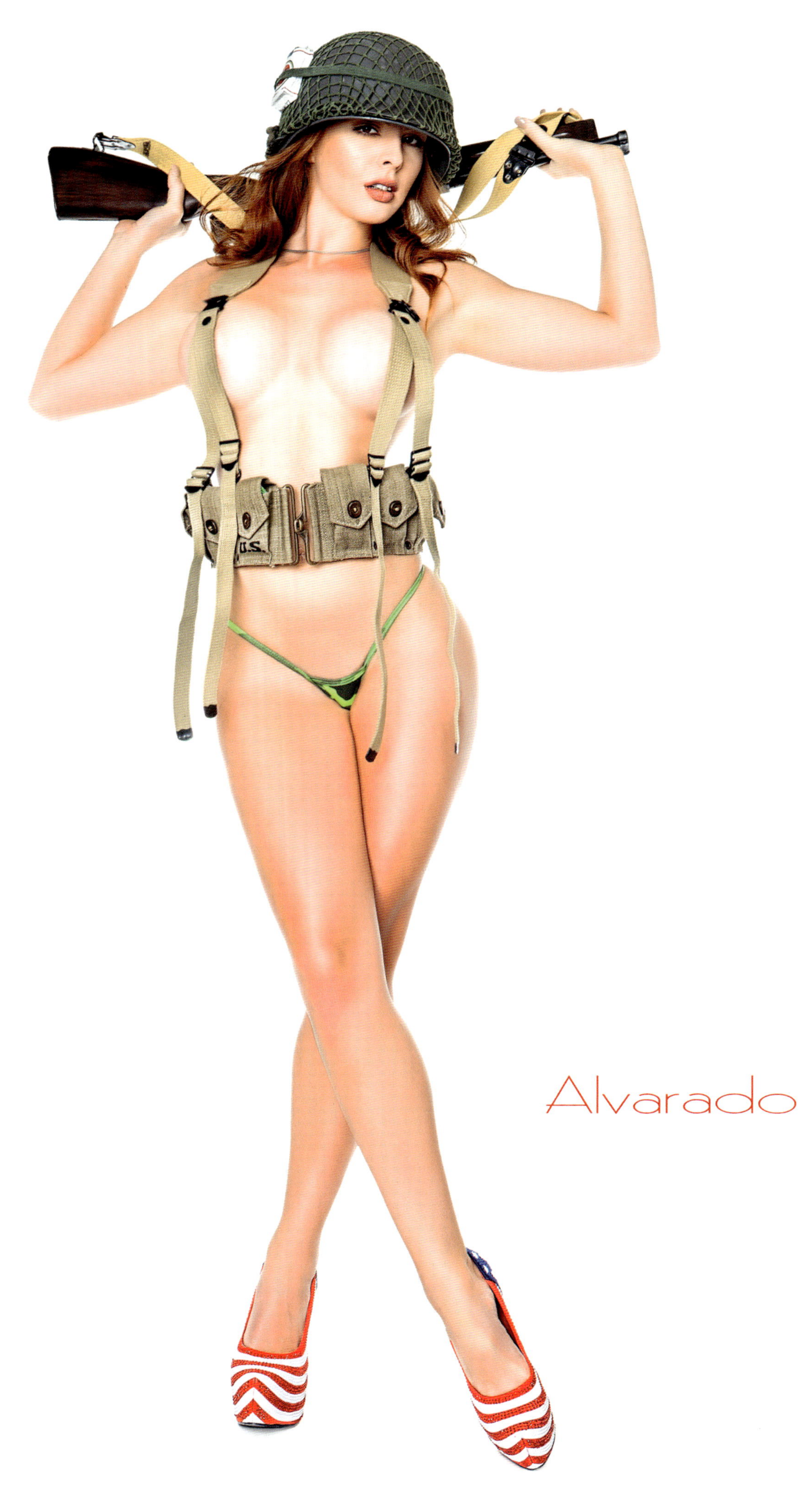

Alvarado

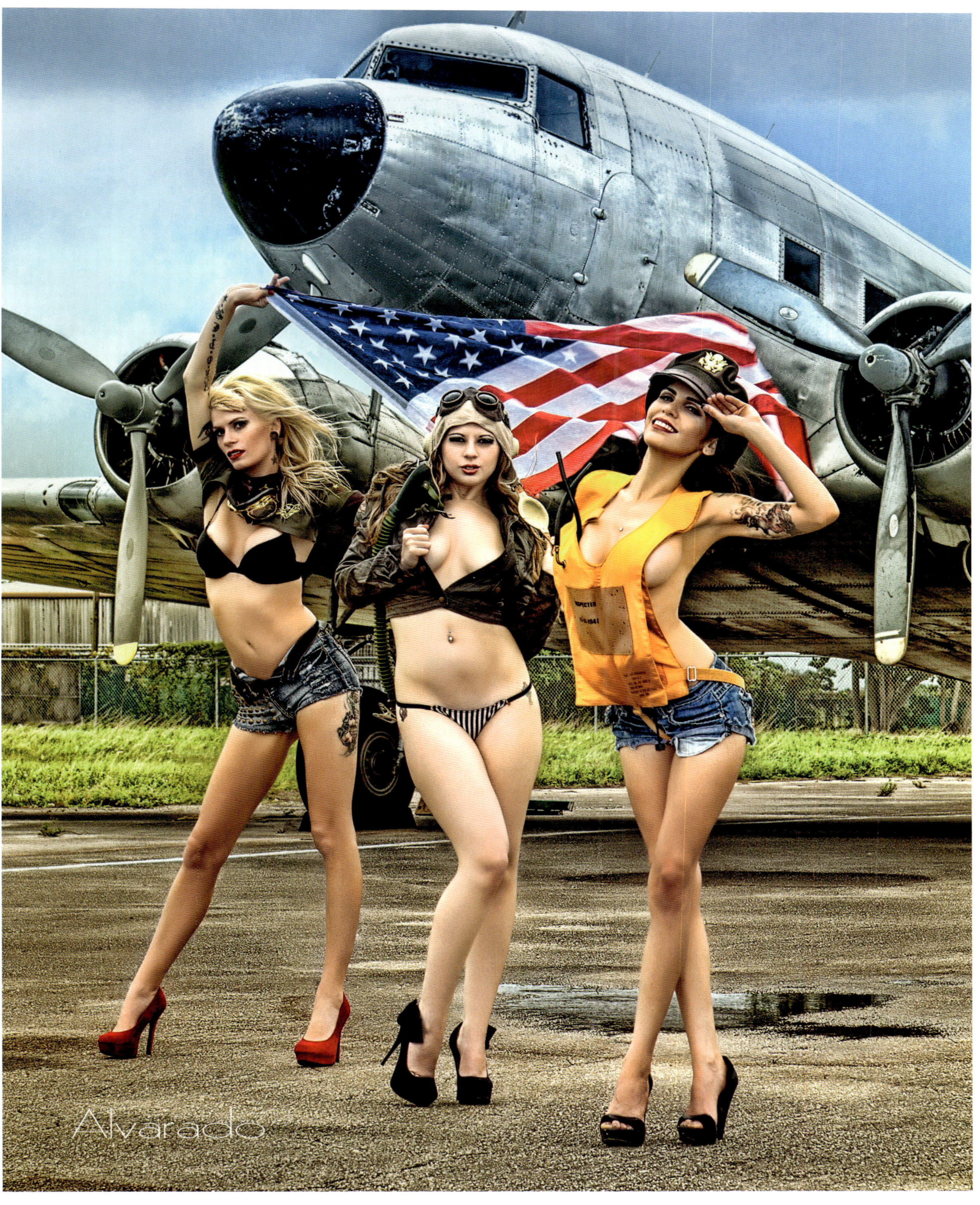
Alvarado

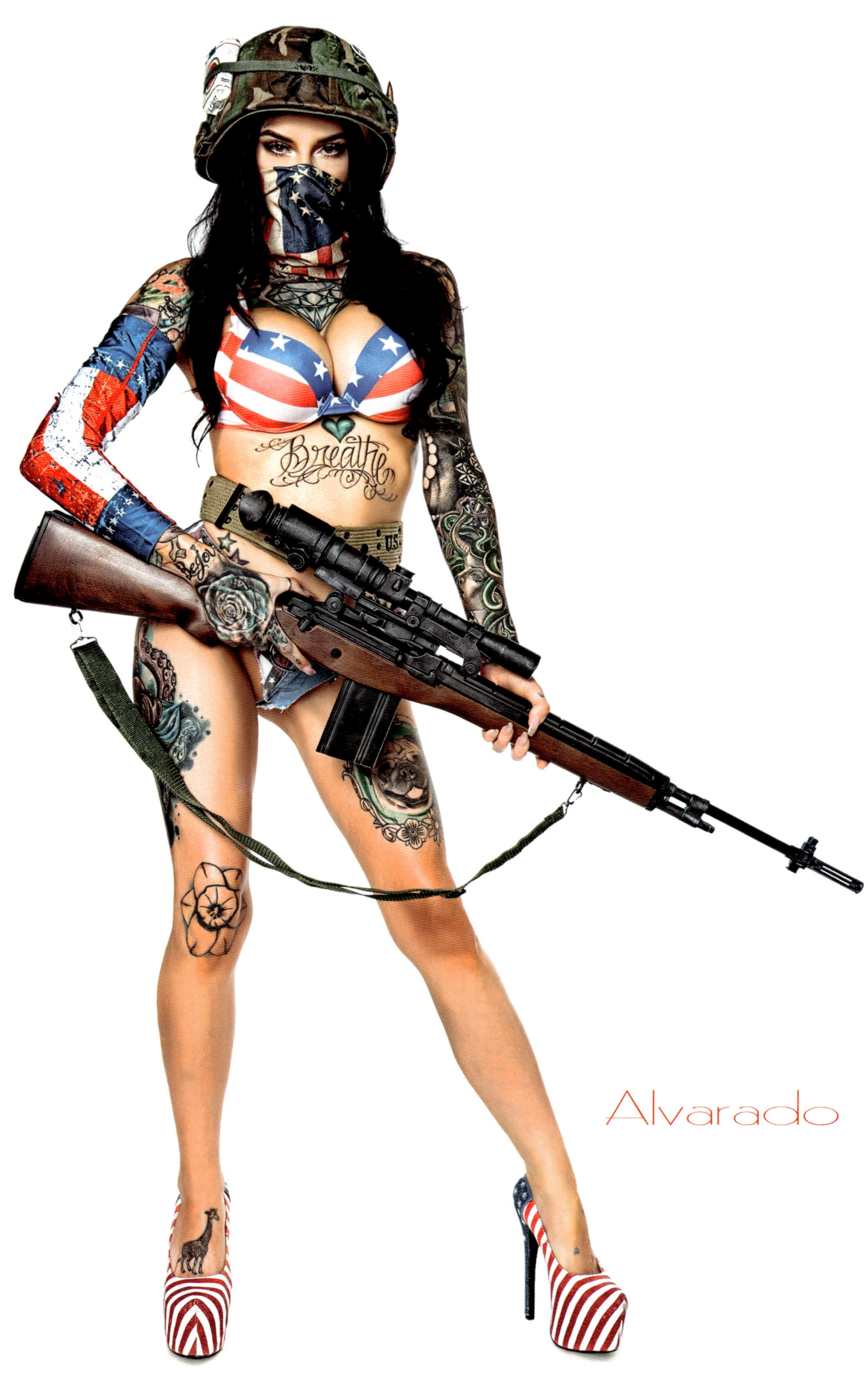

Alvarado

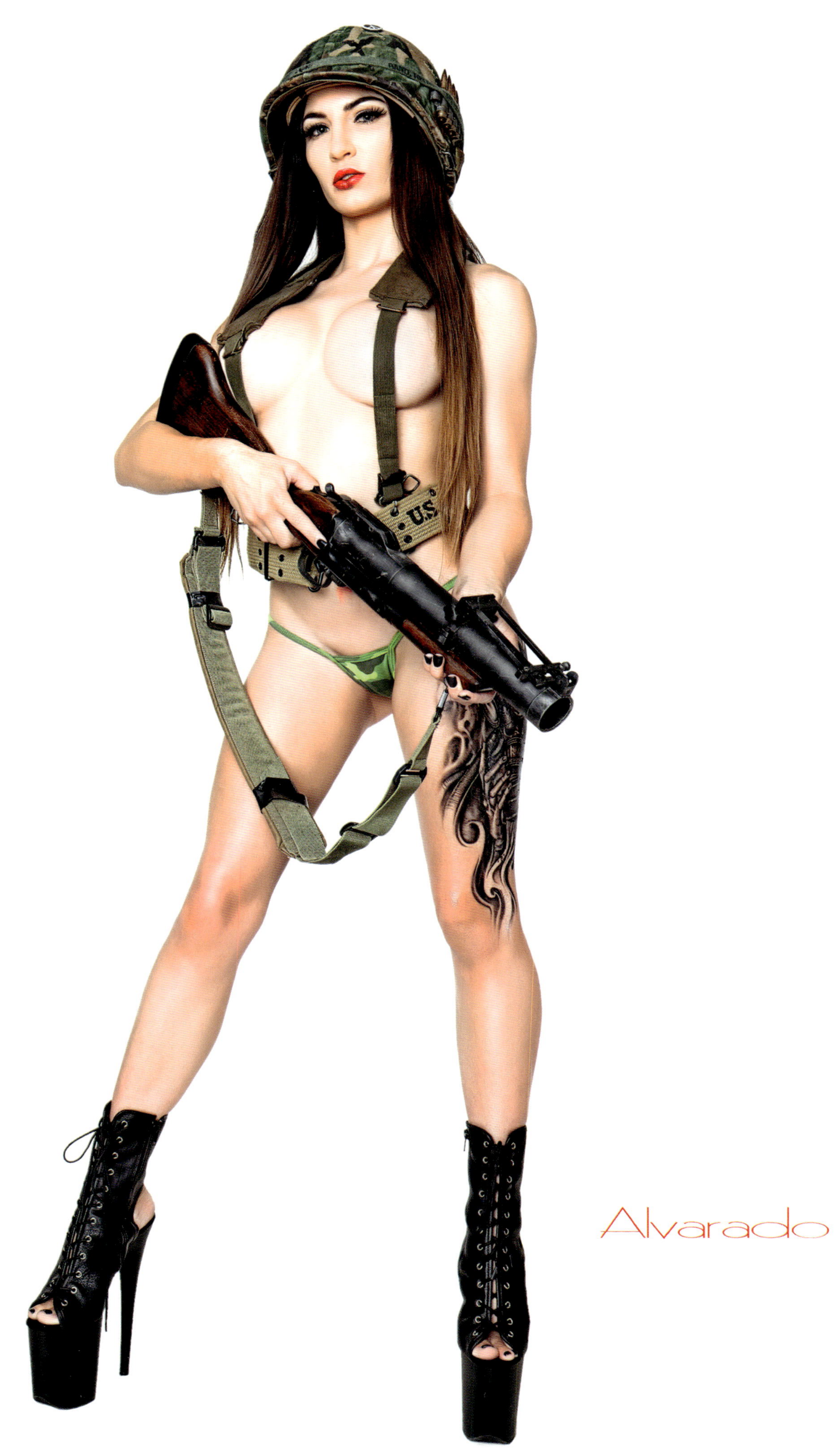

Alvarado

Alvarado

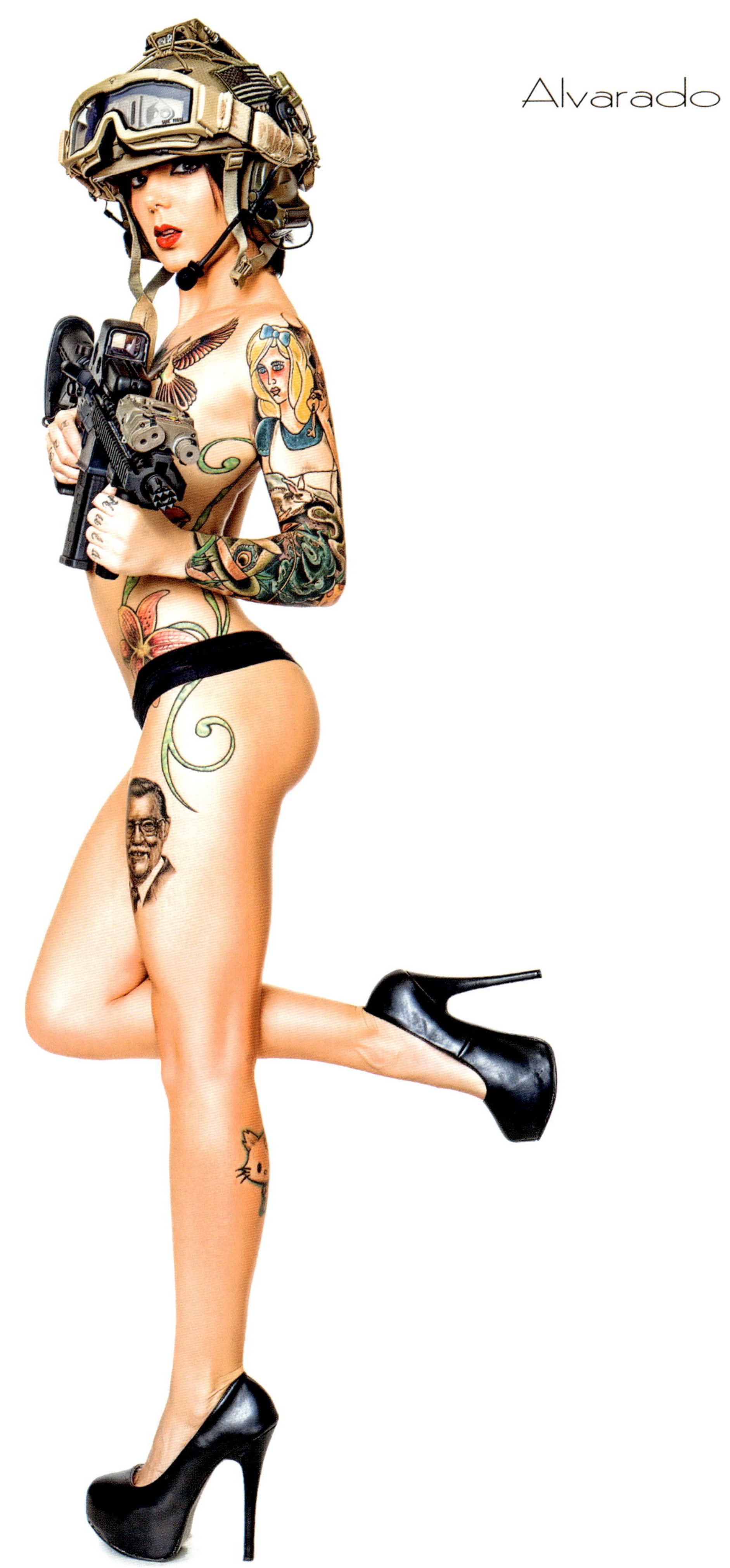

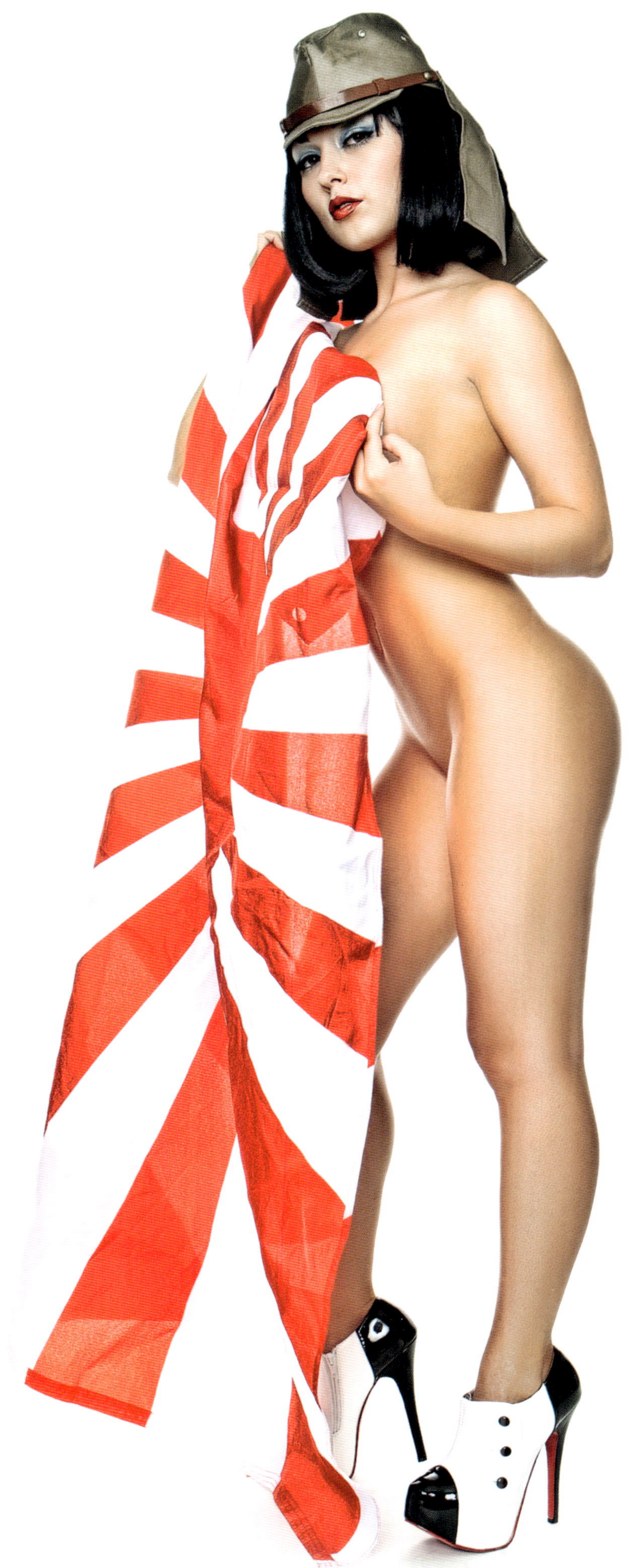

Alvarado

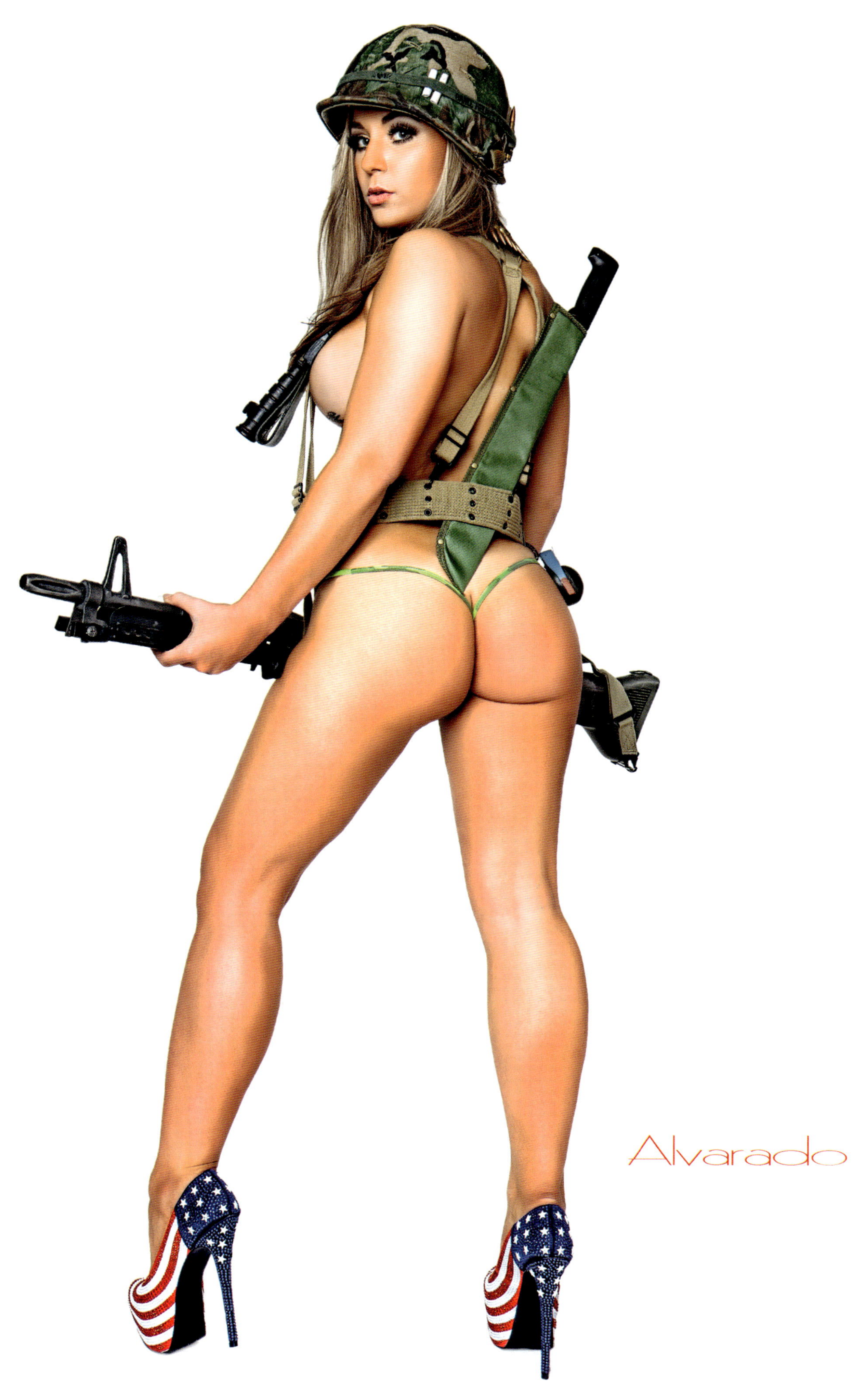

Alvarado

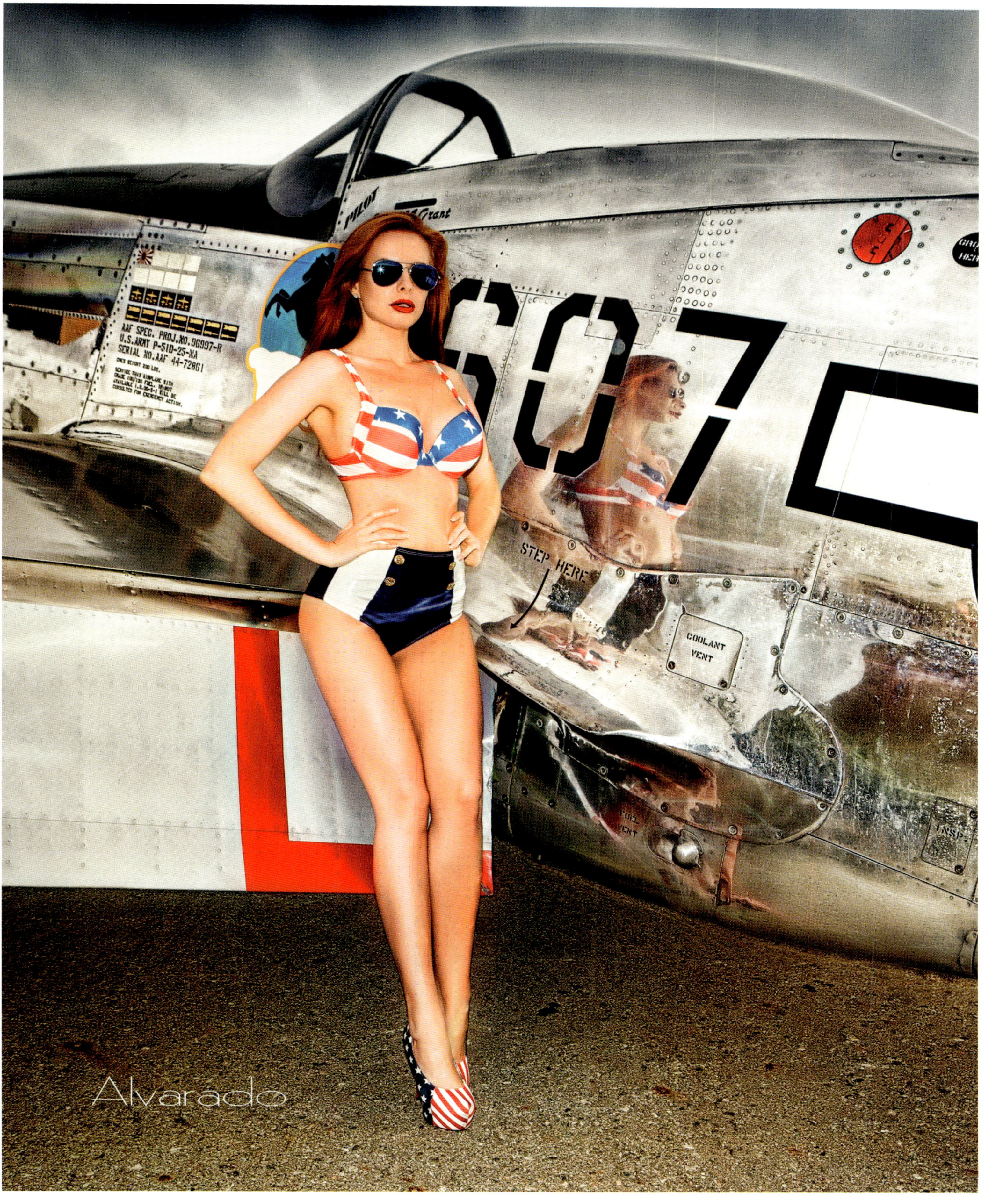
PILOT
607
STEP HERE
COOLANT VENT
Alvarado

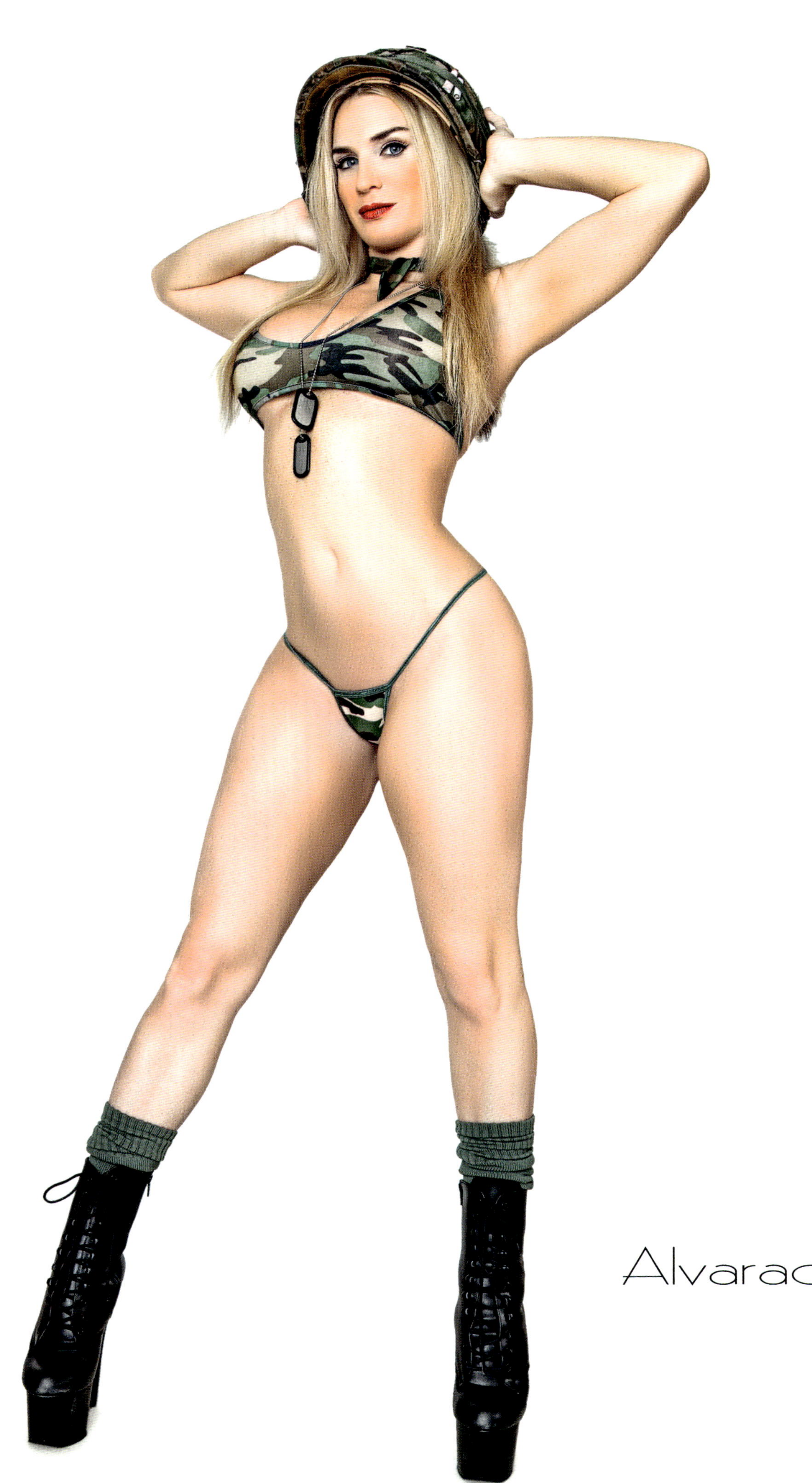

Alvarado

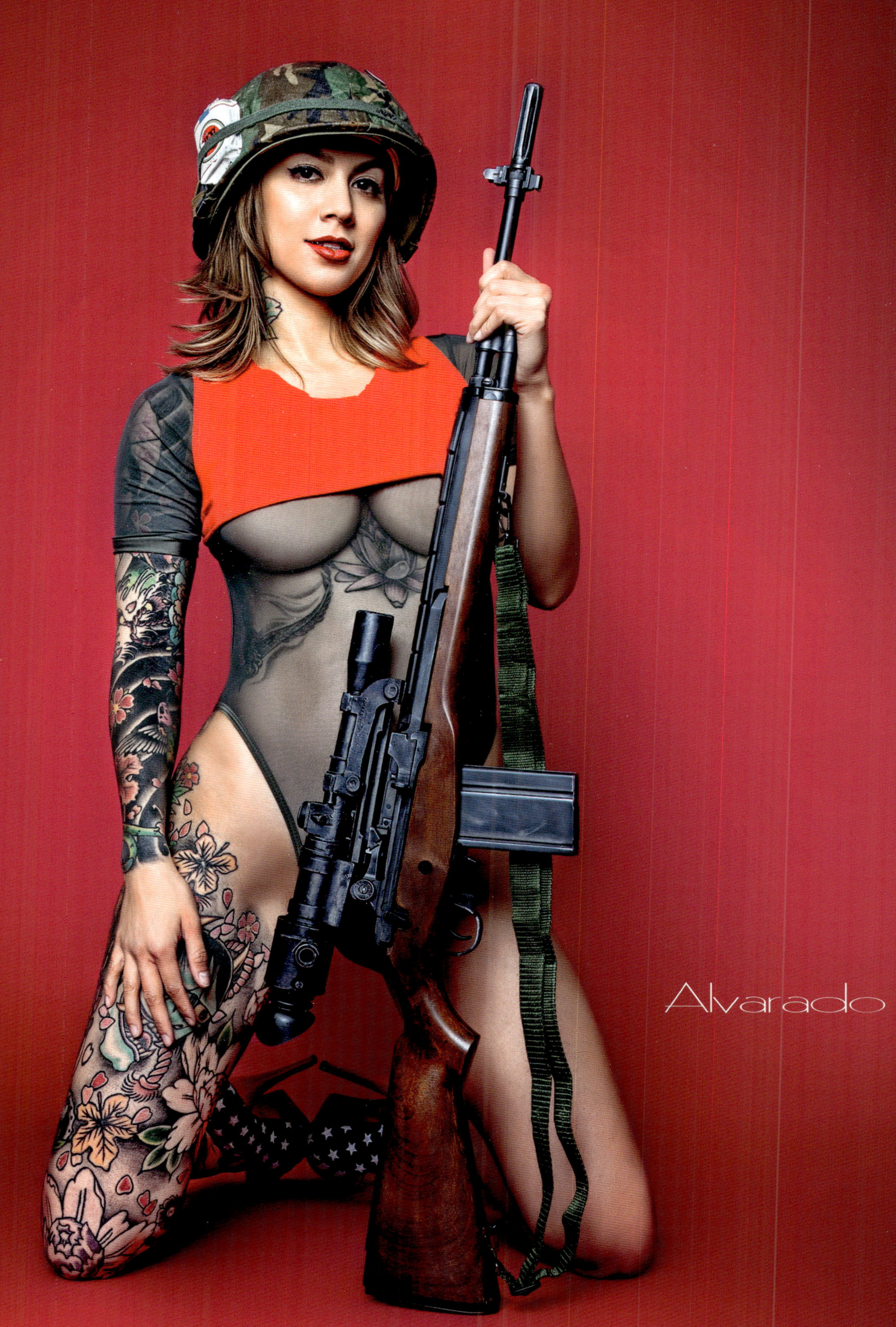
Alvarado

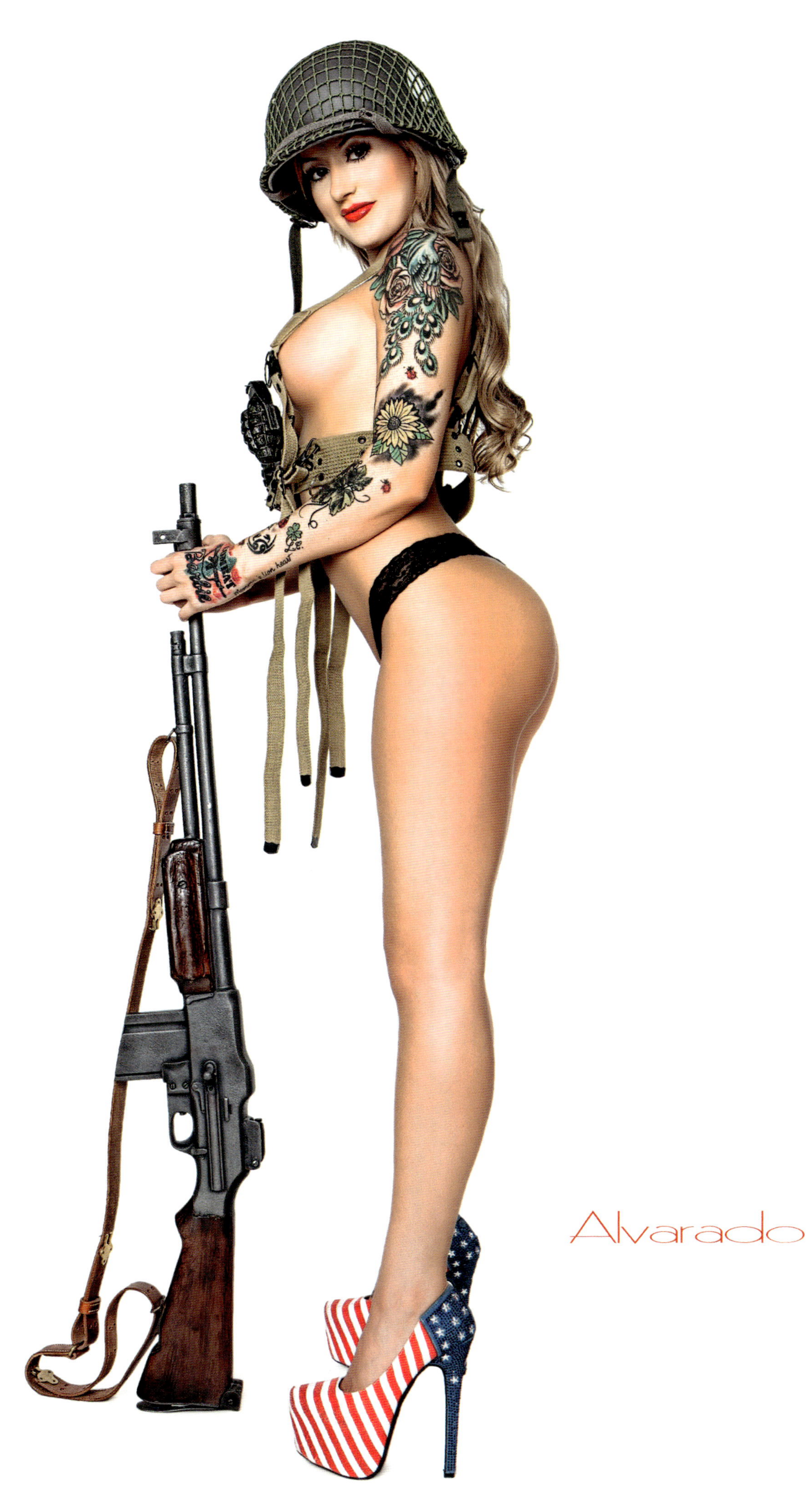

Alvarado

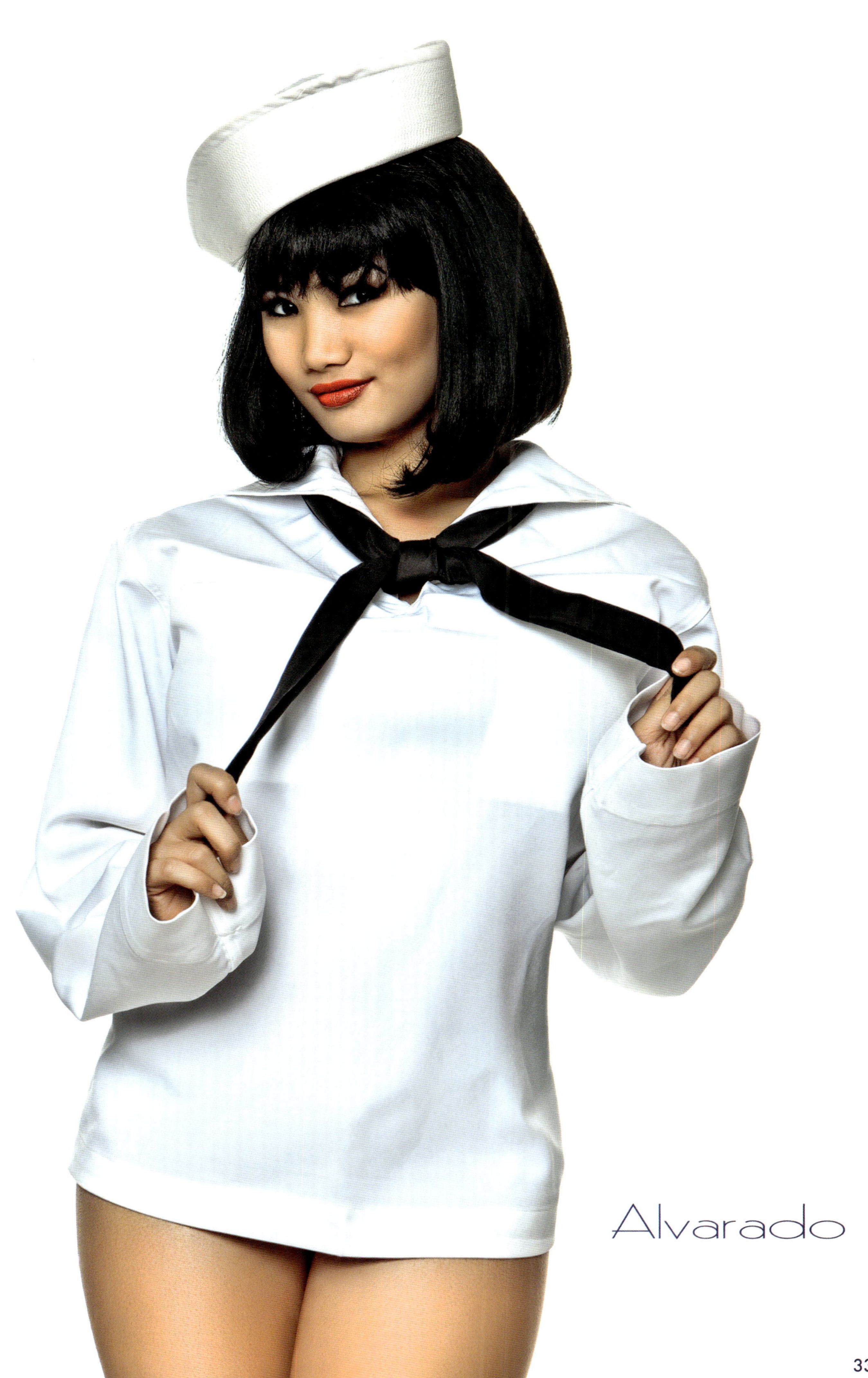

Alvarado

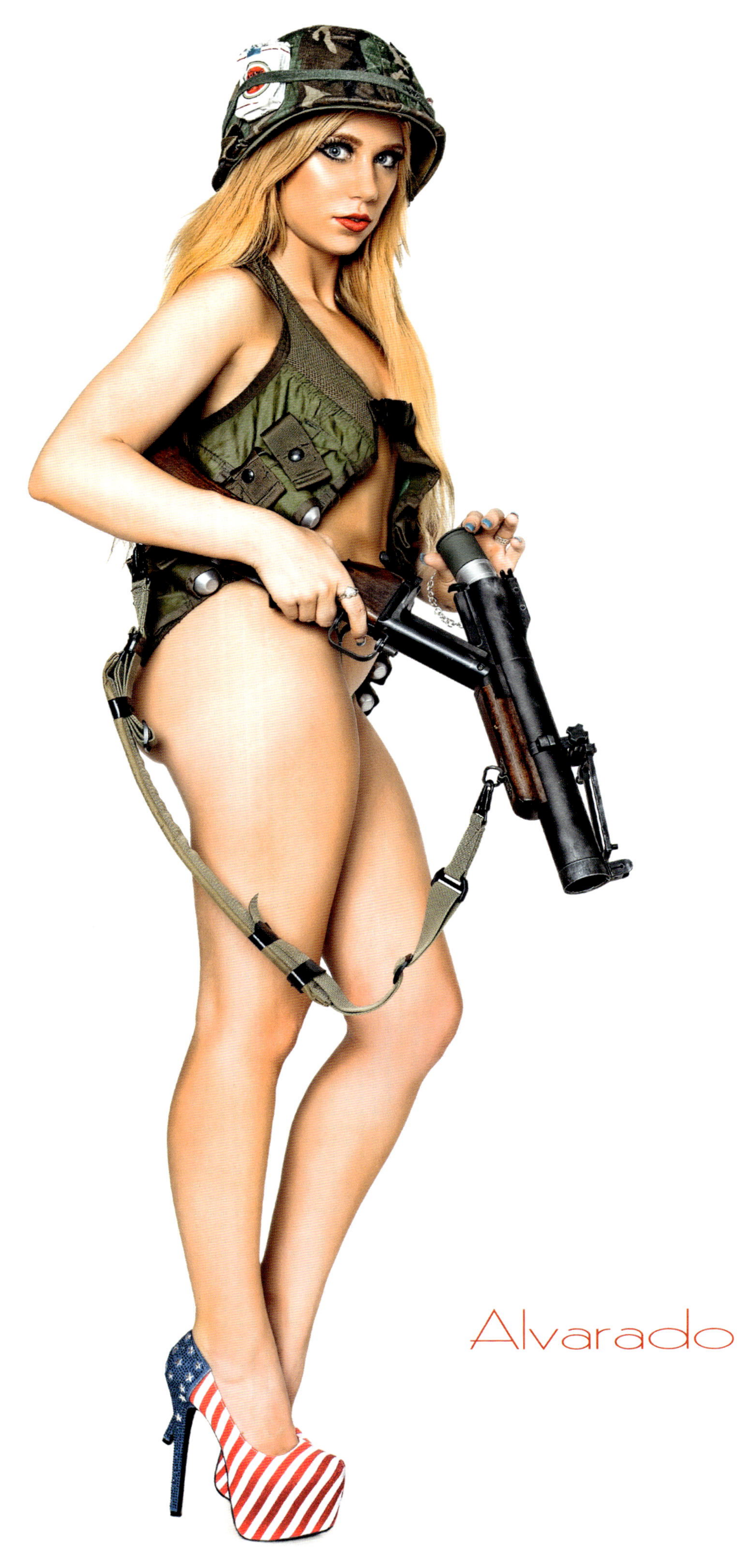

Alvarado

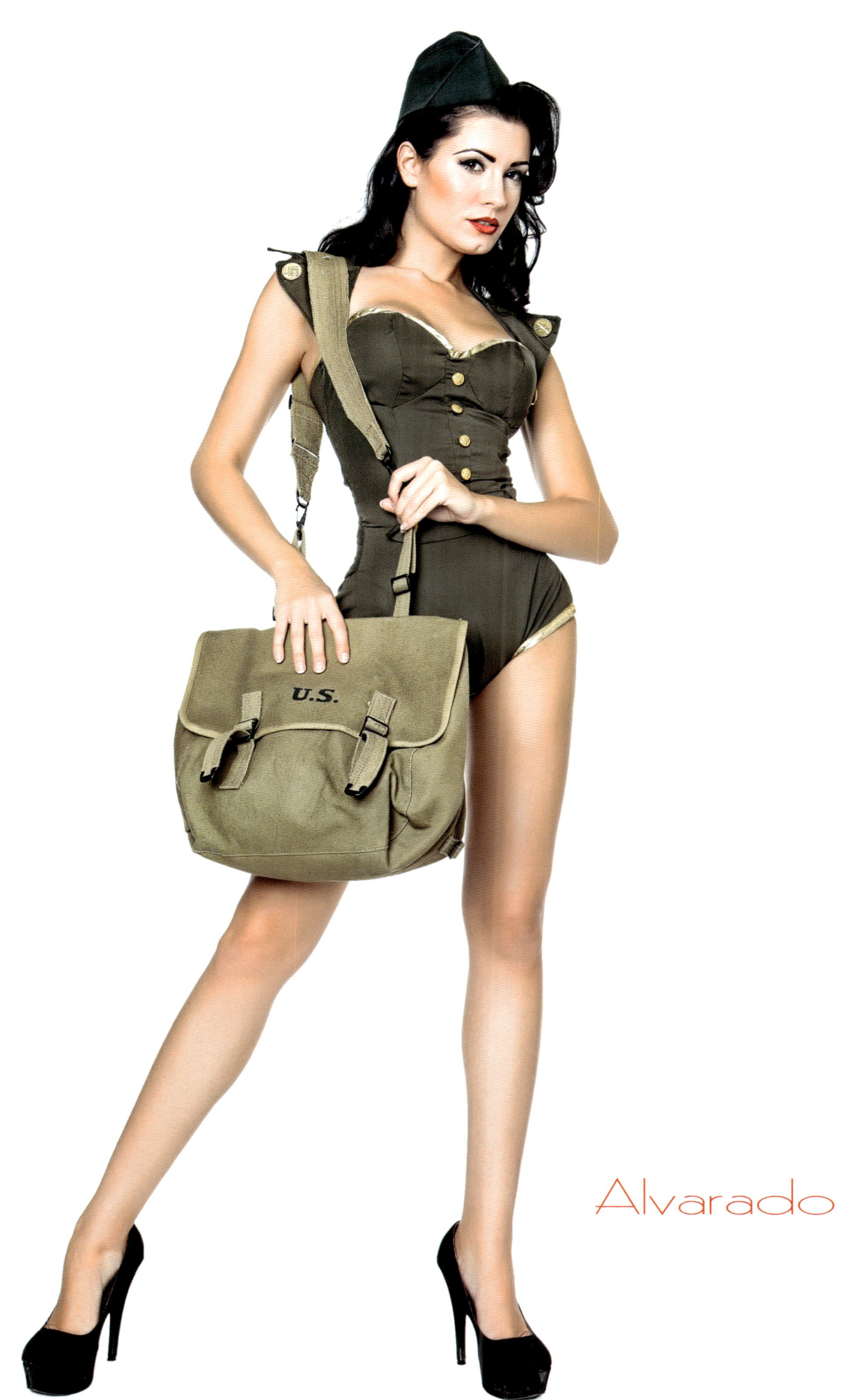

Alvarado

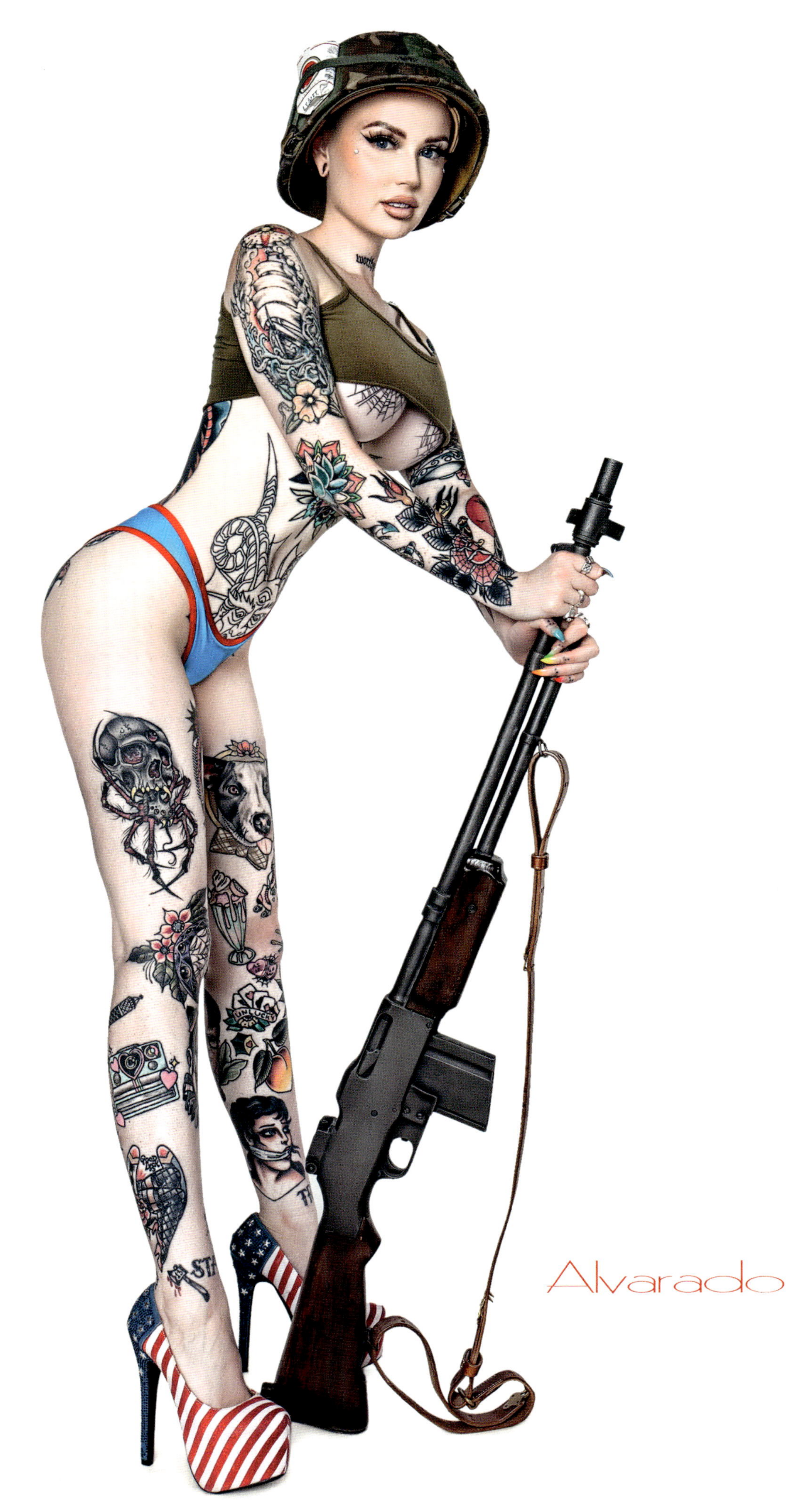

Alvarado

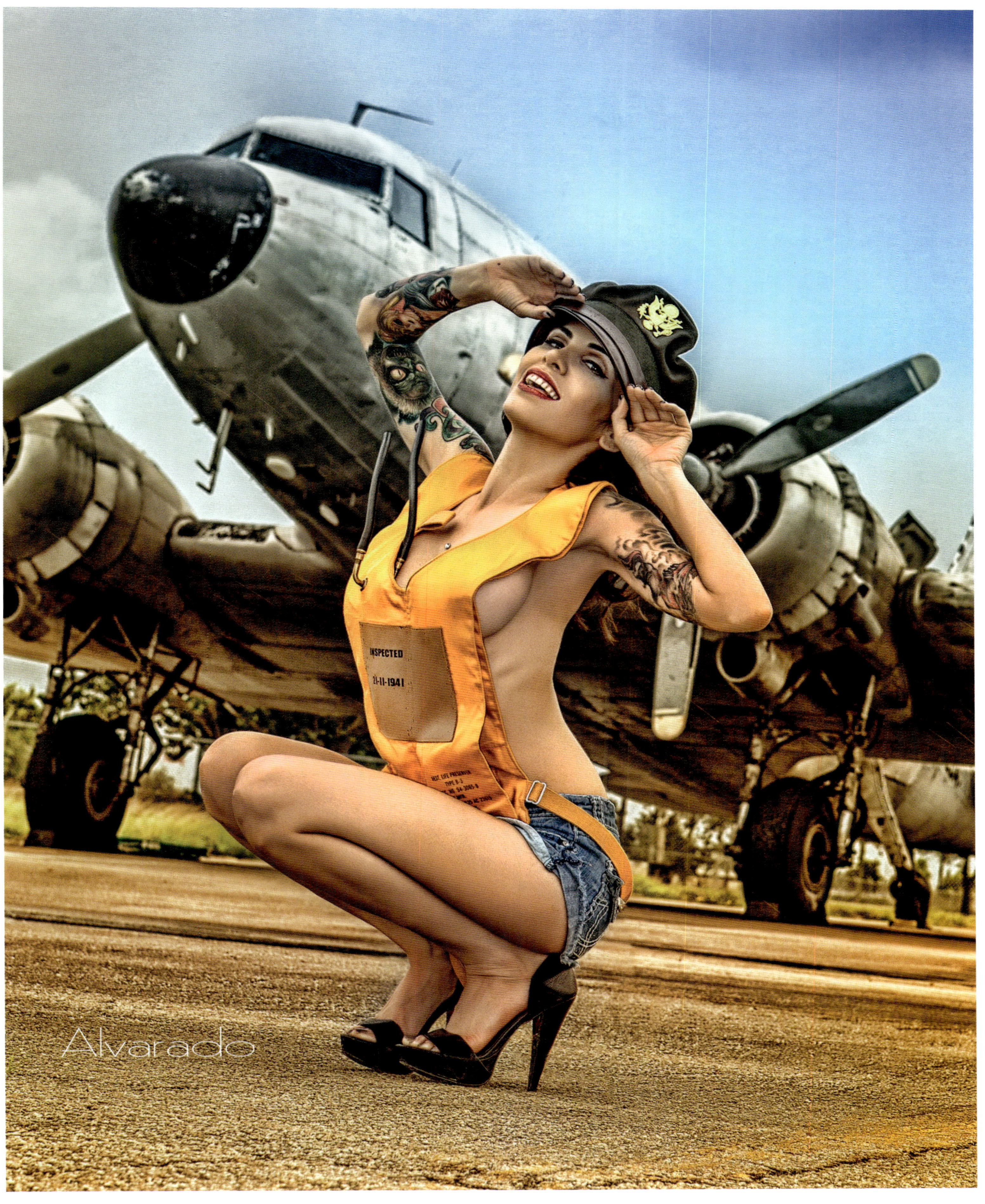
INSPECTED
21-11-1941
Alvarado

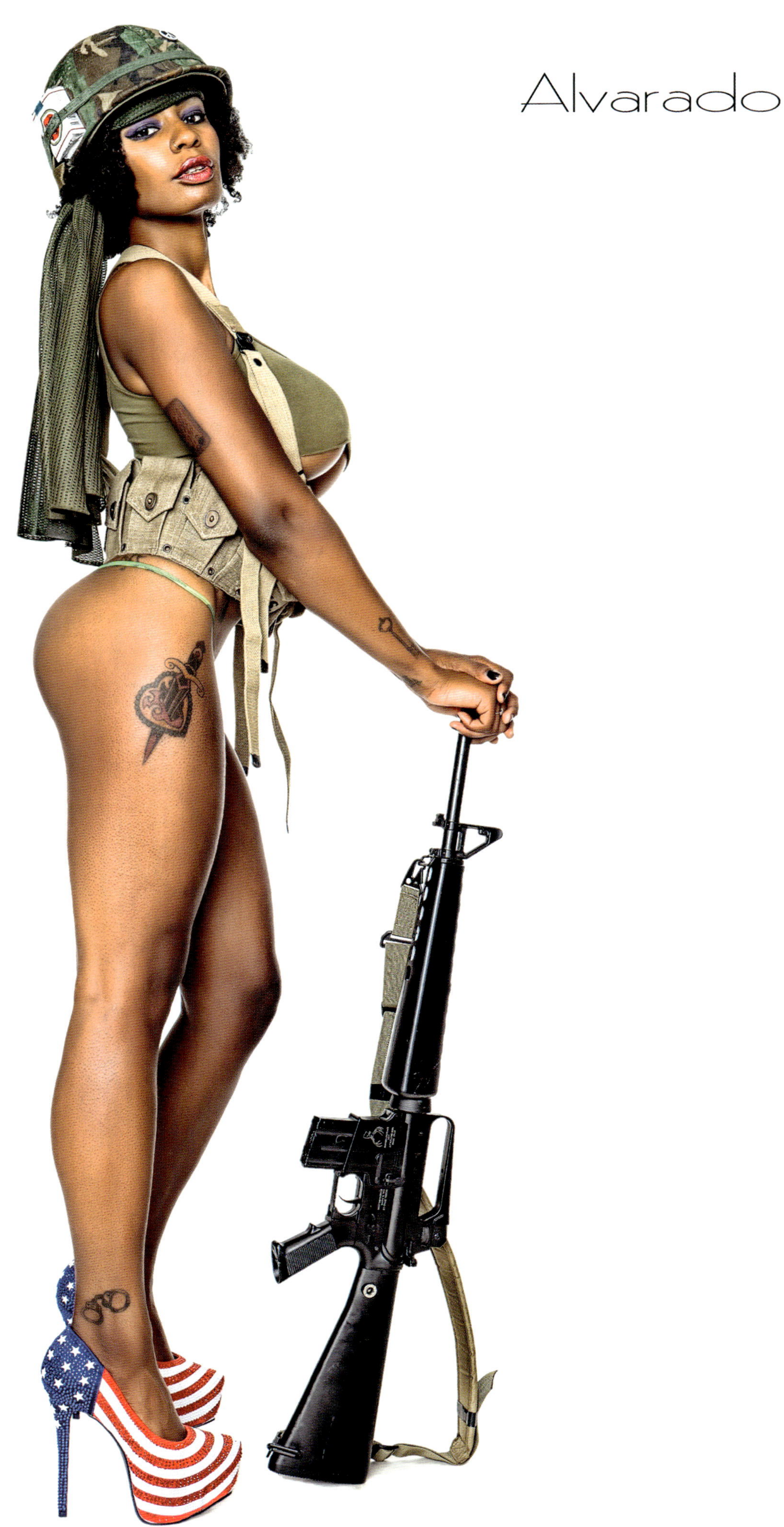

Alvarado

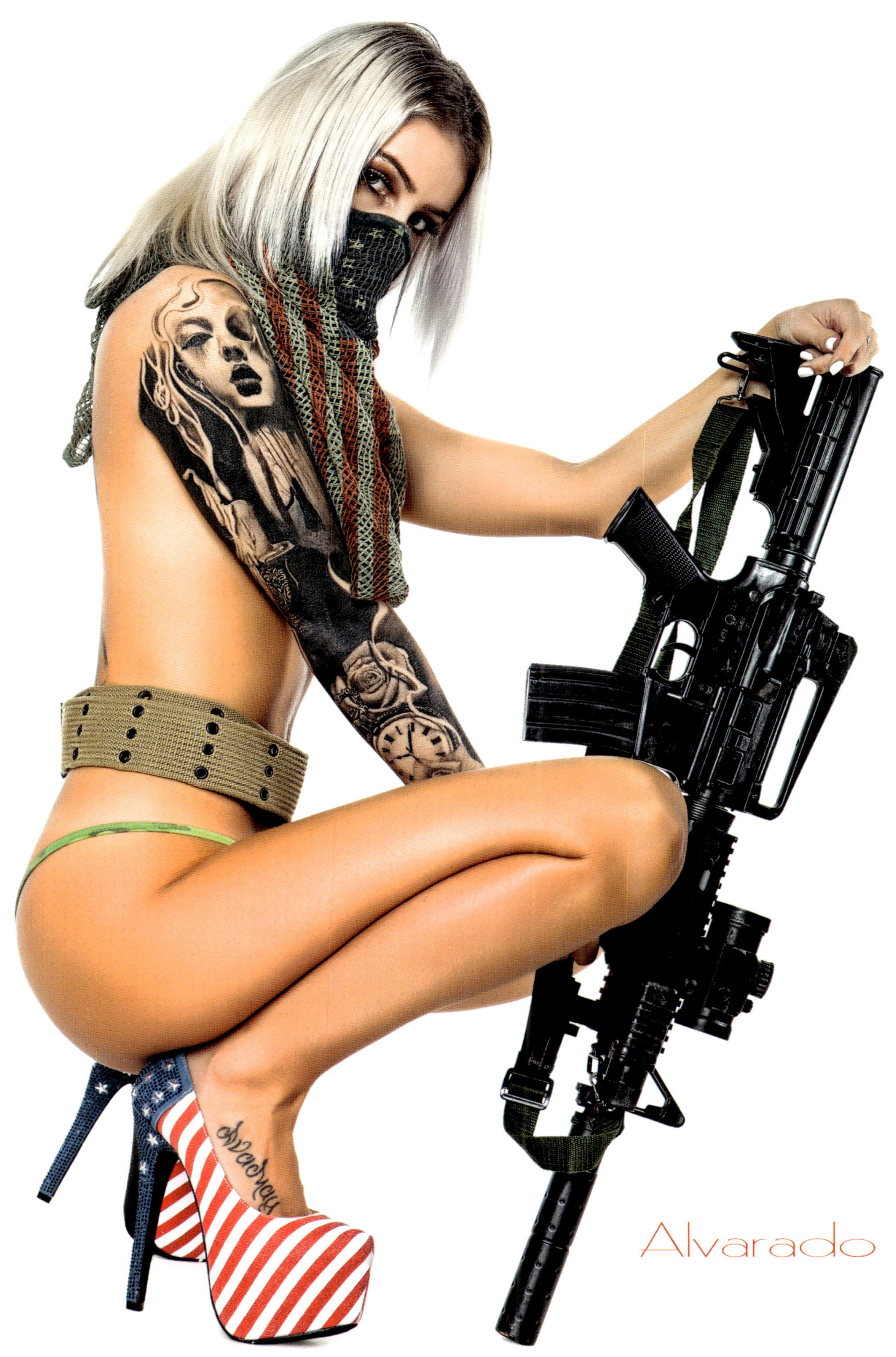

Alvarado

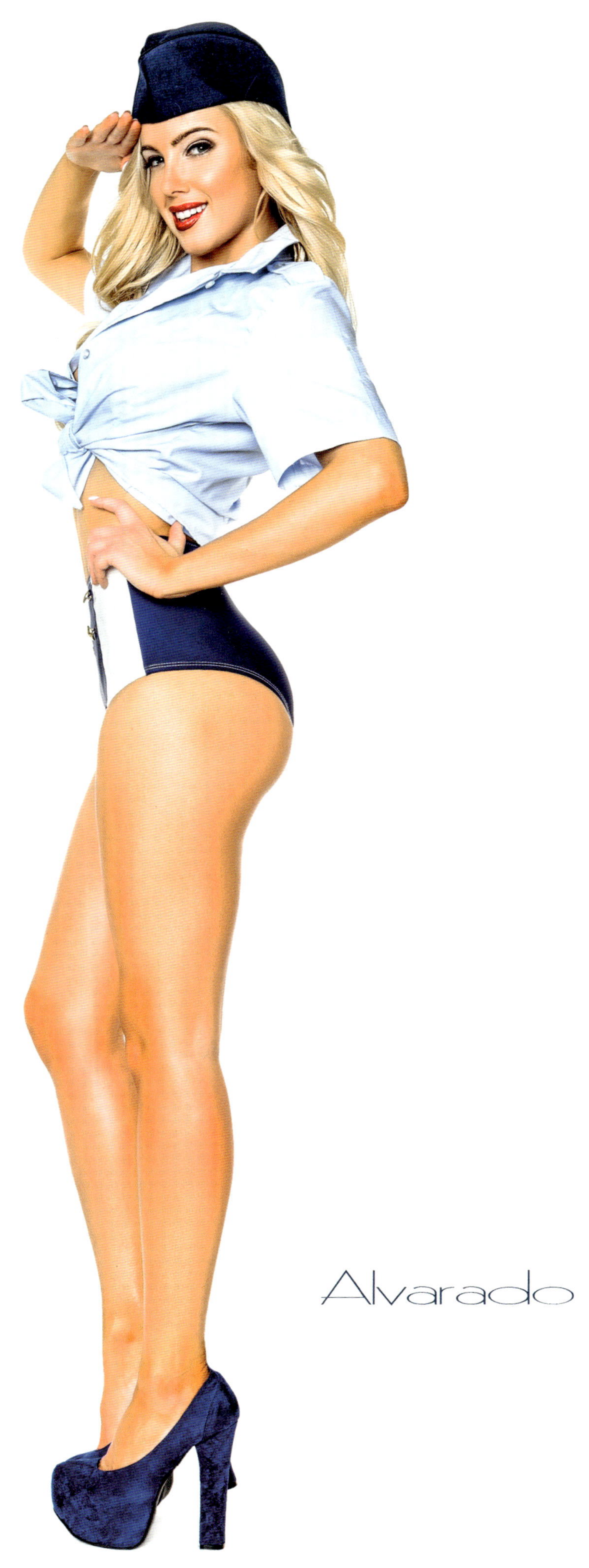

Alvarado

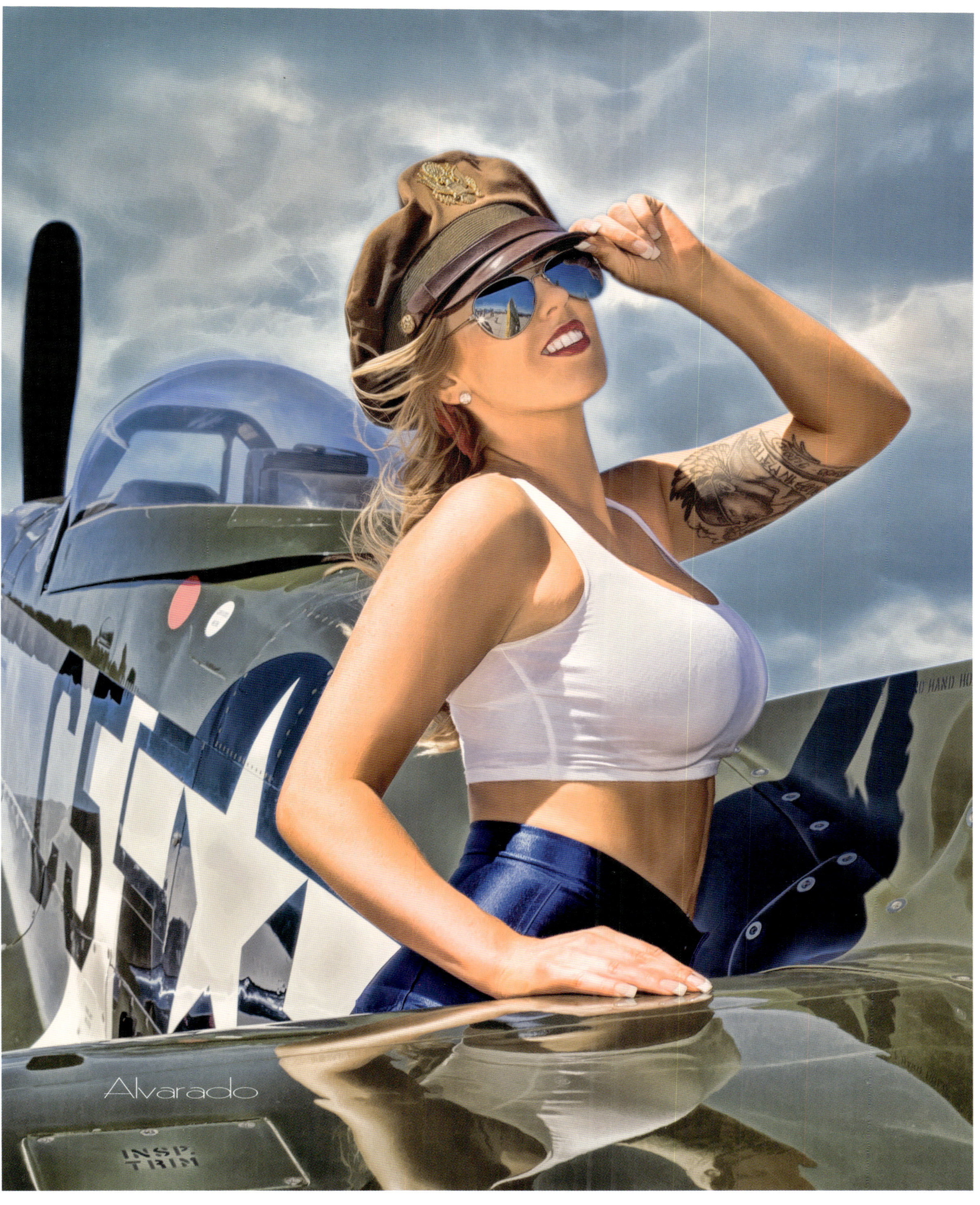
Alvarado
INSP.
TRIM

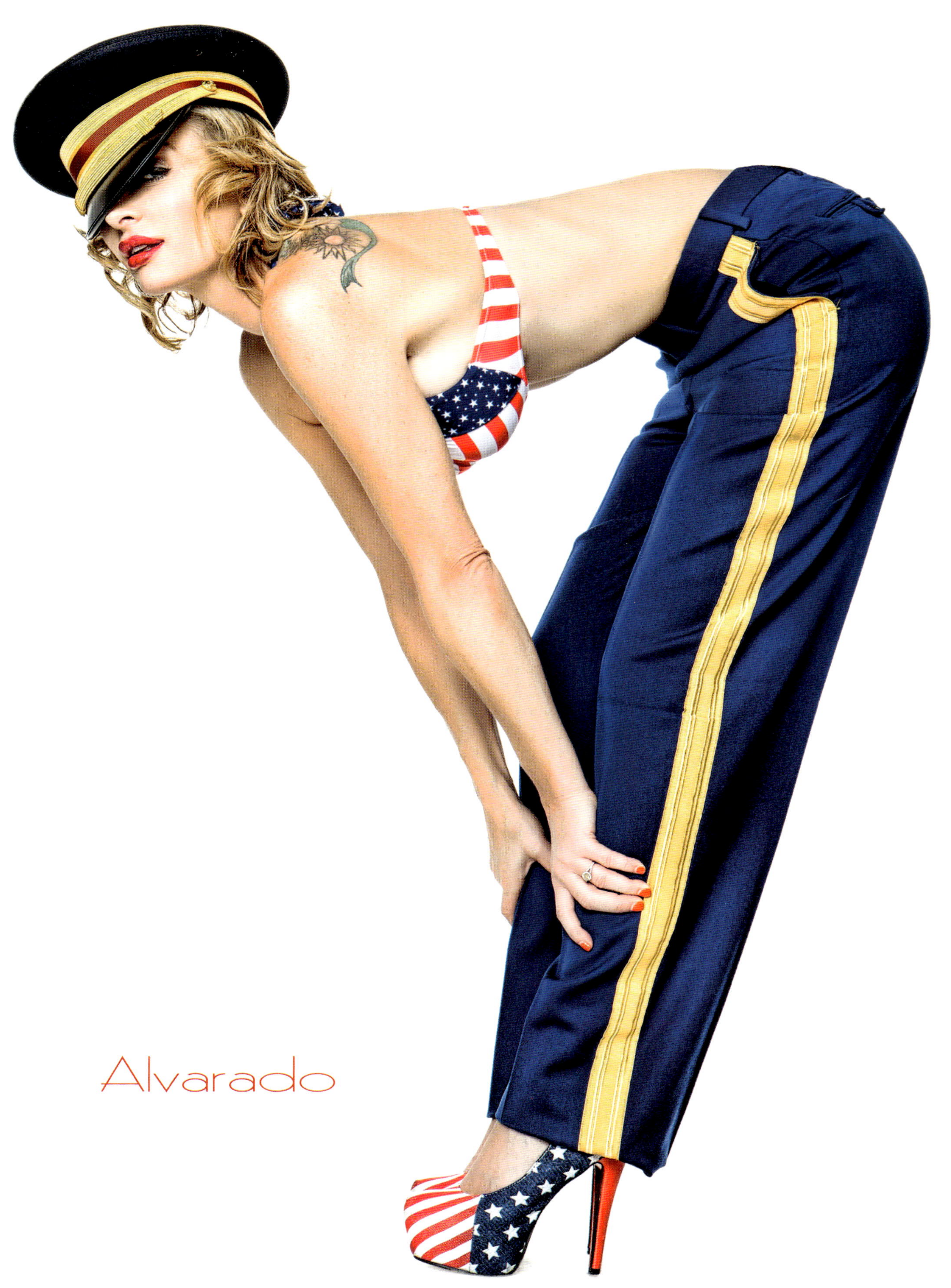

Alvarado

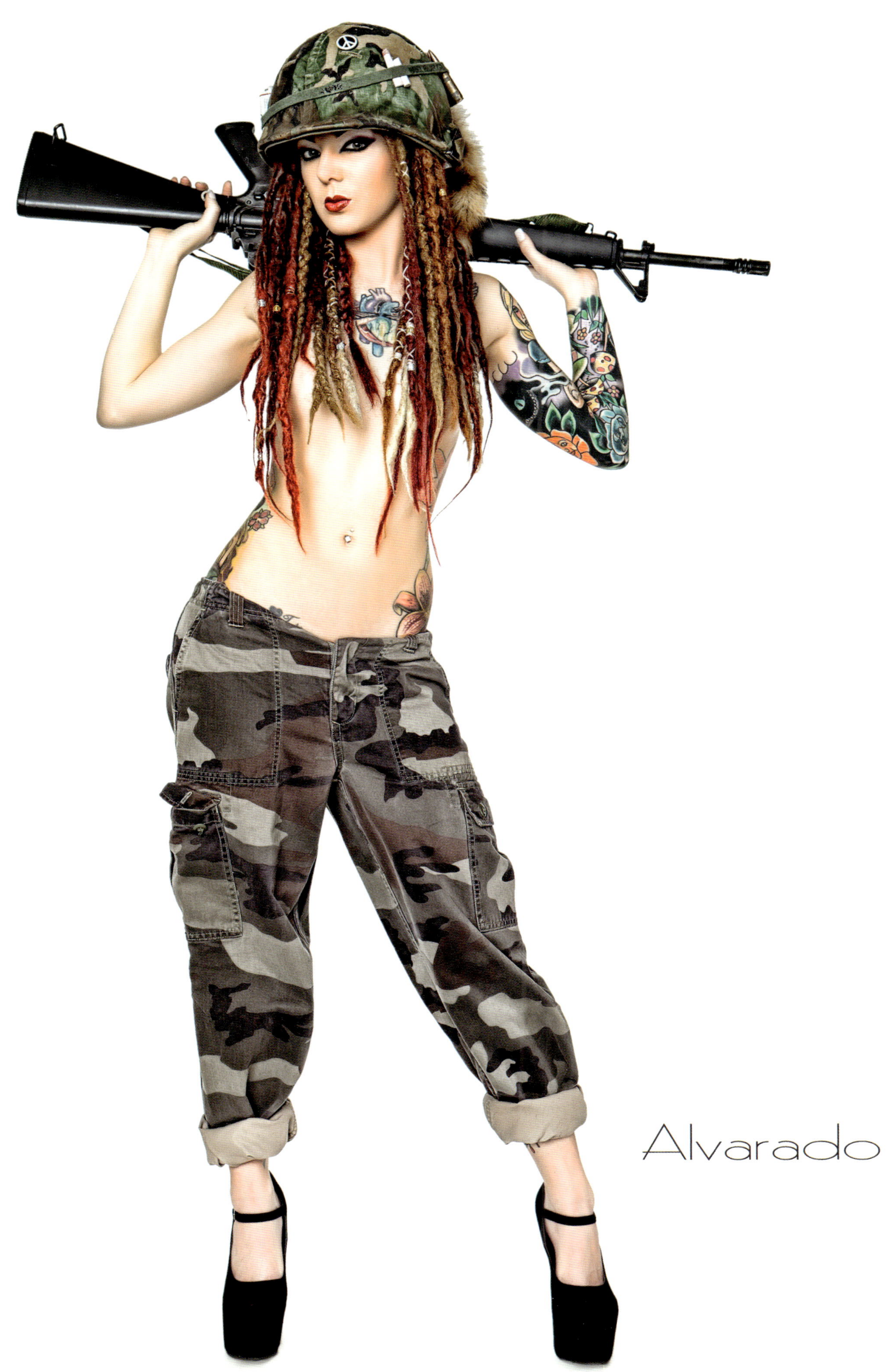

Alvarado

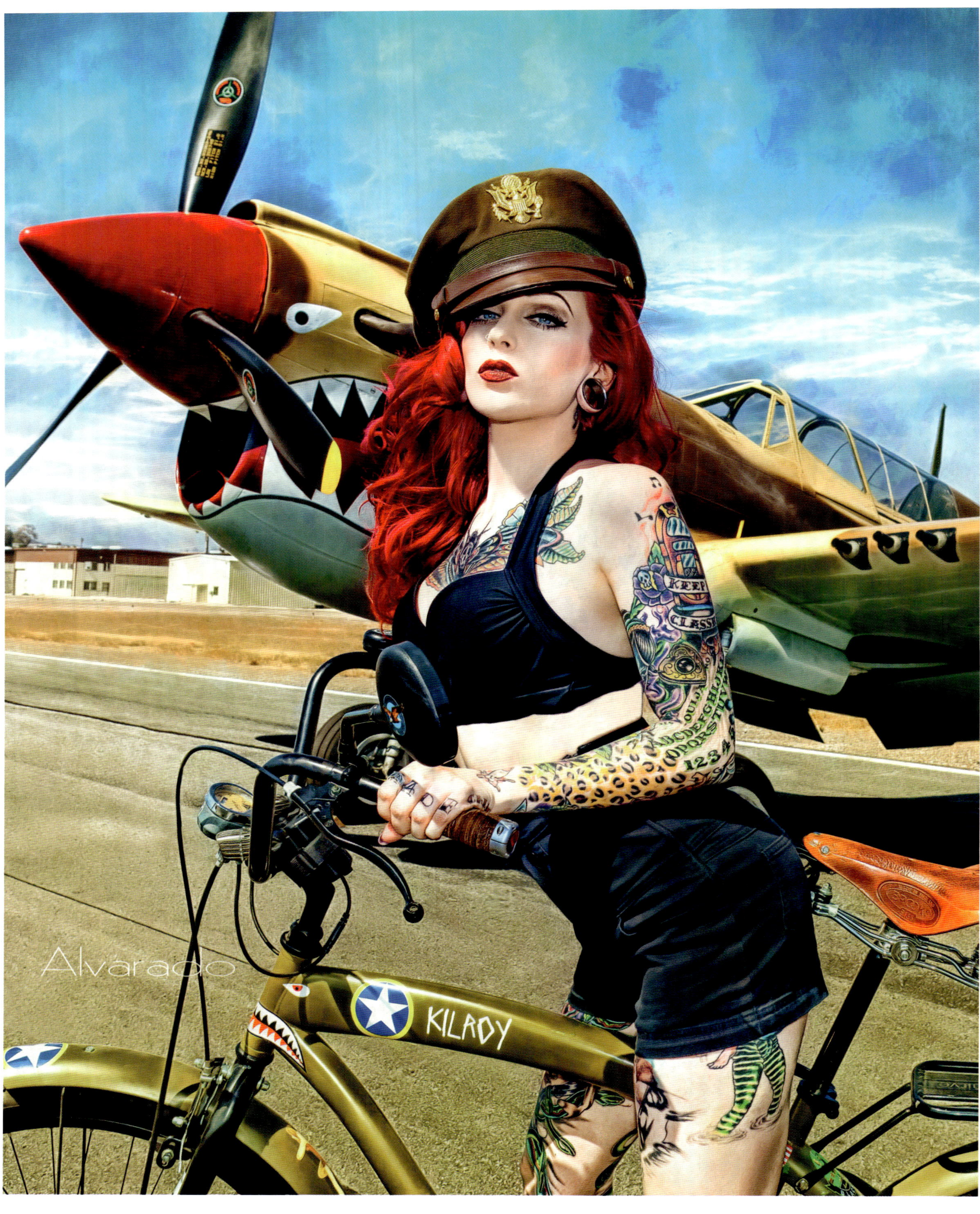
Alvarado
KILROY

Alvarado

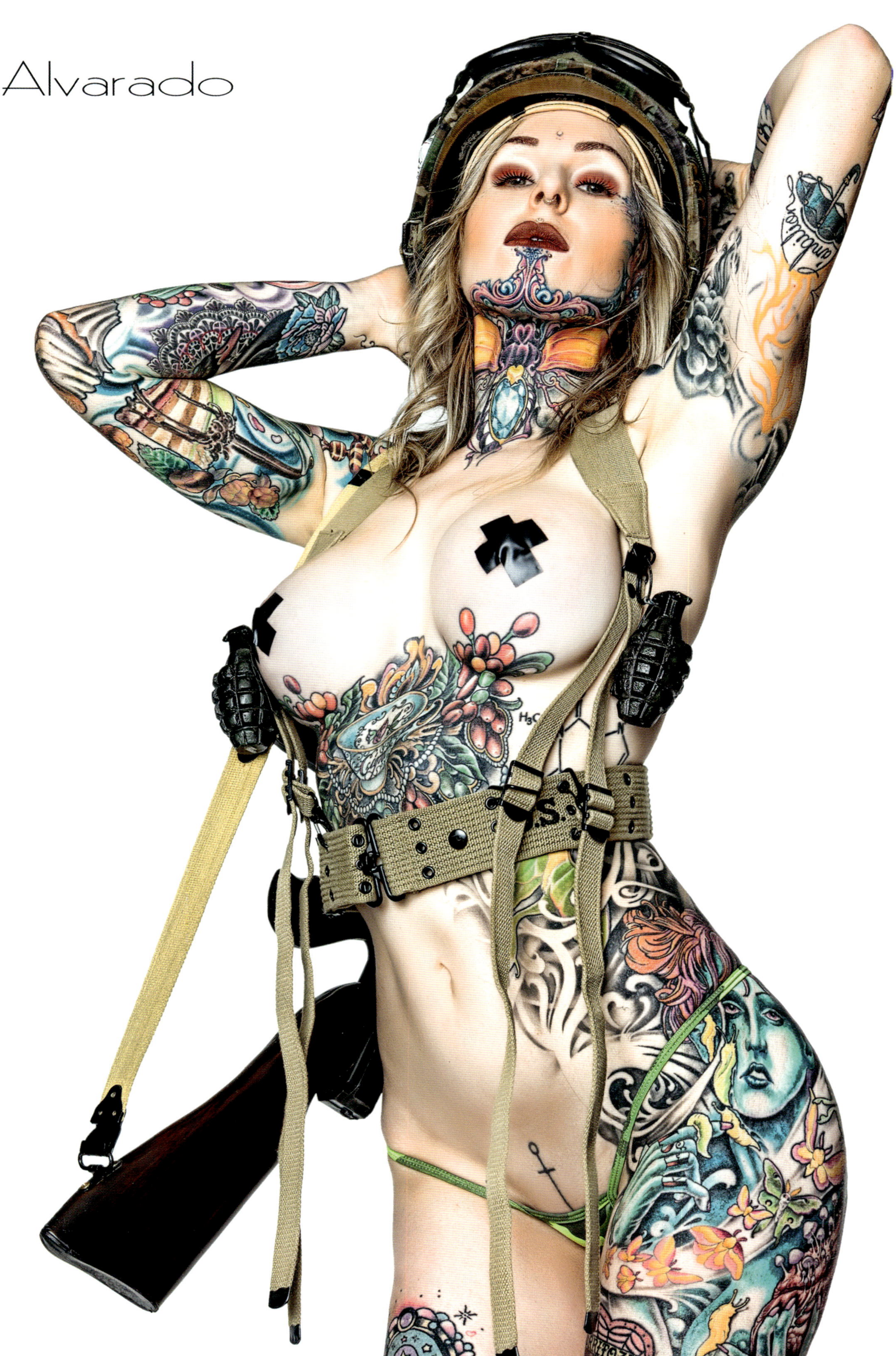

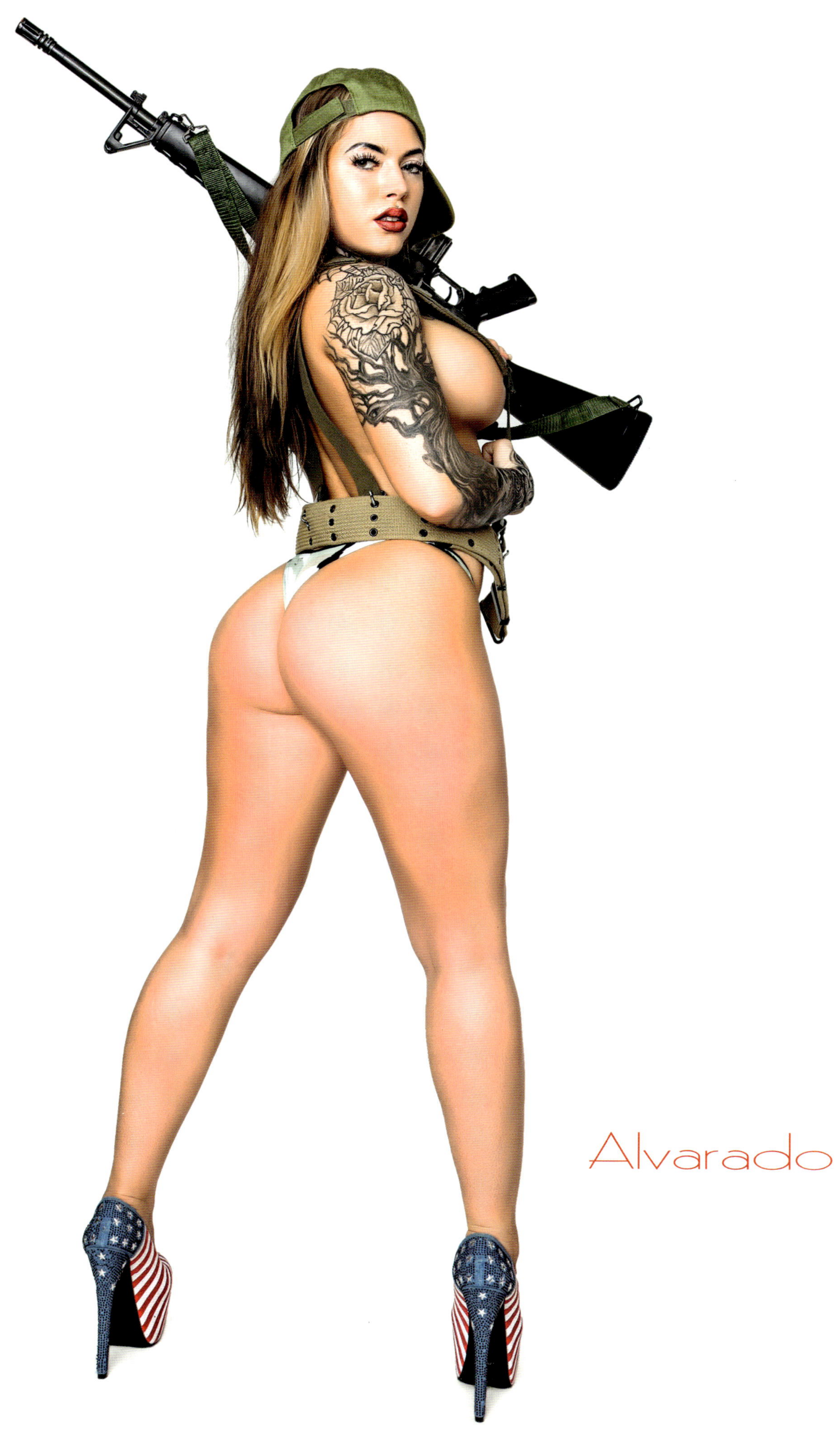

Alvarado

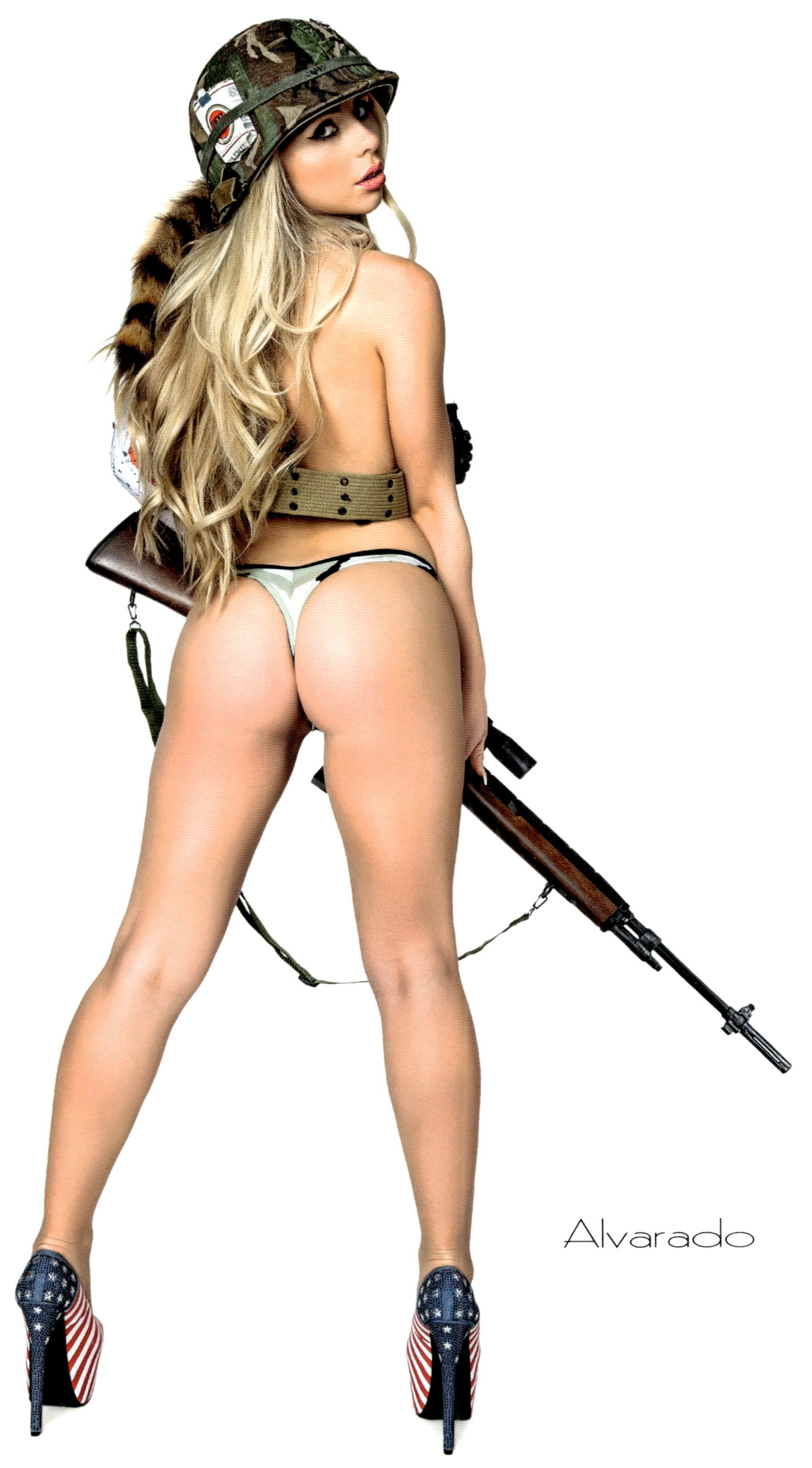

Alvarado

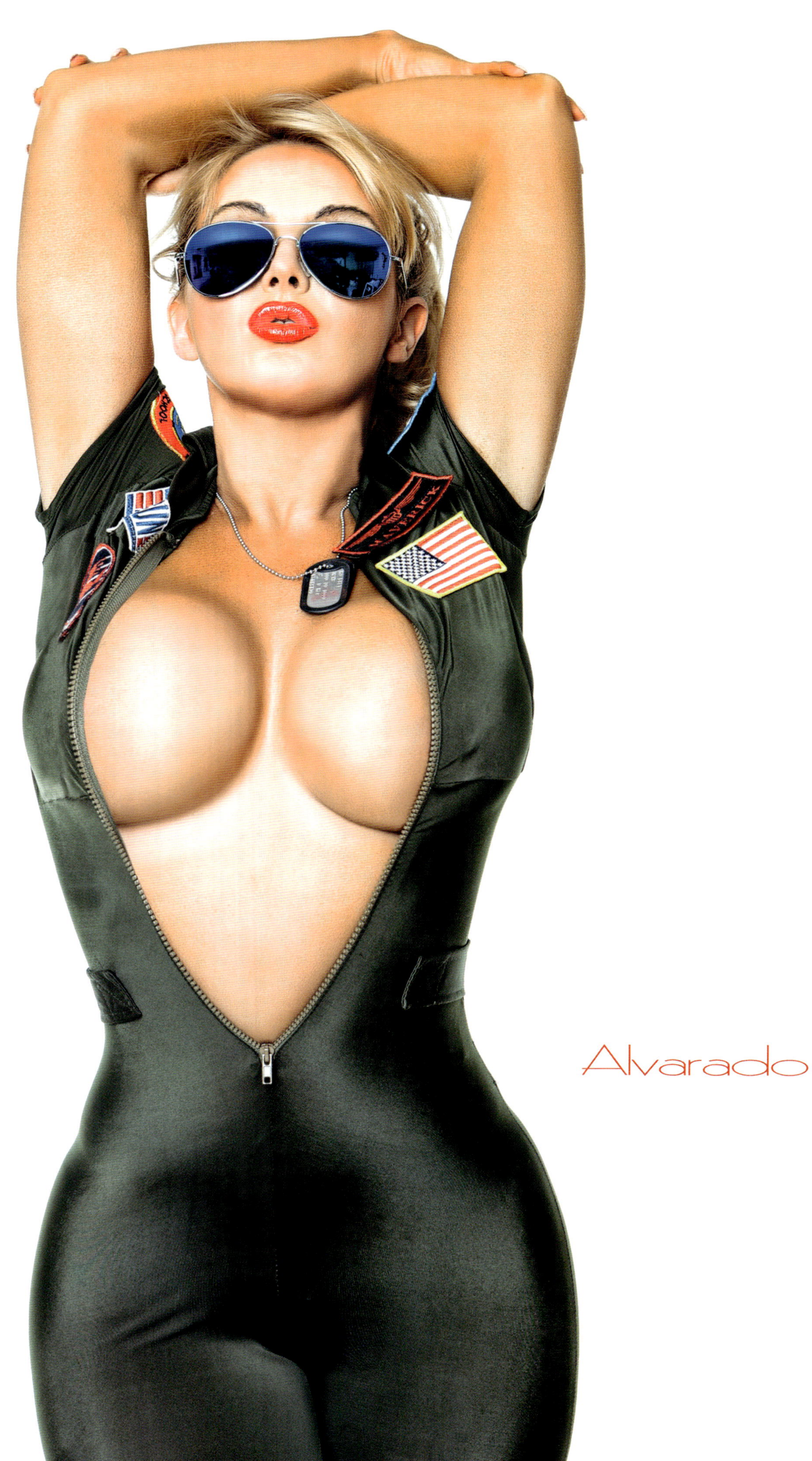

Alvarado

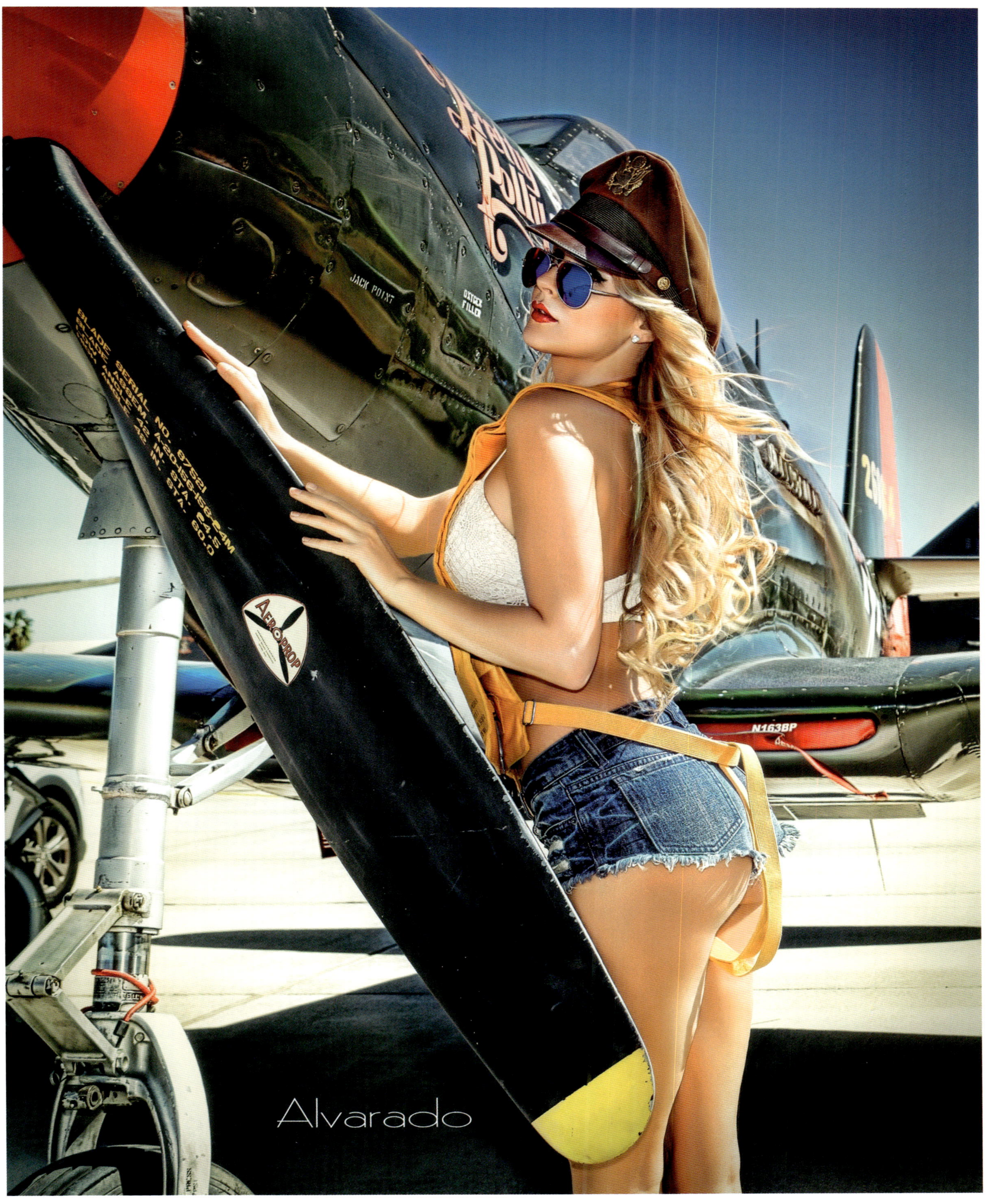

Alvarado

Alvarado

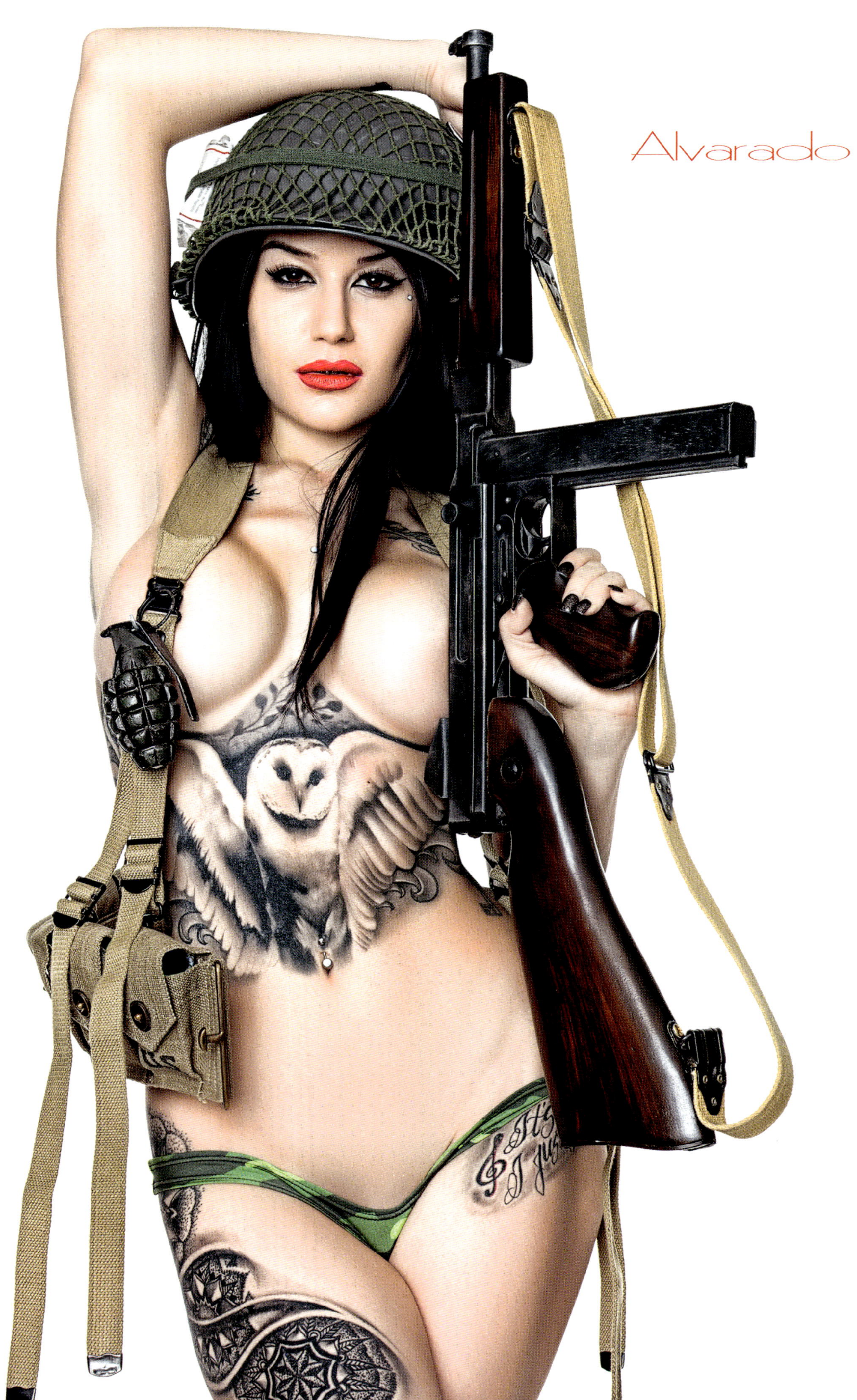

Alvarado

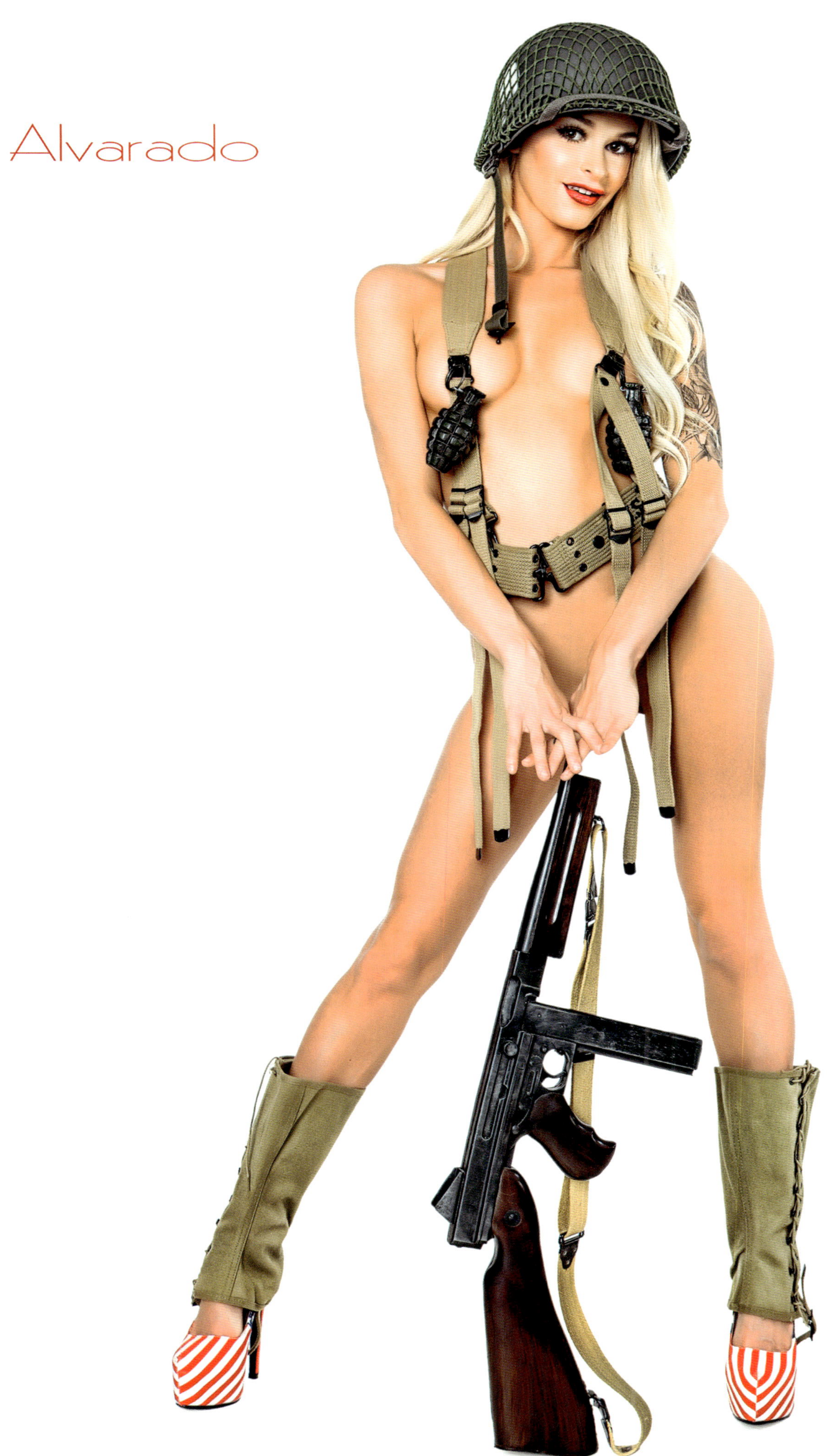

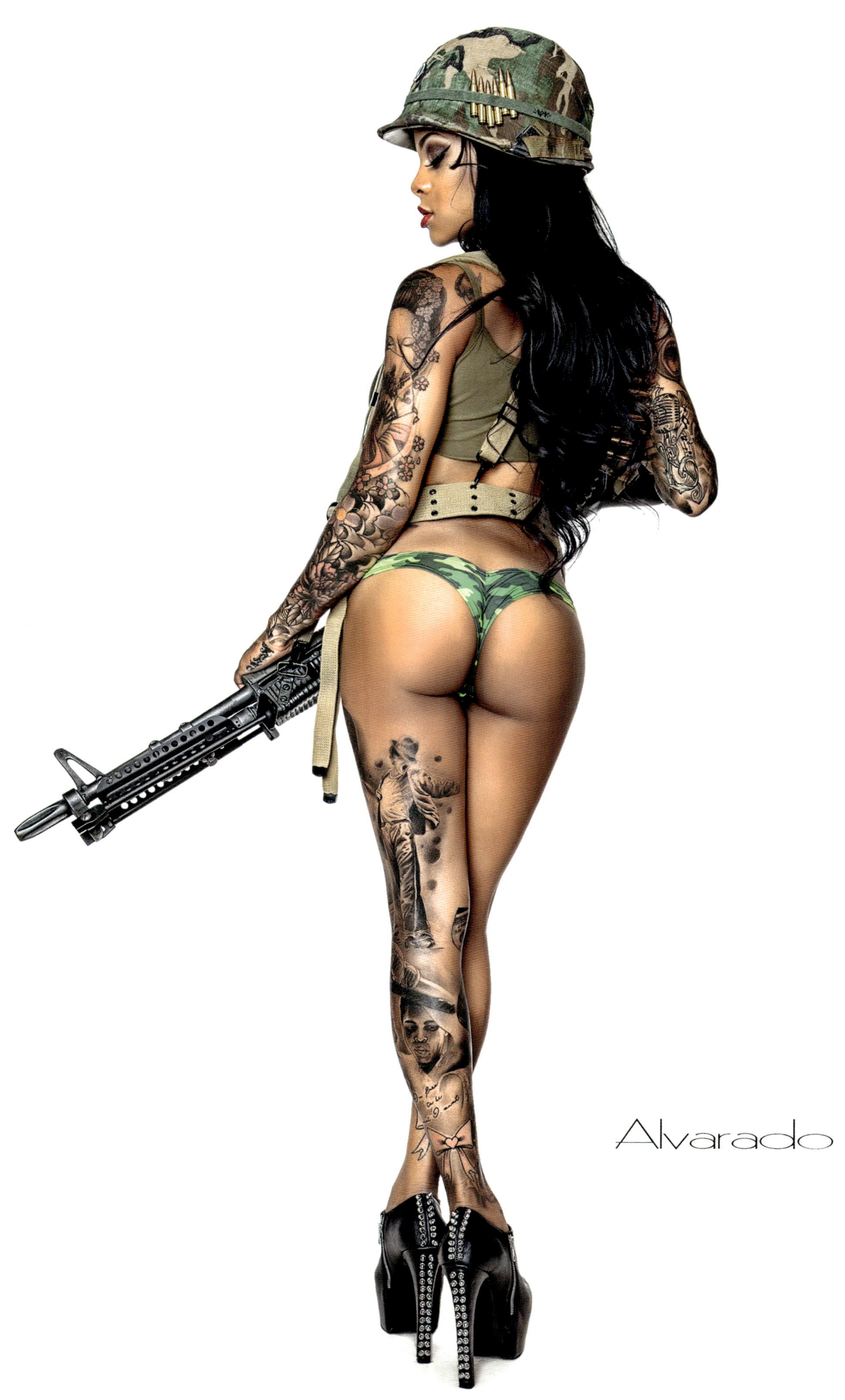

Alvarado

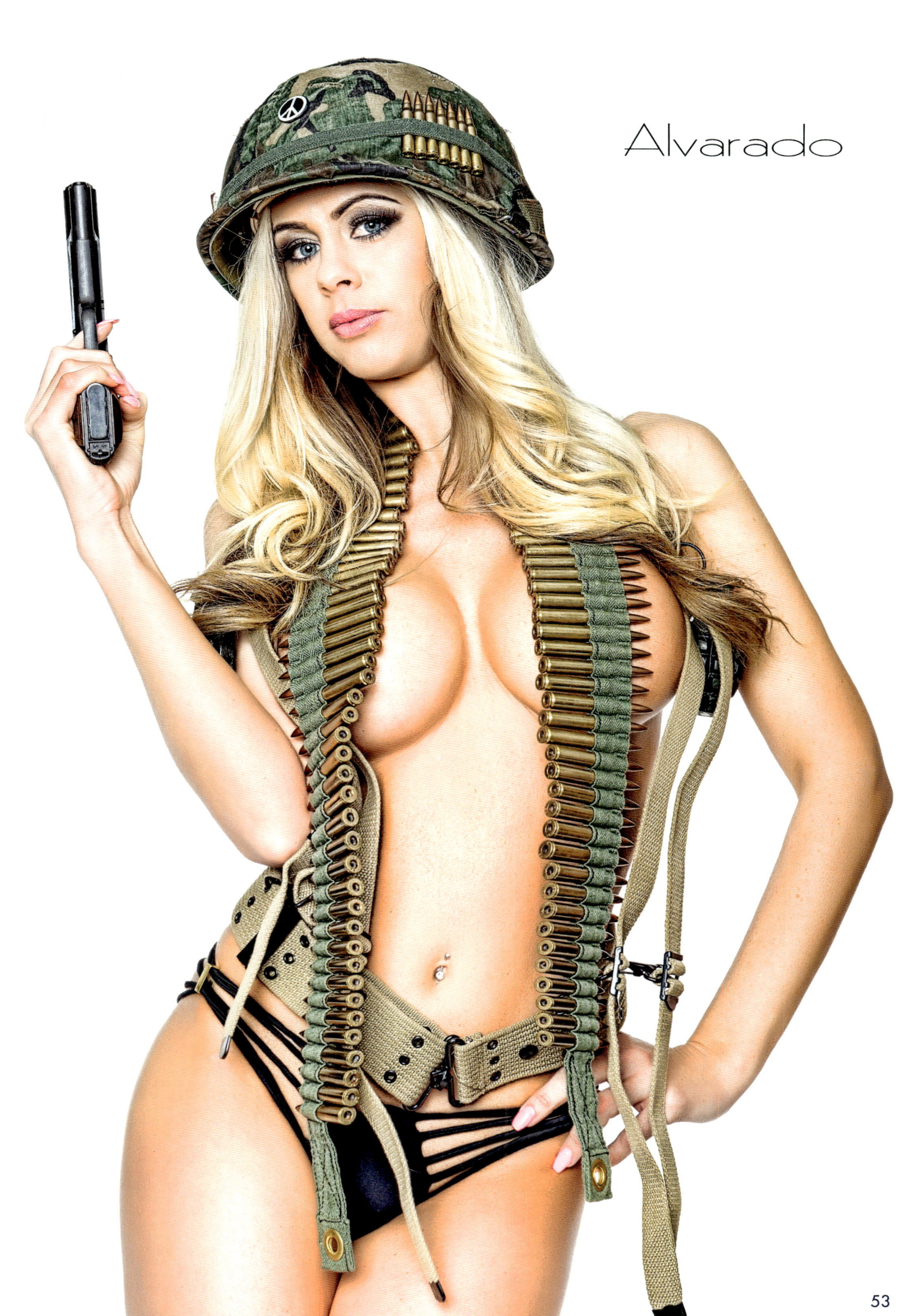

Alvarado

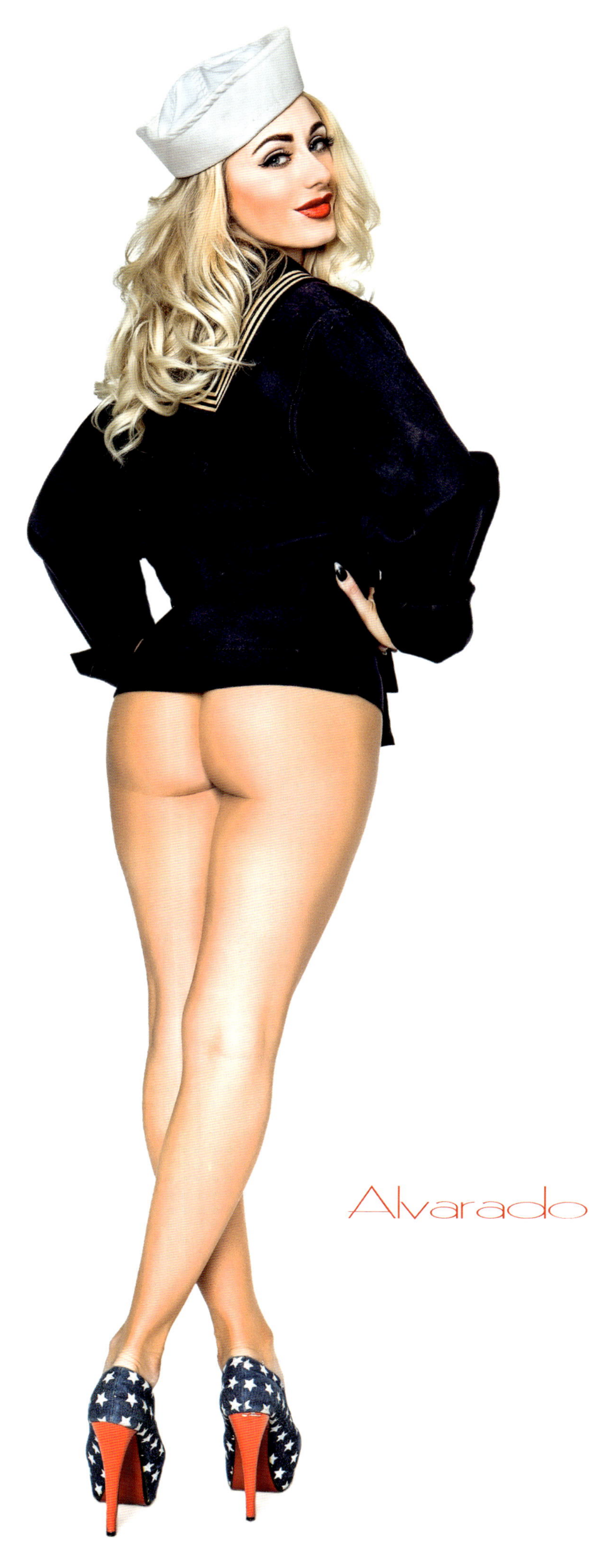

Alvarado

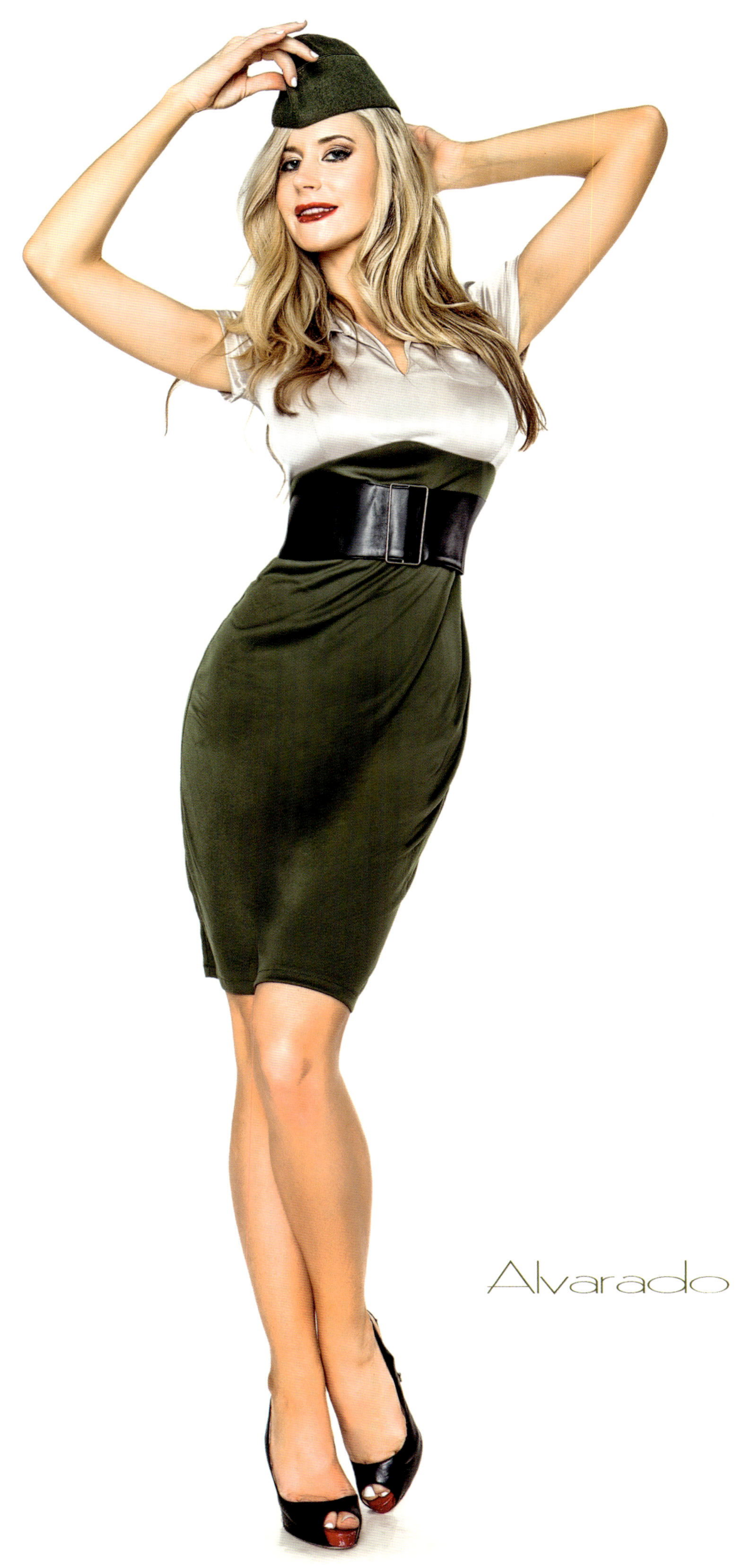

Alvarado

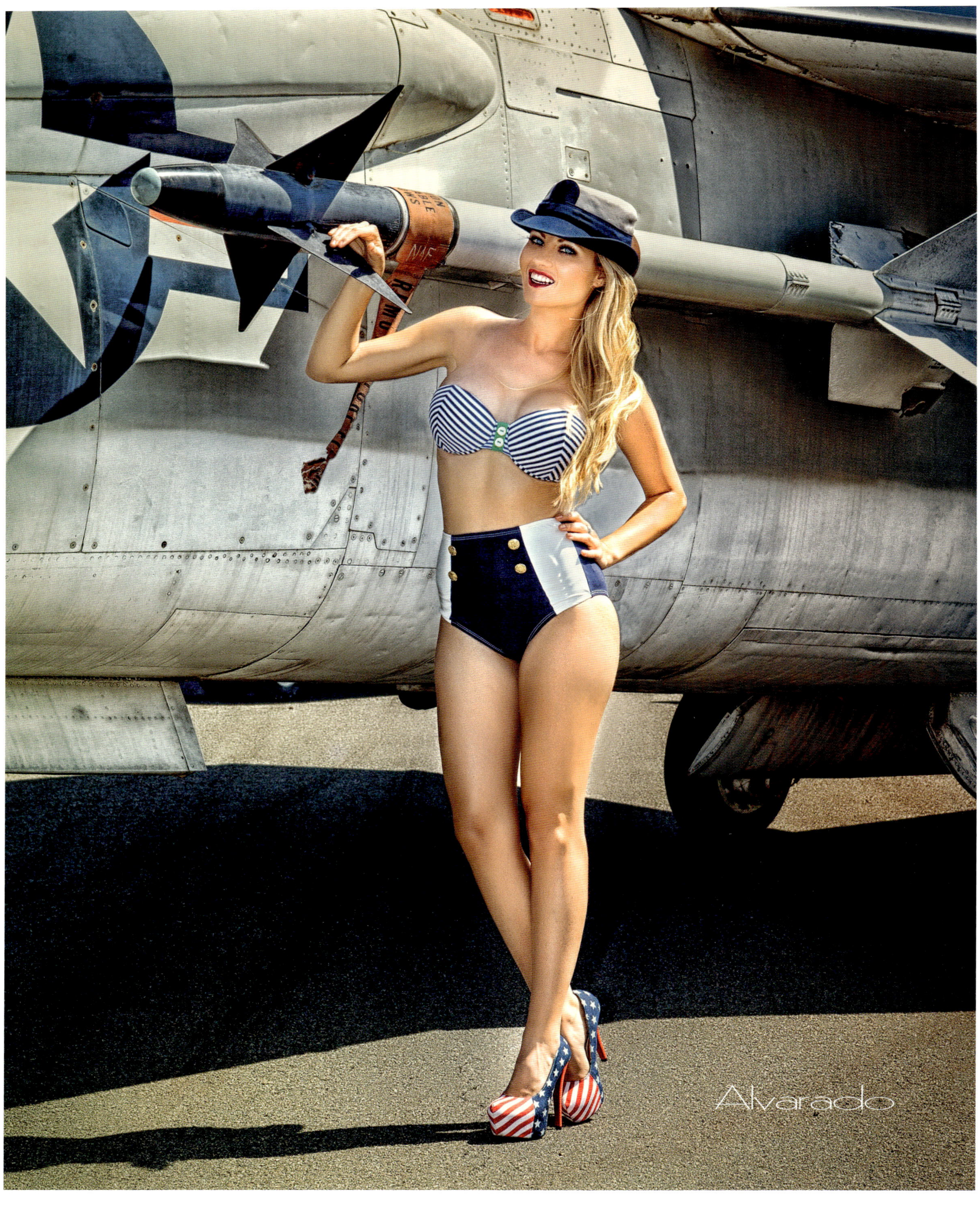
Alvarado

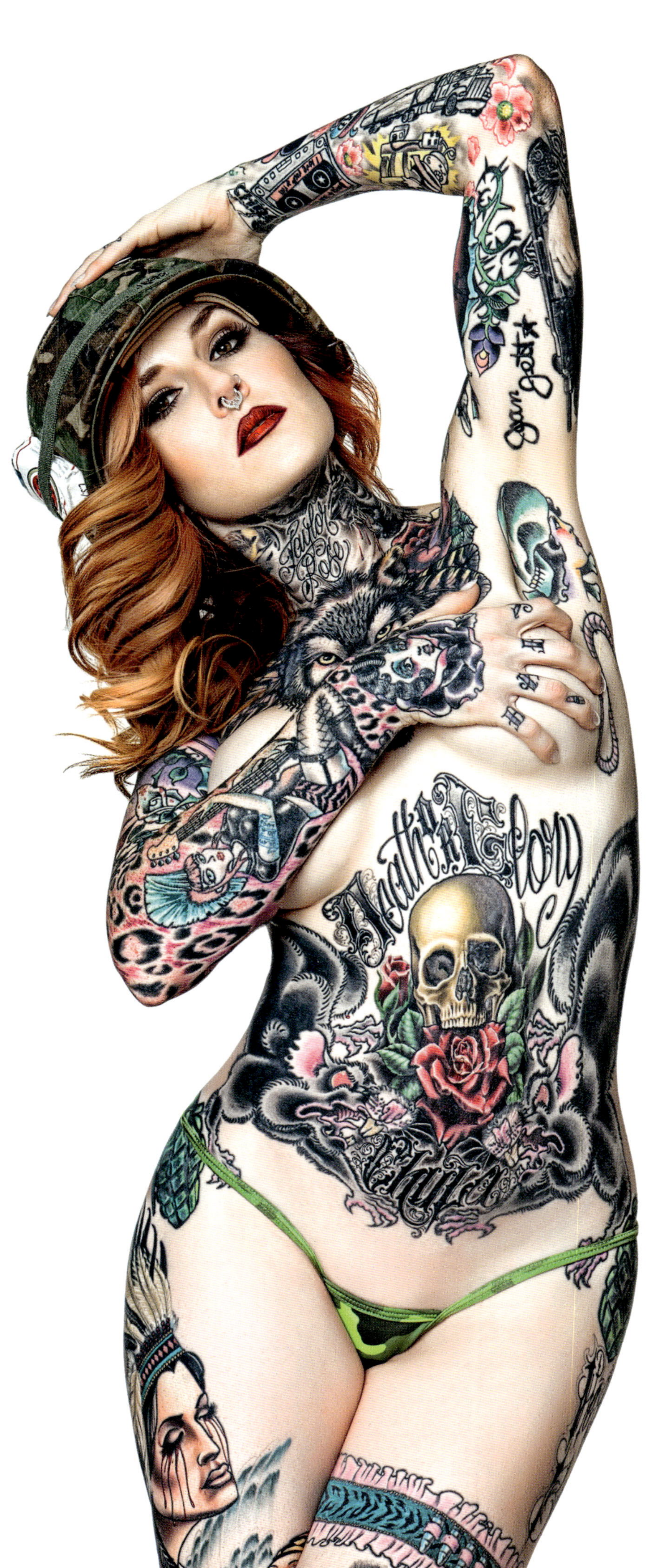

Alvarado

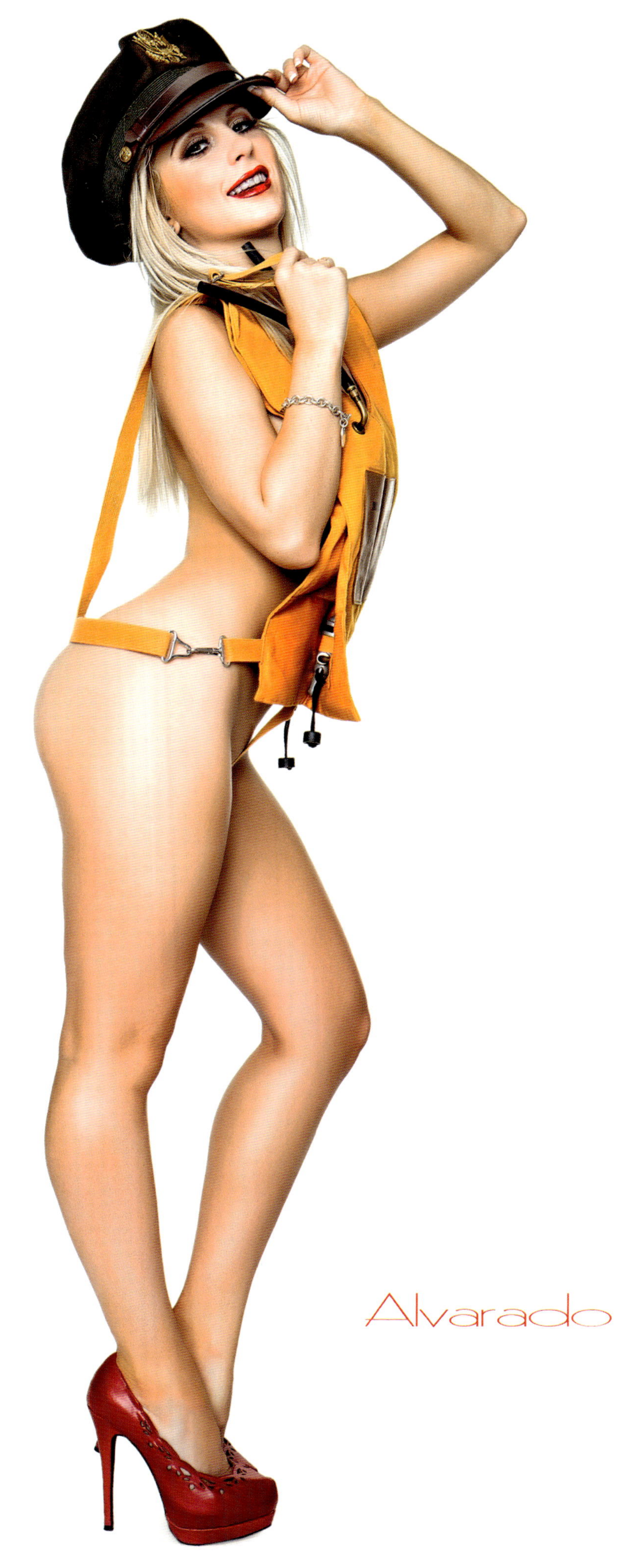

Alvarado

Alvarado

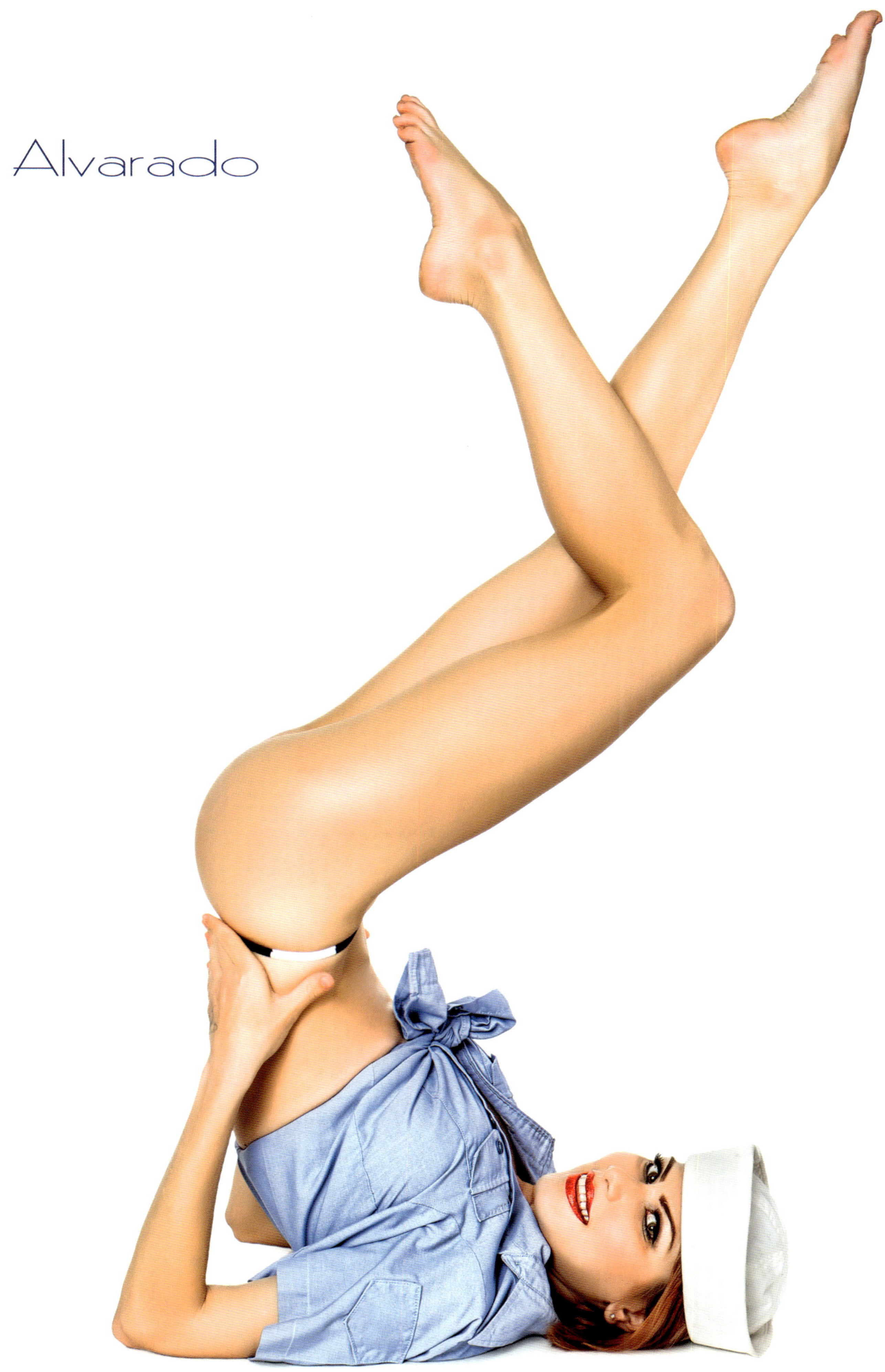

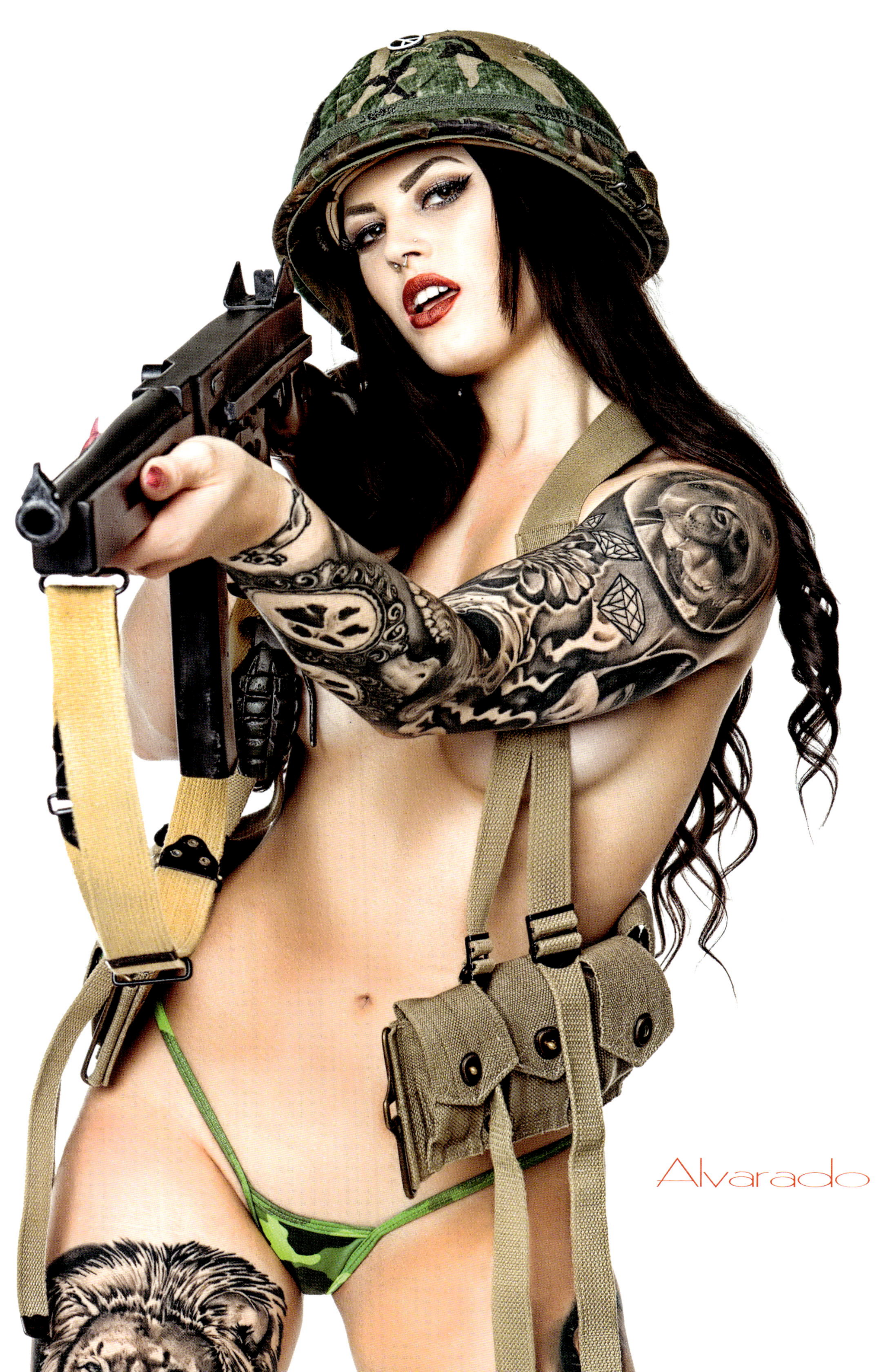

Alvarado

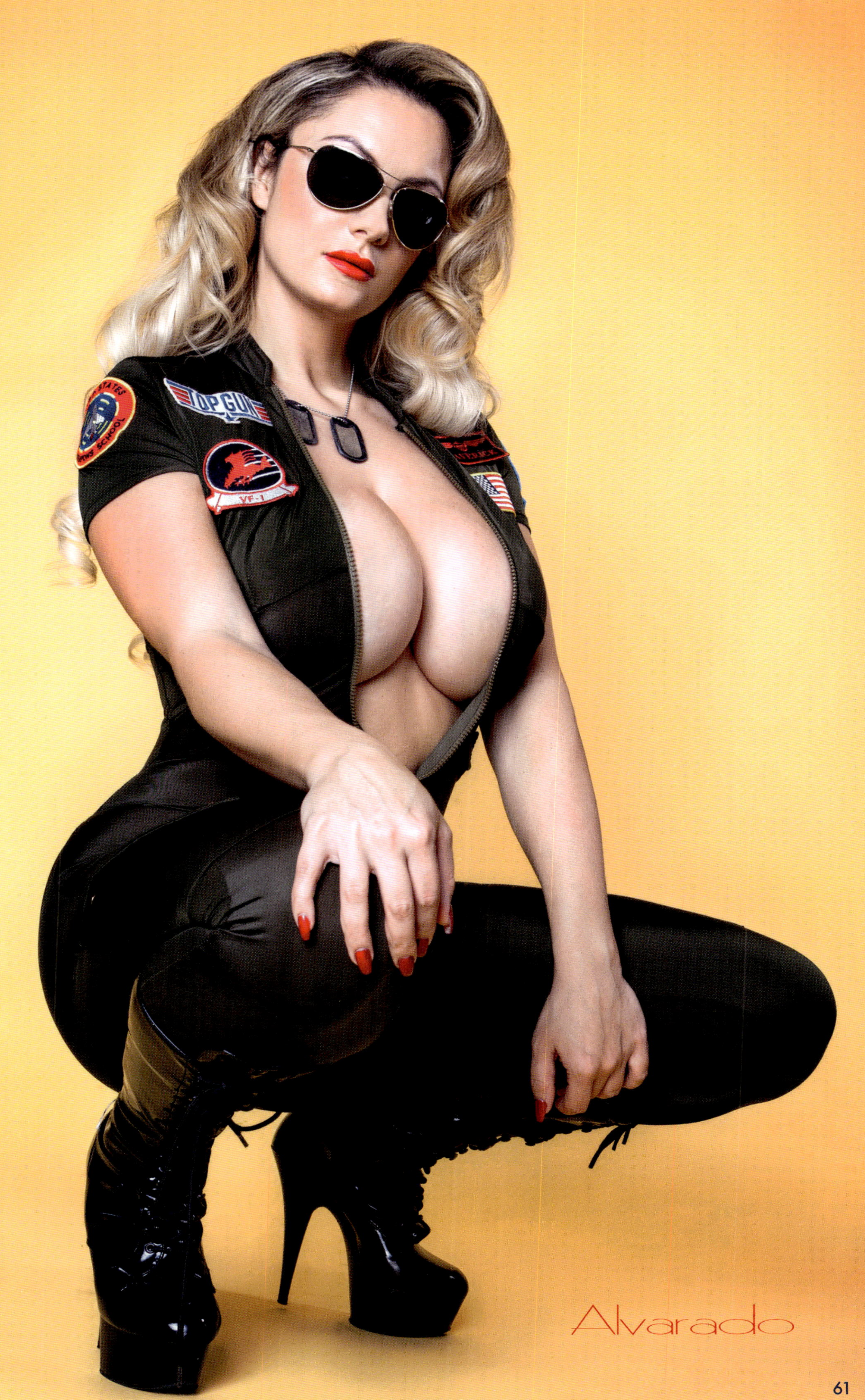

Alvarado

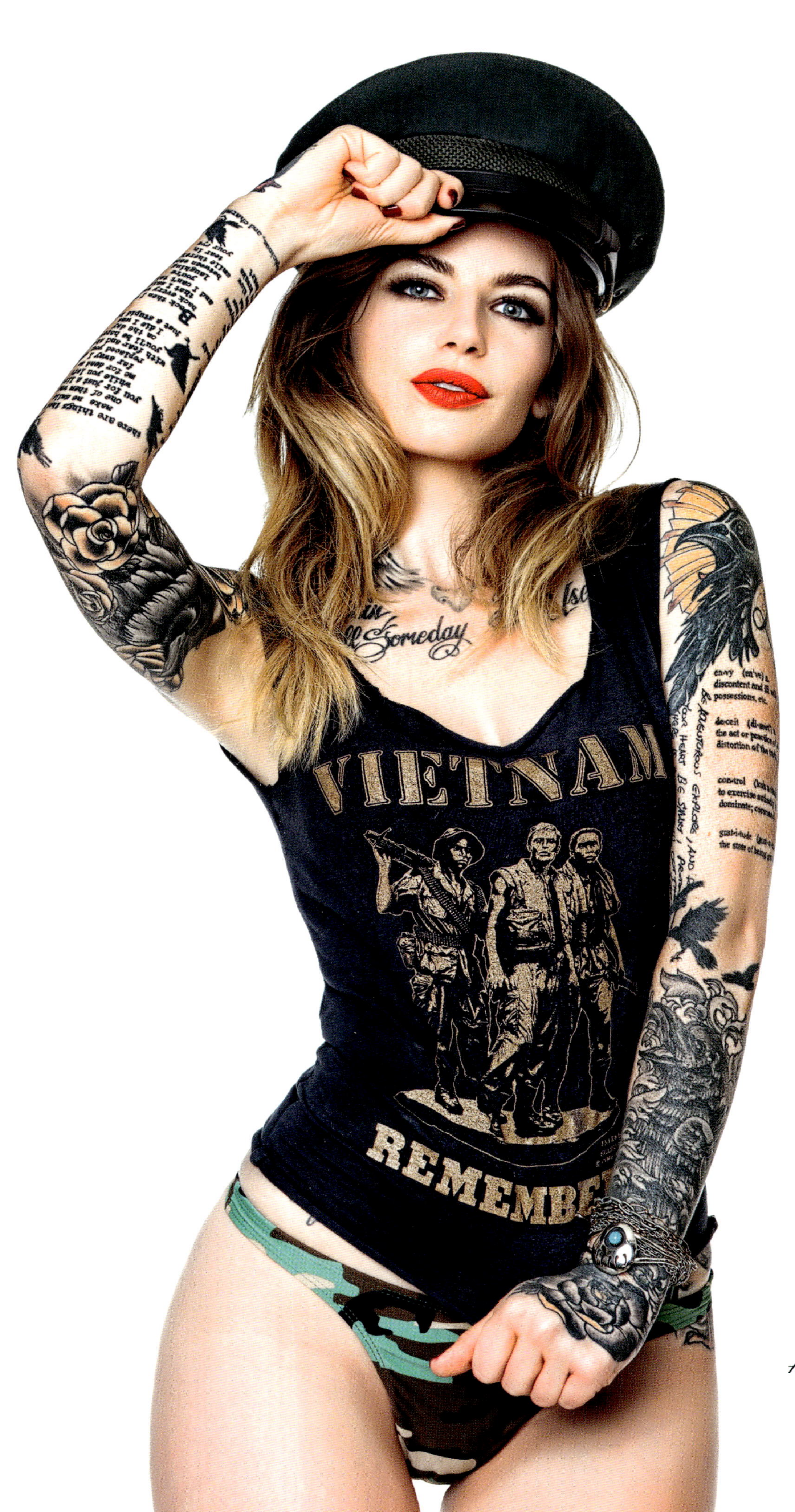

Alvarado

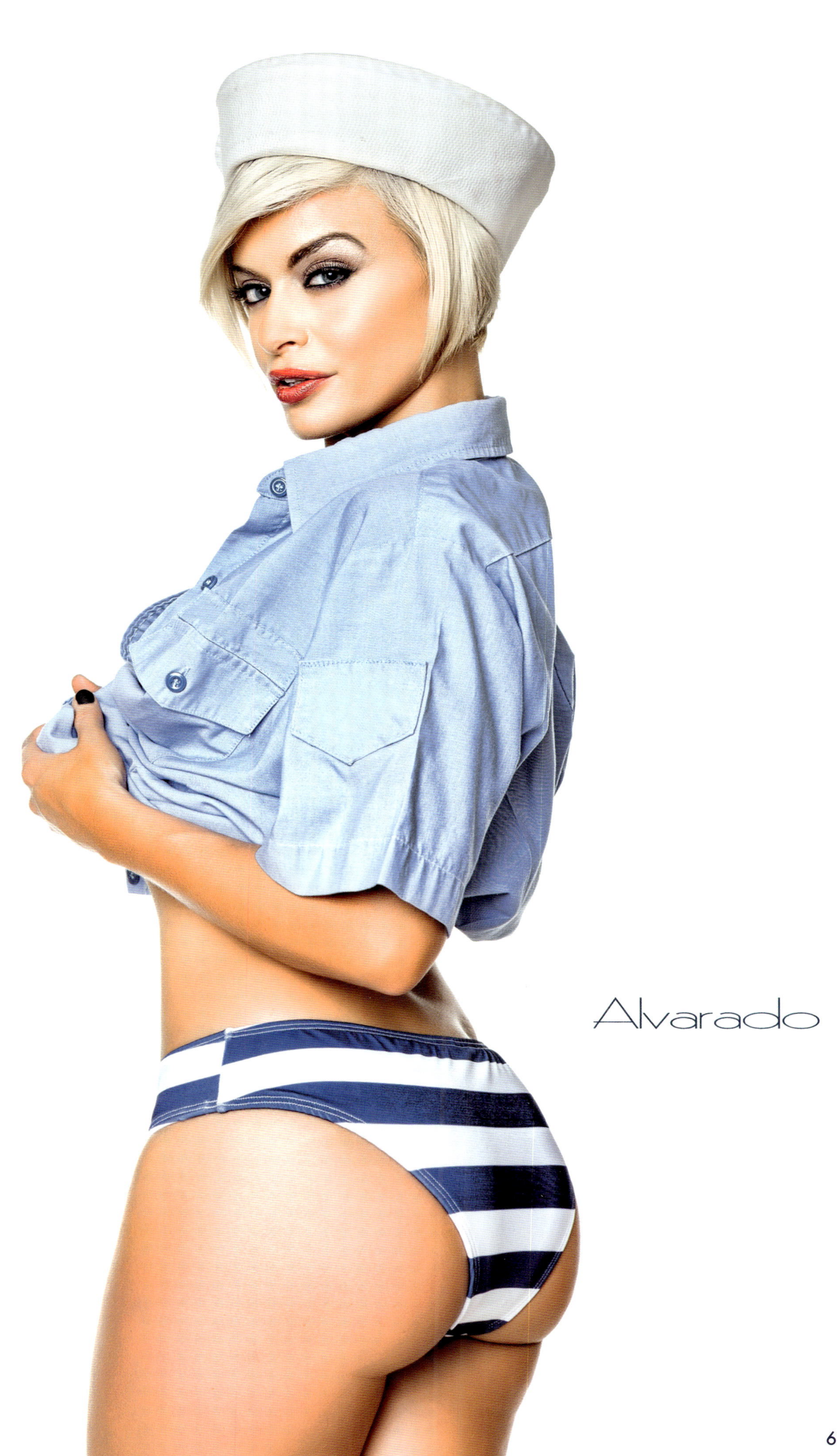

Alvarado

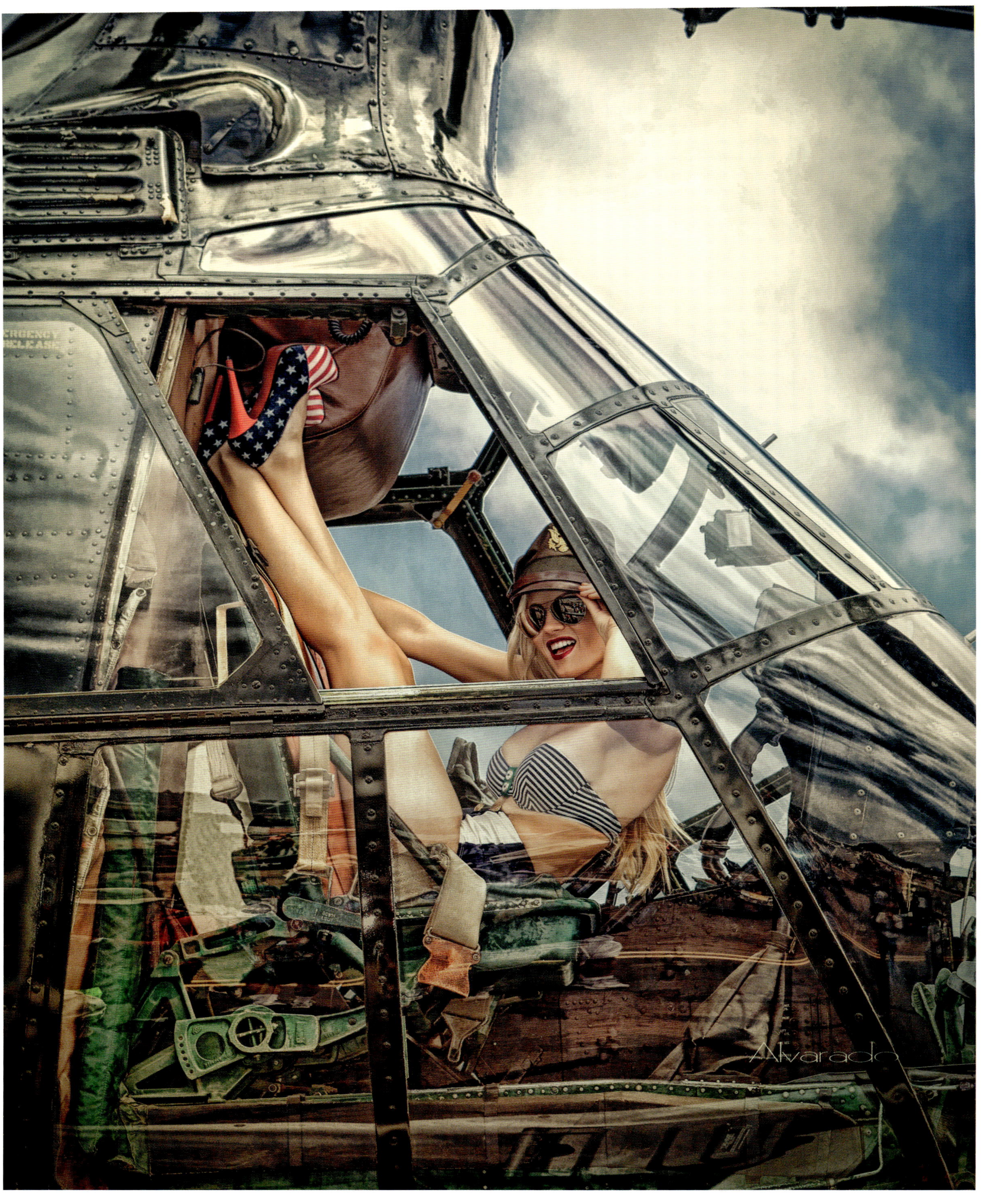
Alvarado

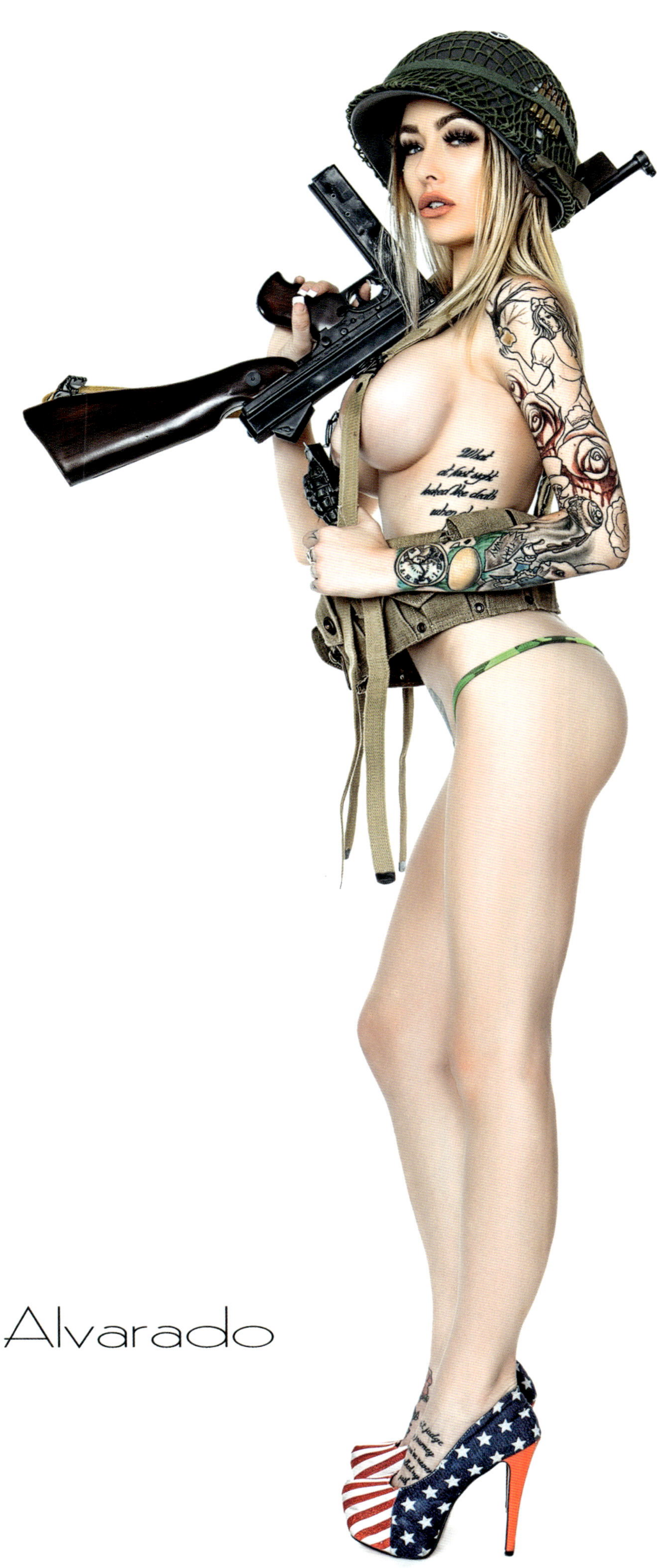

Alvarado

Alvarado

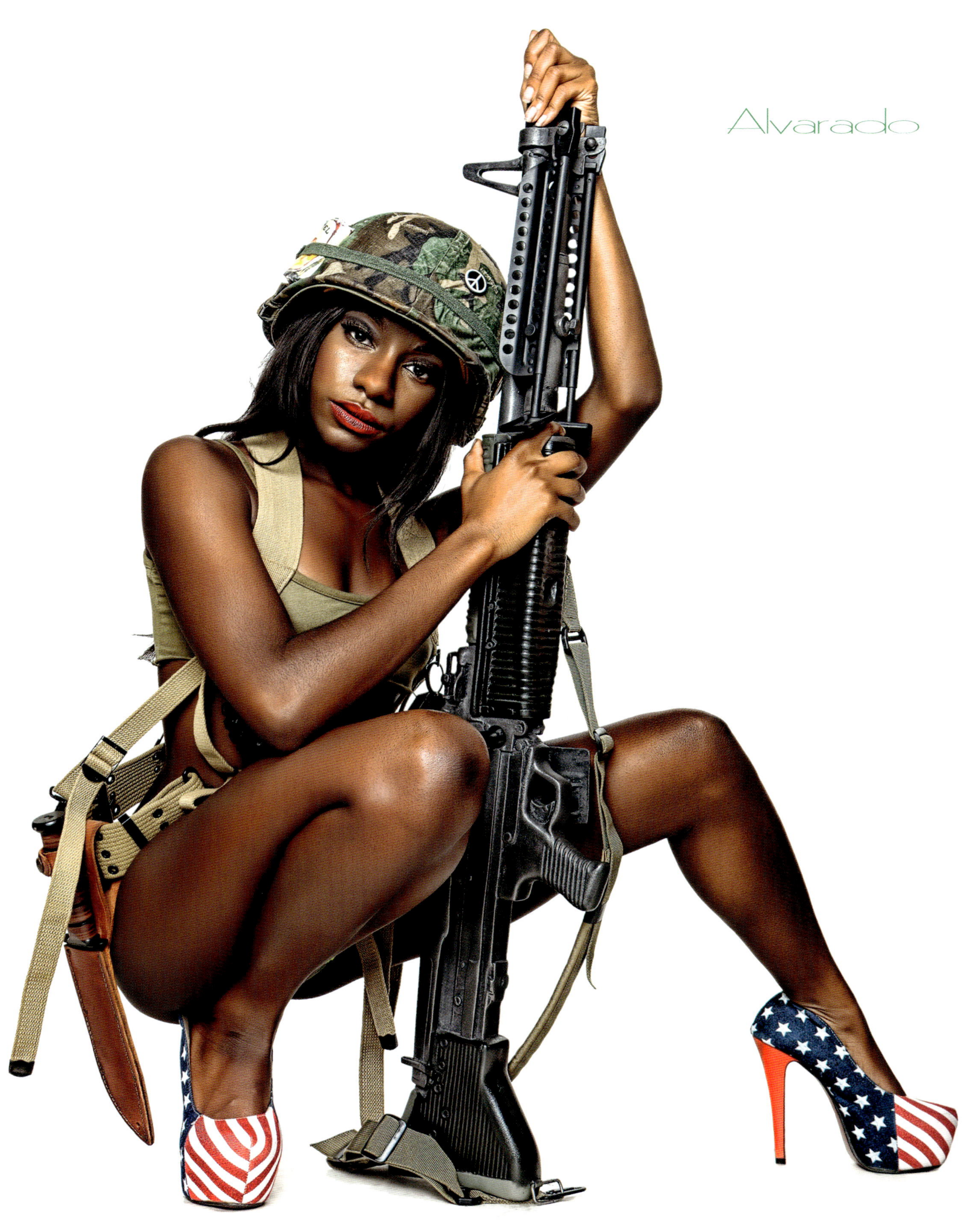

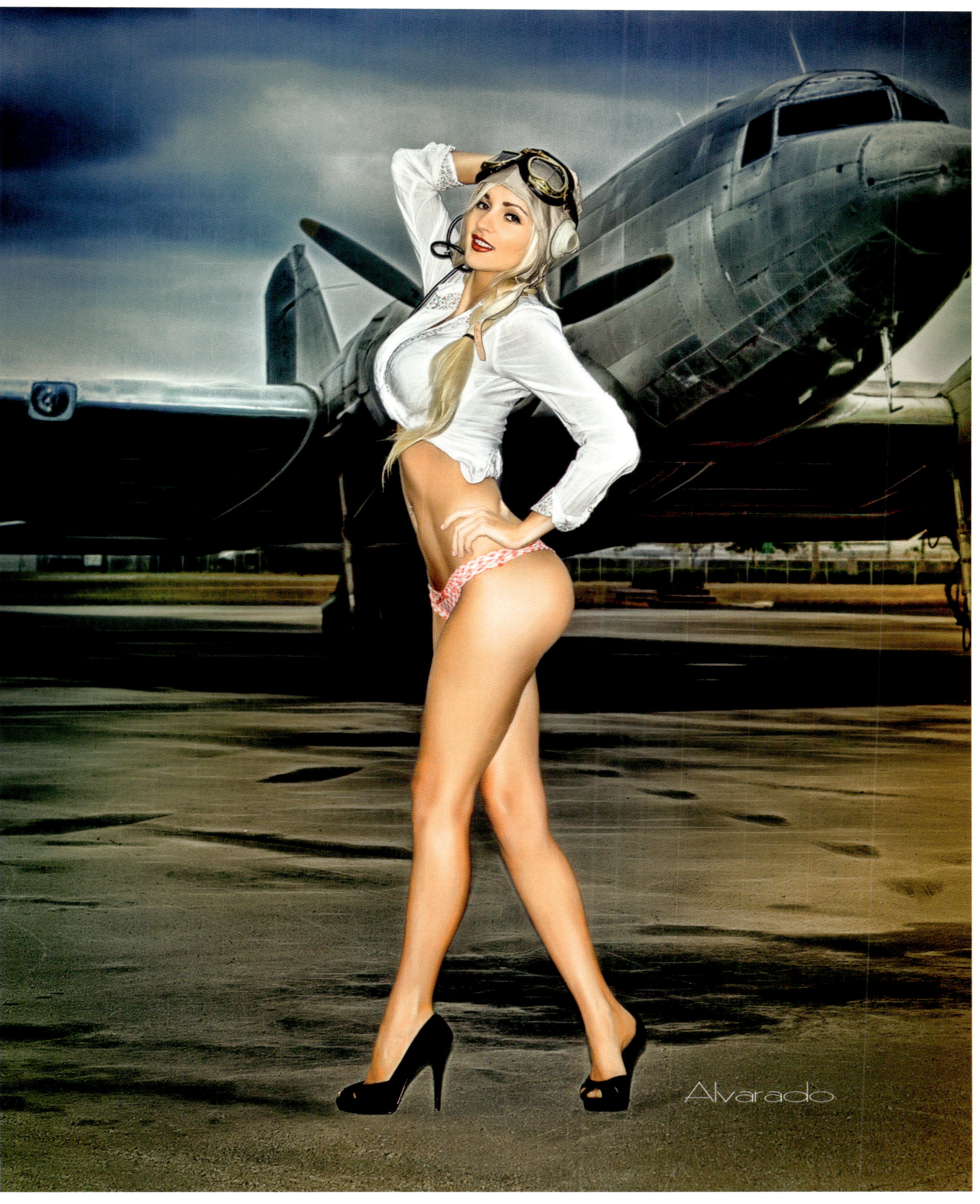
Alvarado

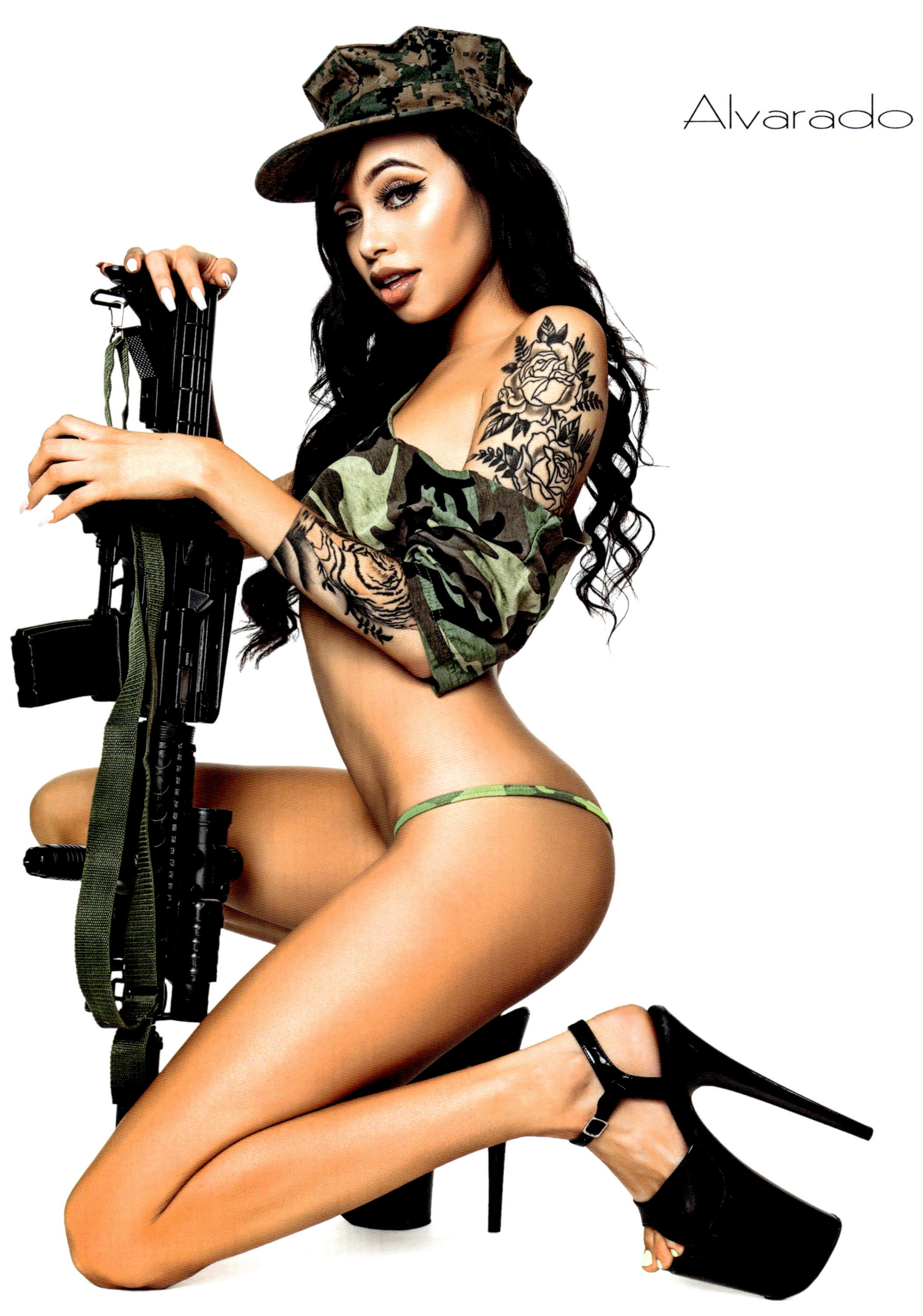

Alvarado

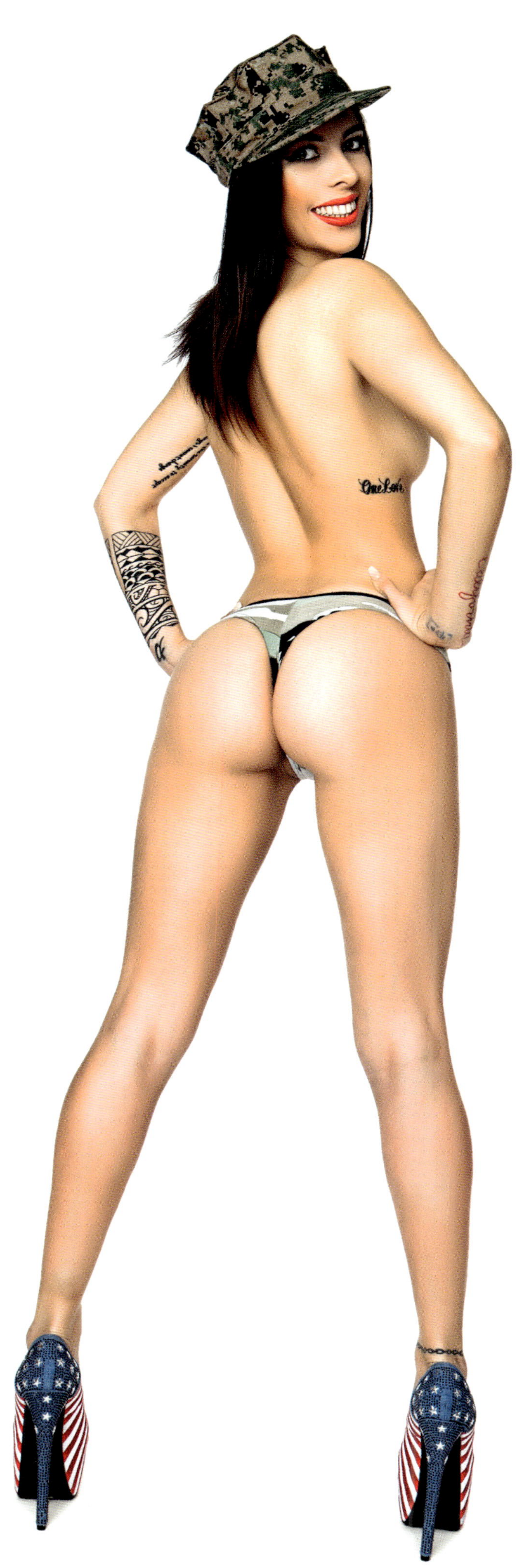

Alvarado

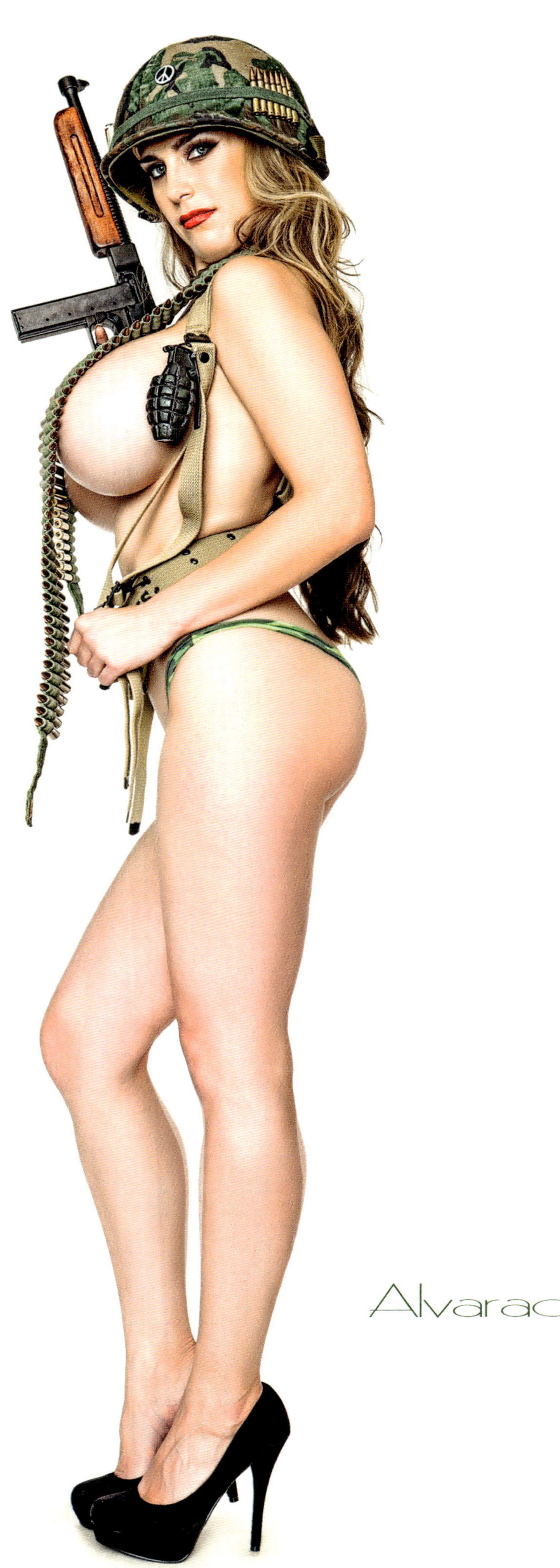

Alvarado

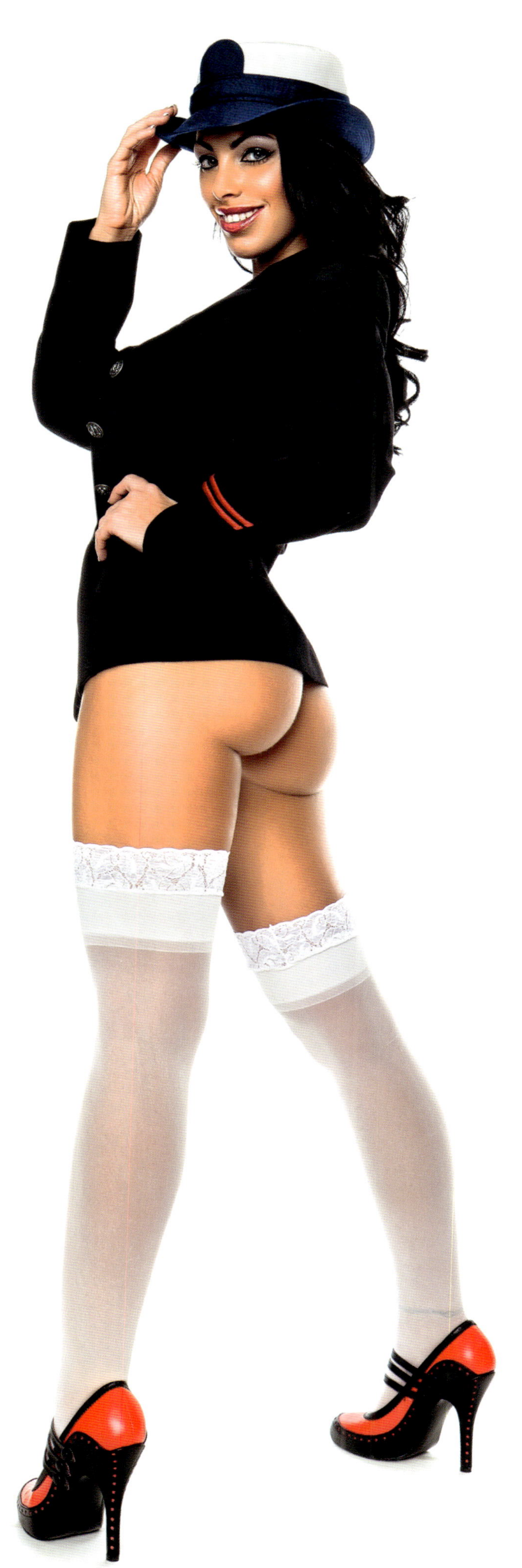

Alvarado

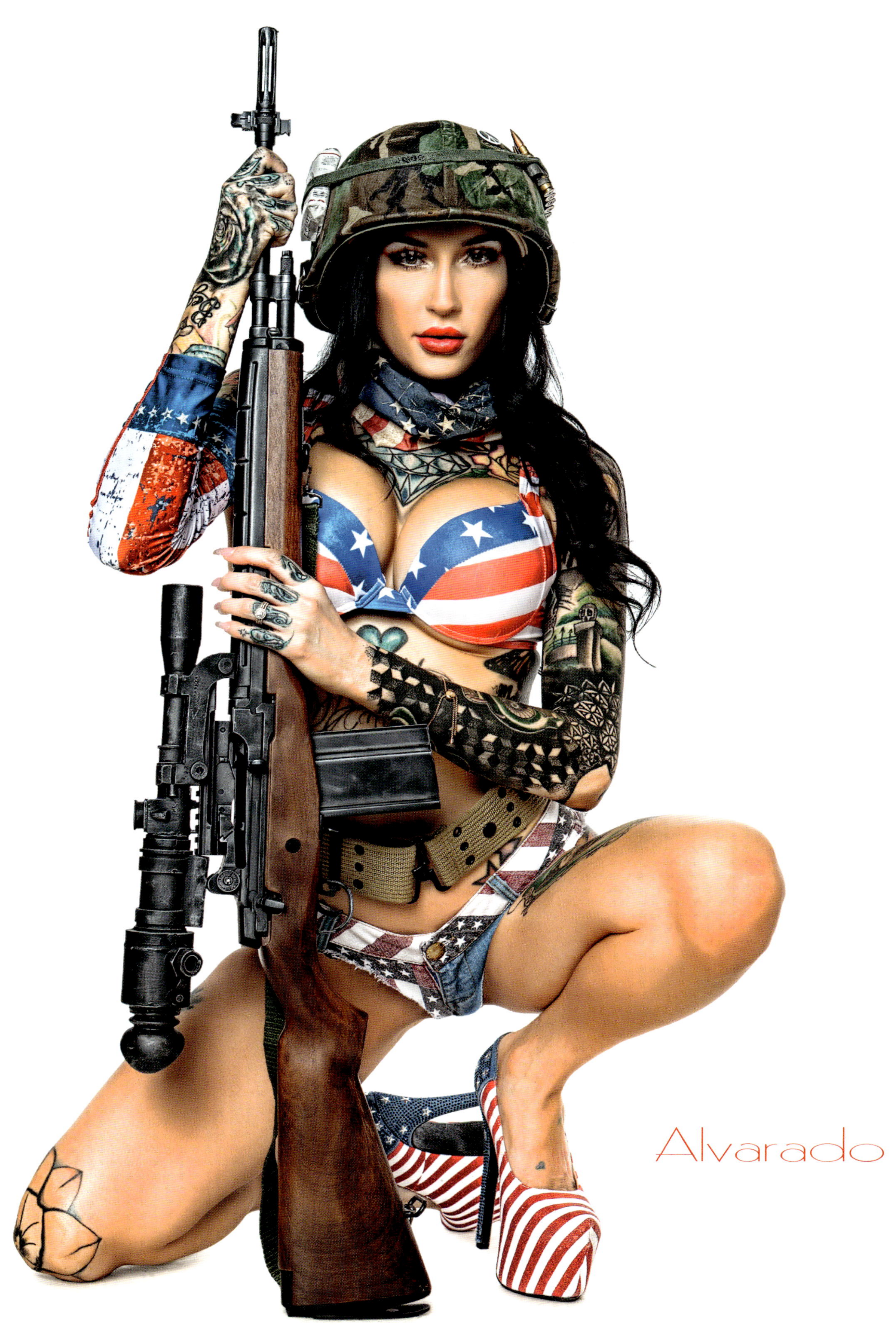

Alvarado

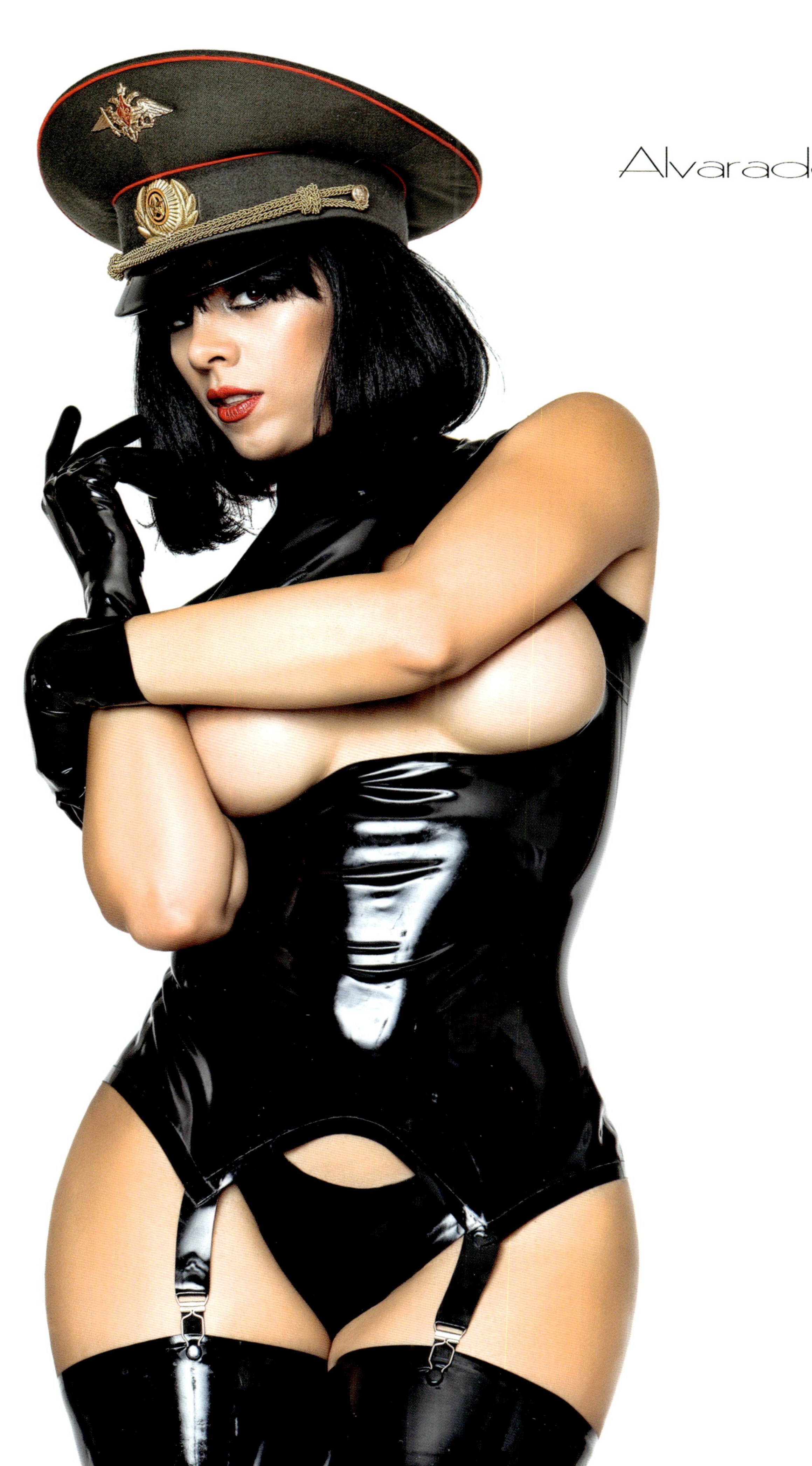

Alvarado

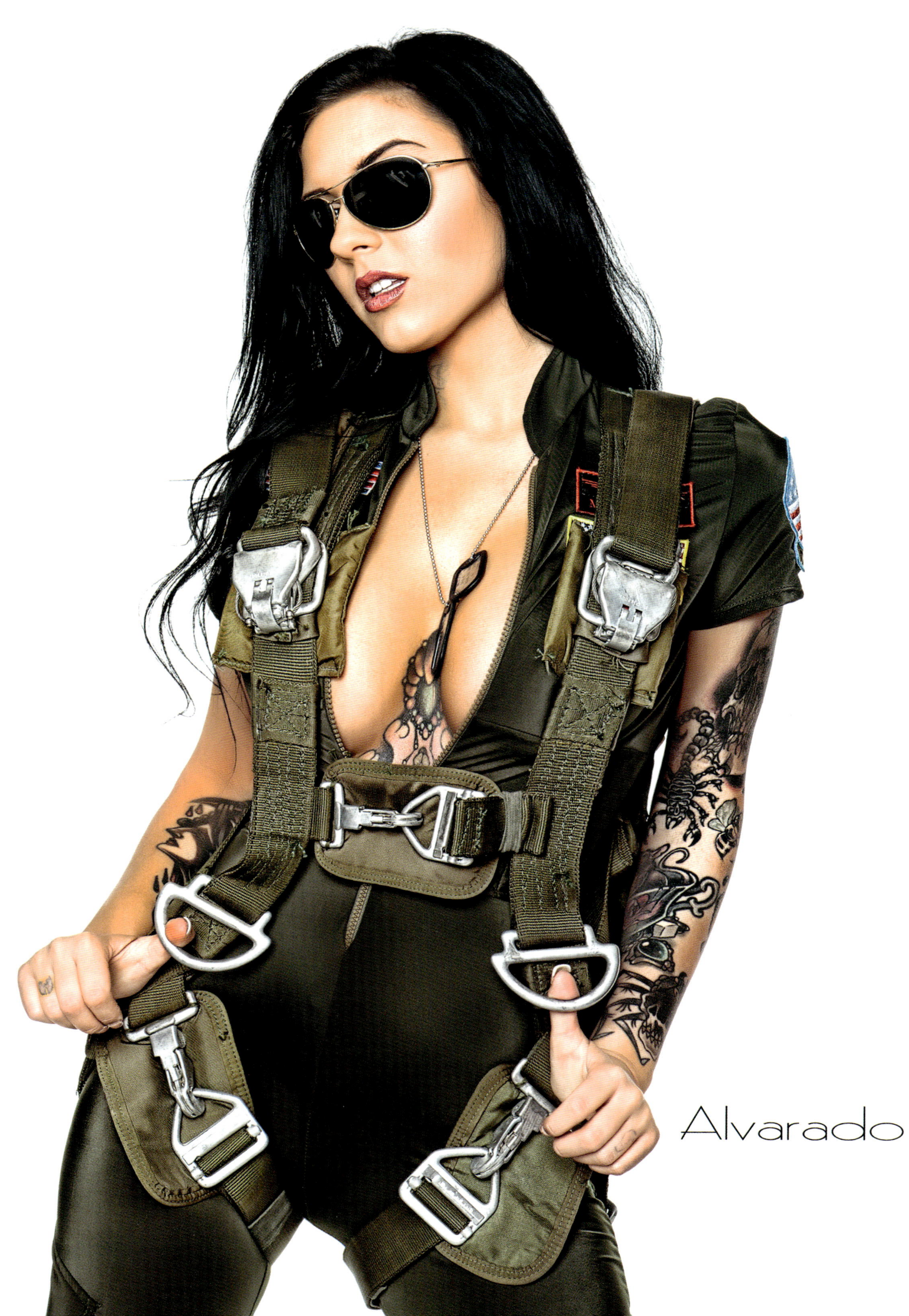

Alvarado

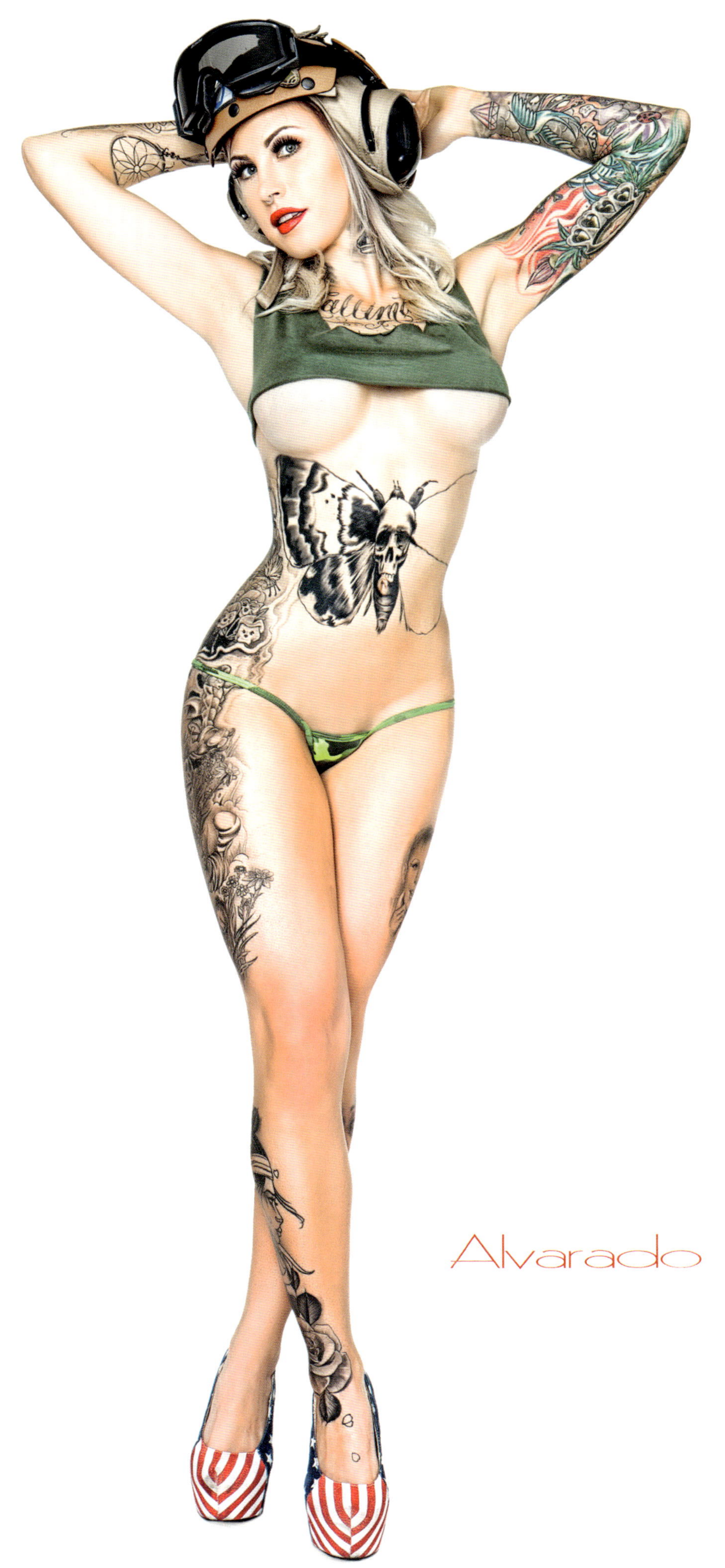

Alvarado

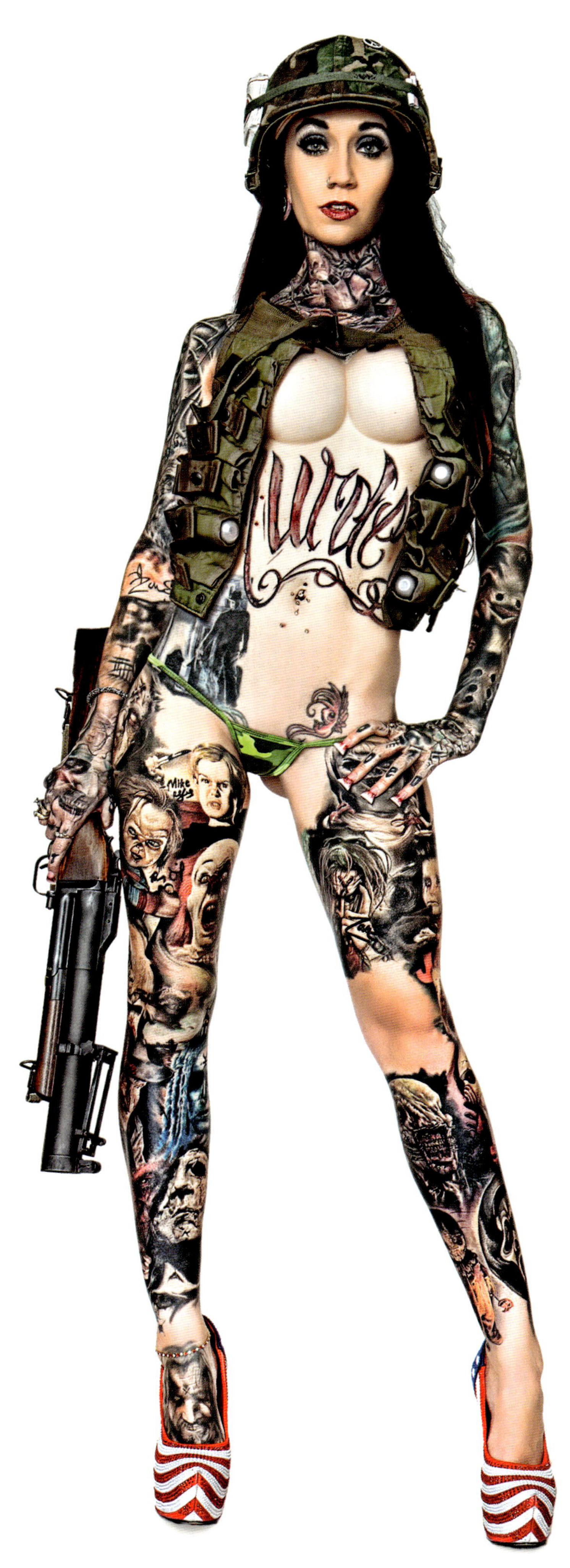

Alvarado

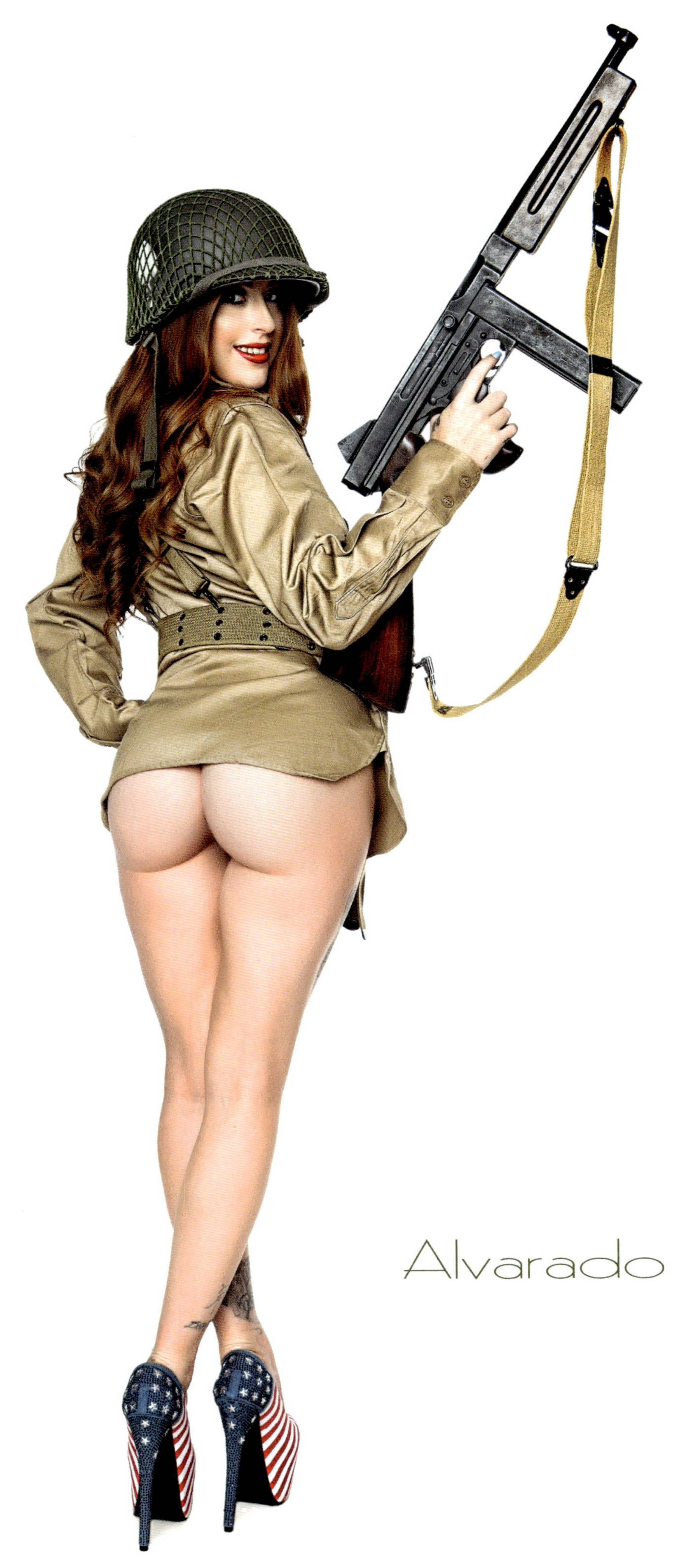

Alvarado

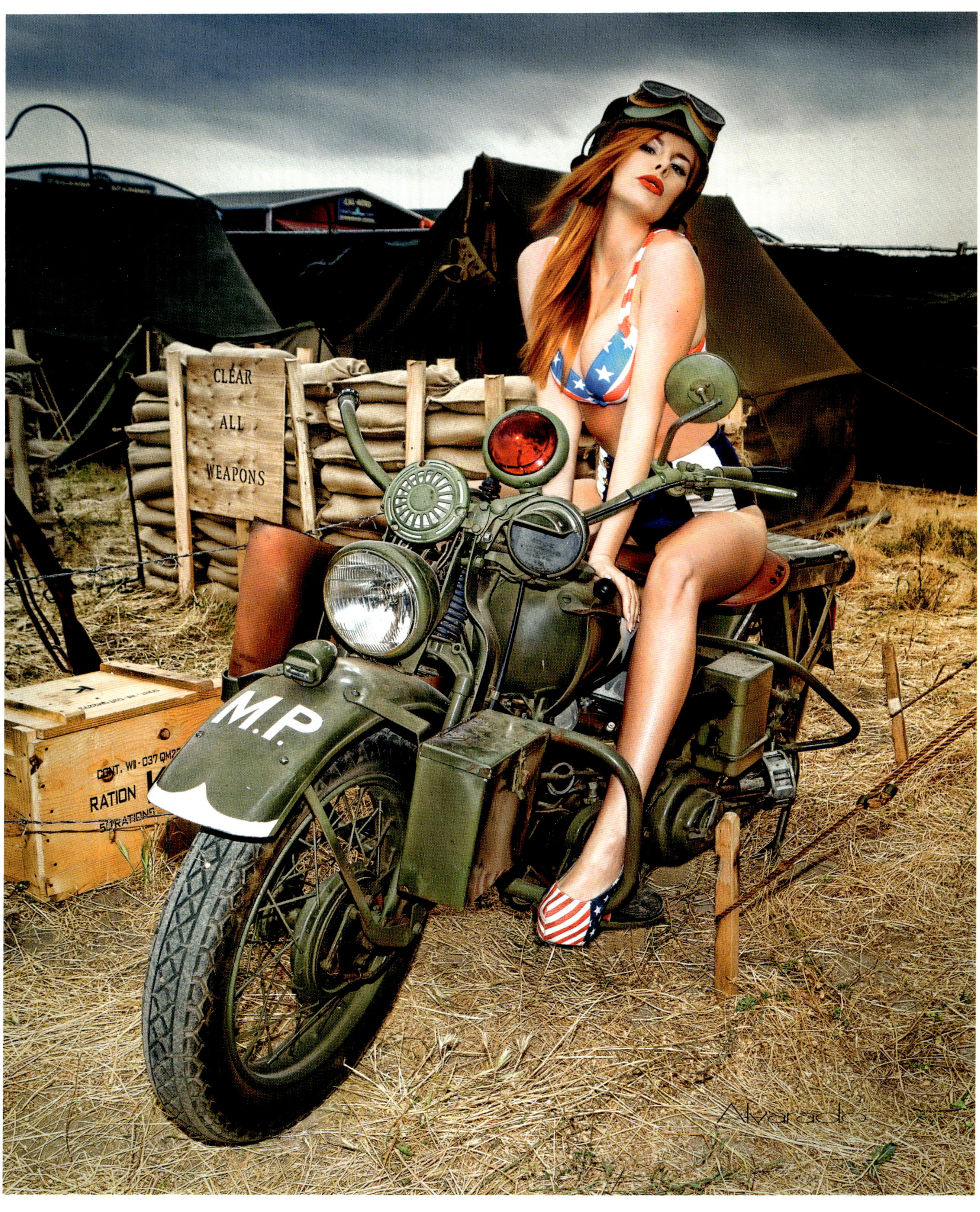
CLEAR
ALL
WEAPONS
M.P
RATION
Alvarado

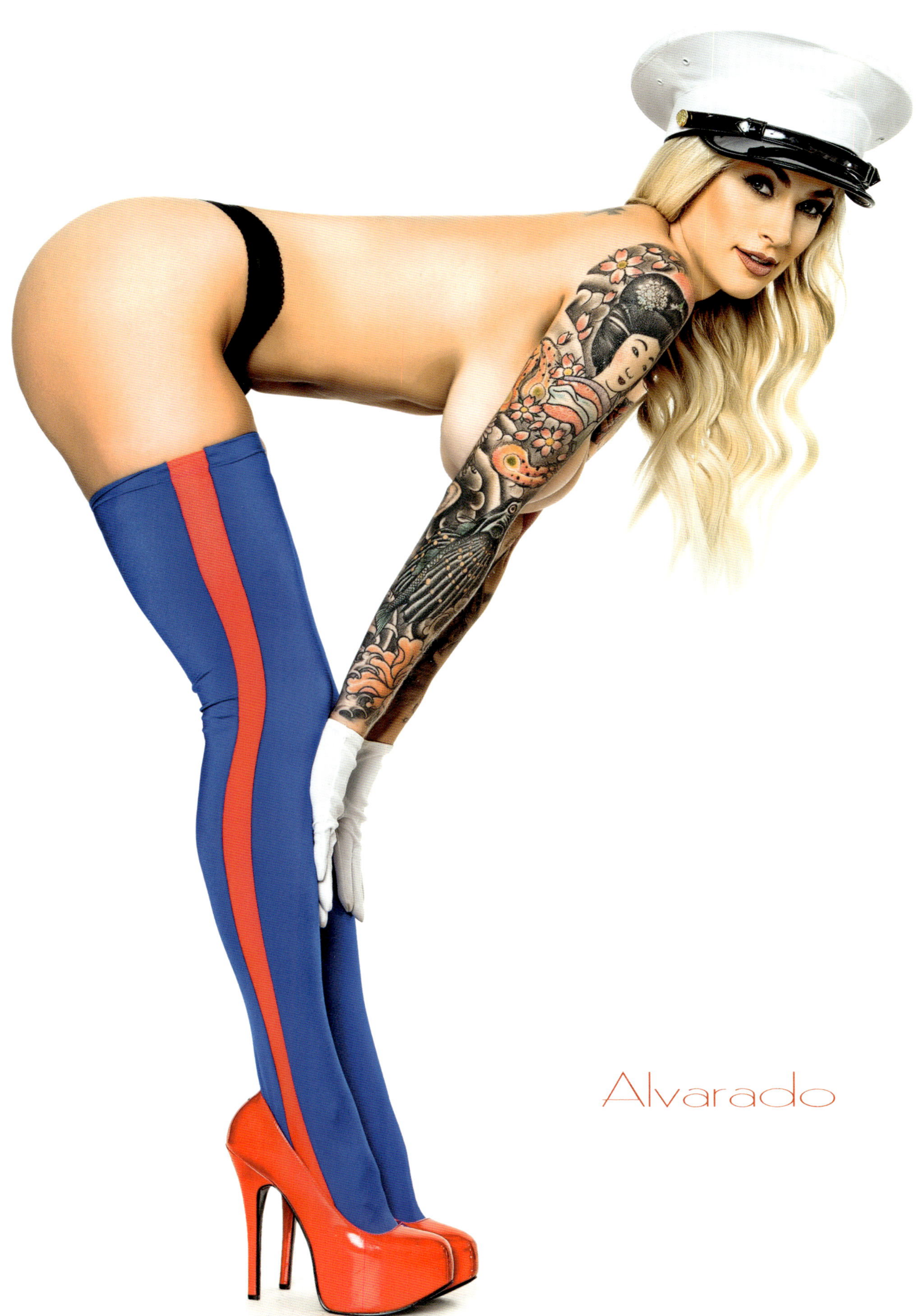

Alvarado

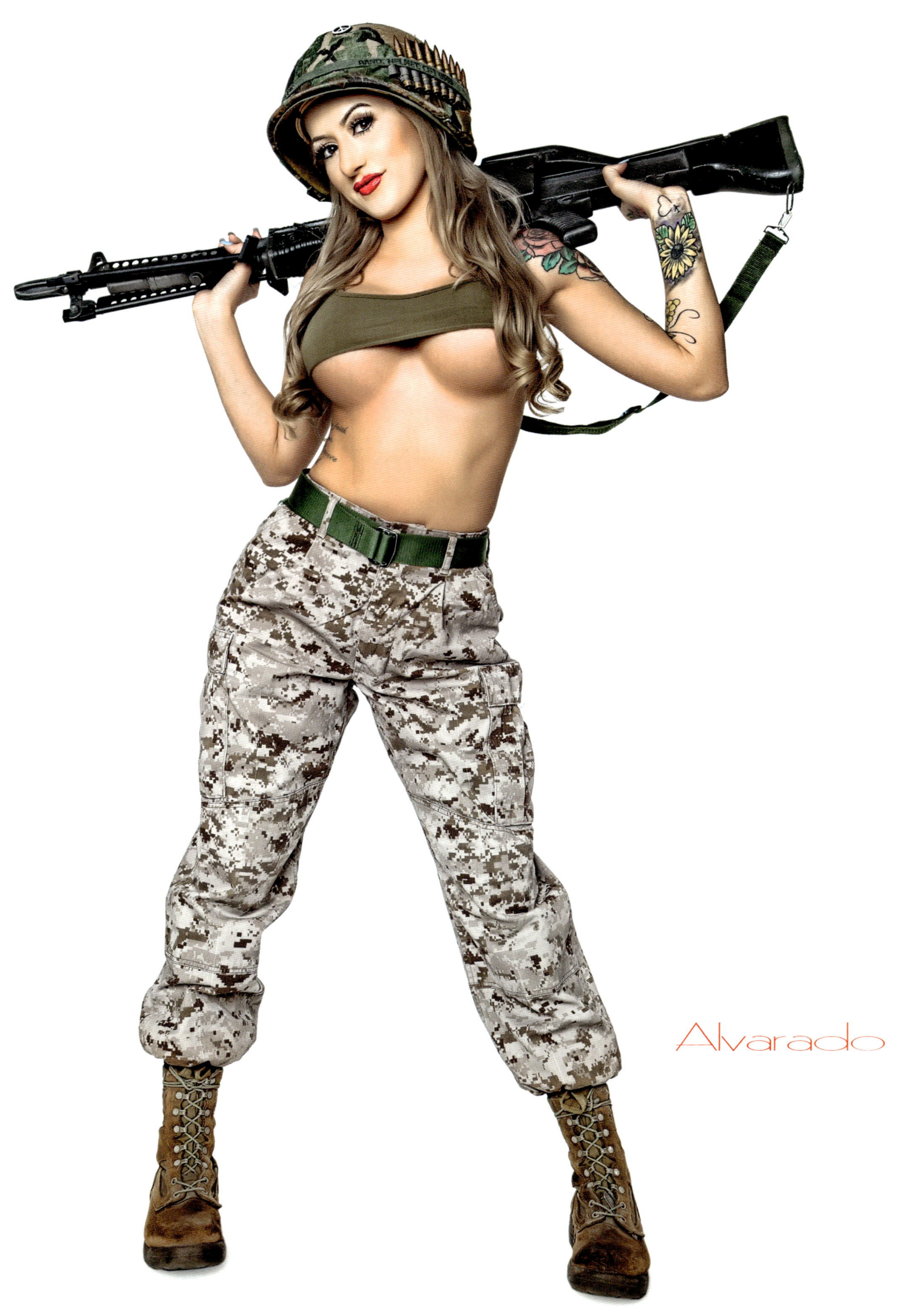

Alvarado

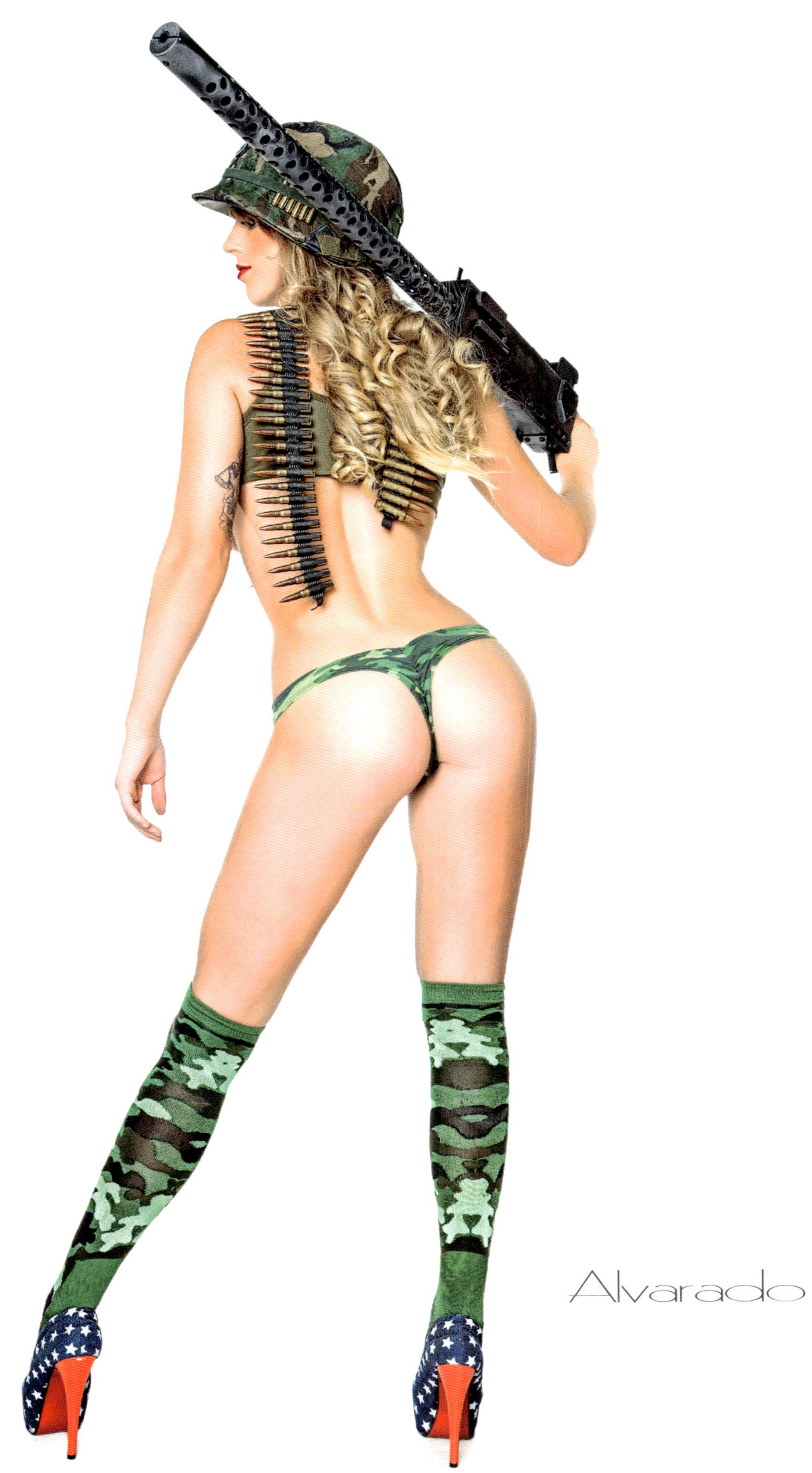
Alvarado

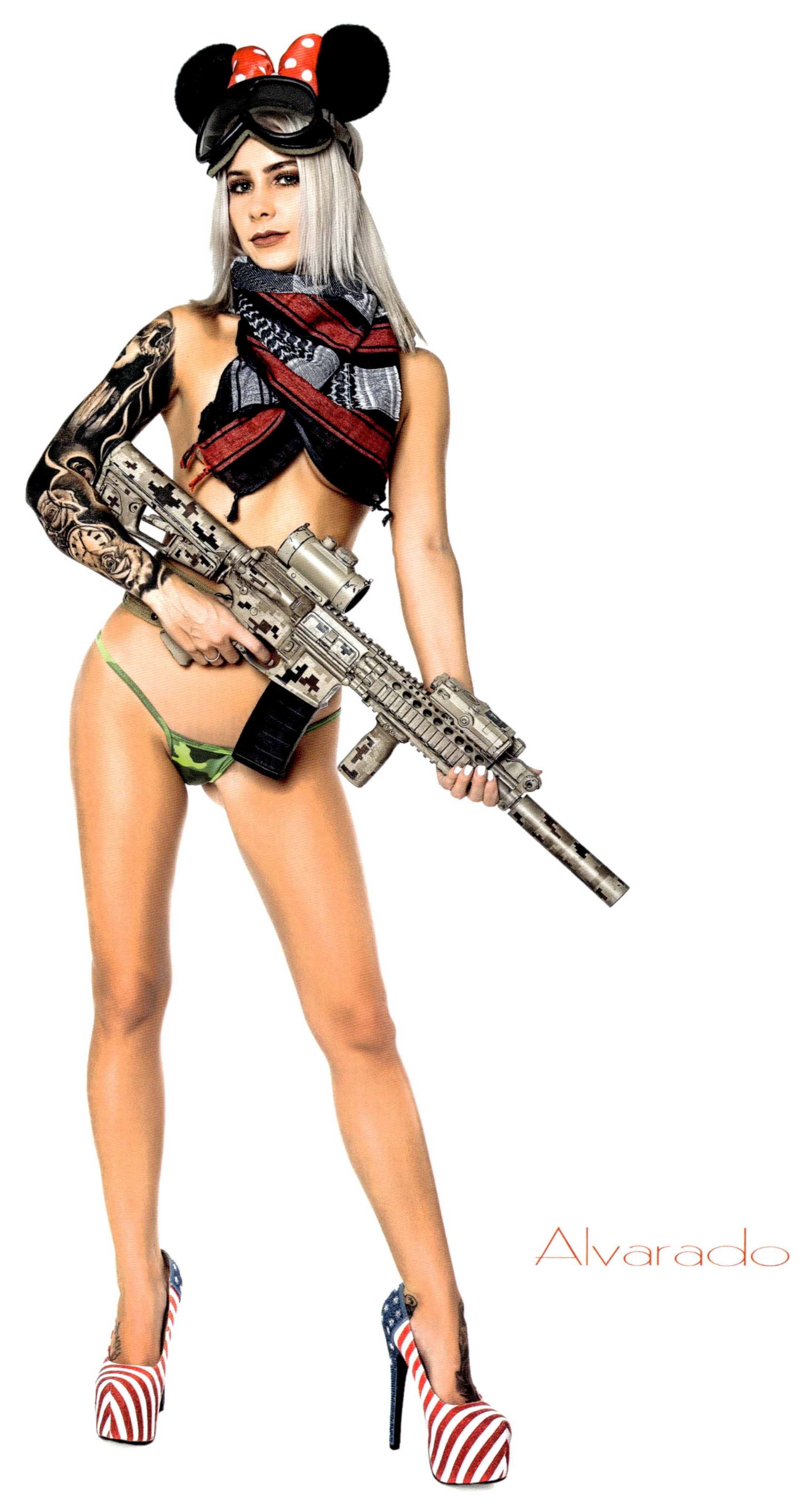

Alvarado

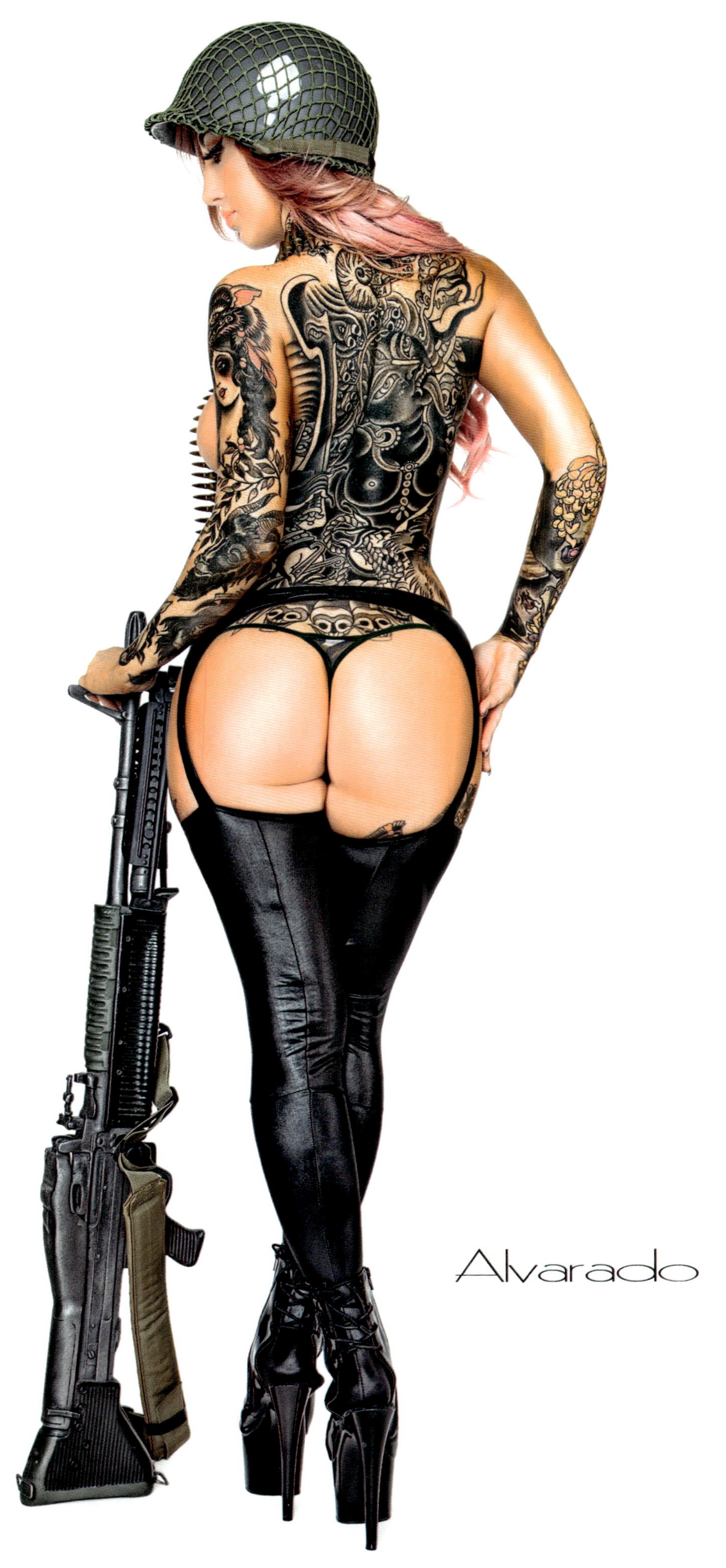

Alvarado

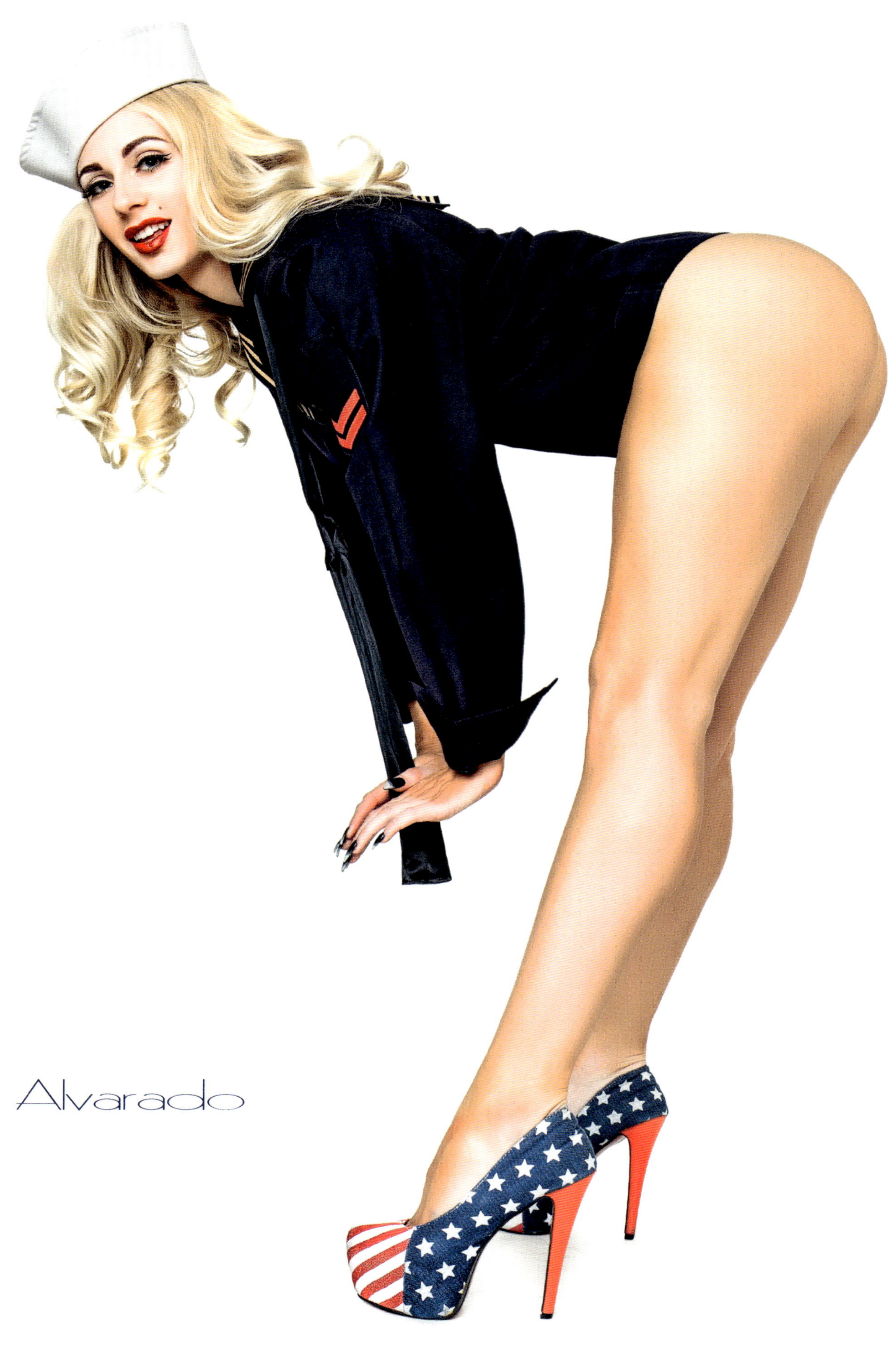

Alvarado

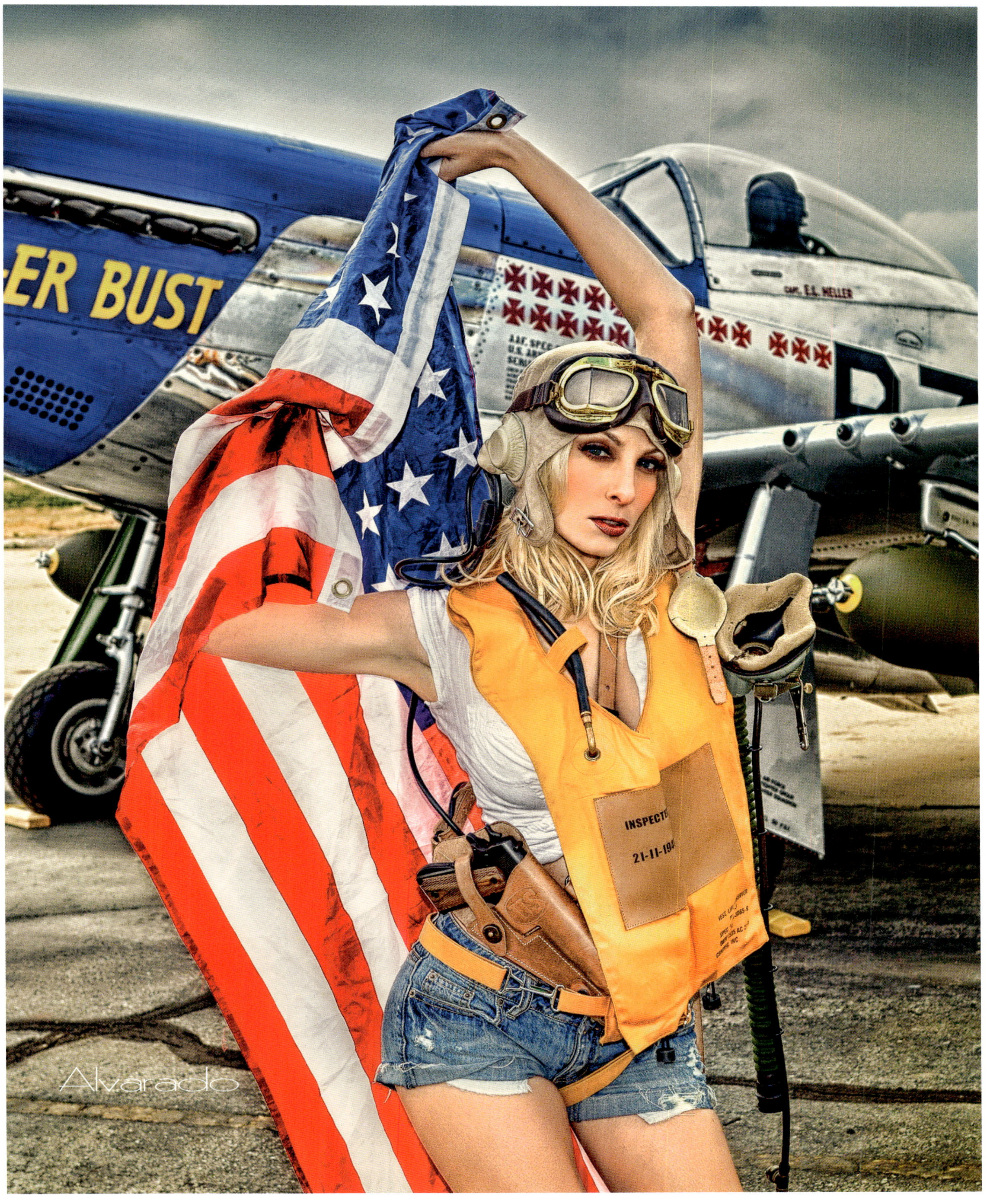
ER BUST
Alvarado

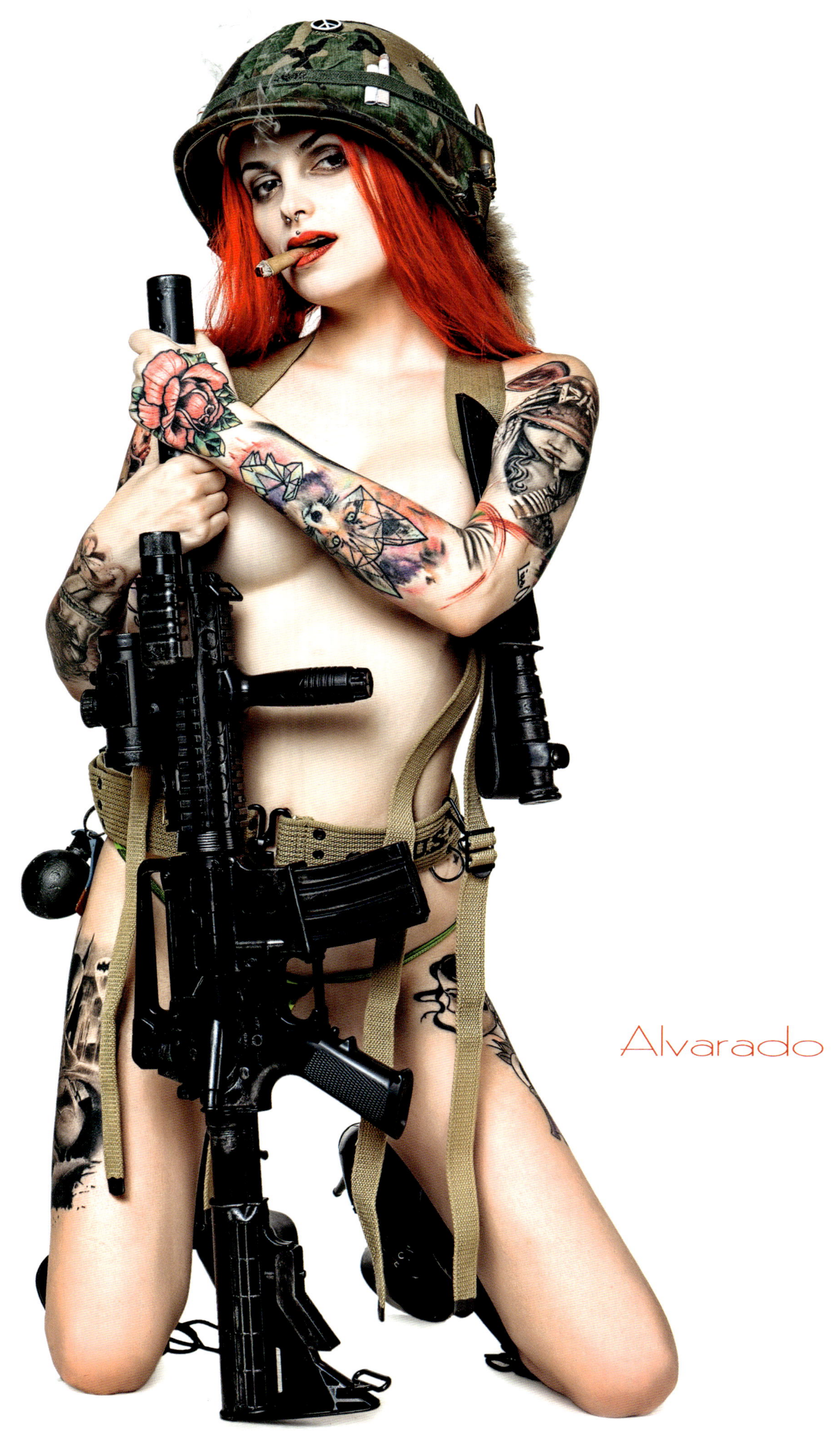

Alvarado

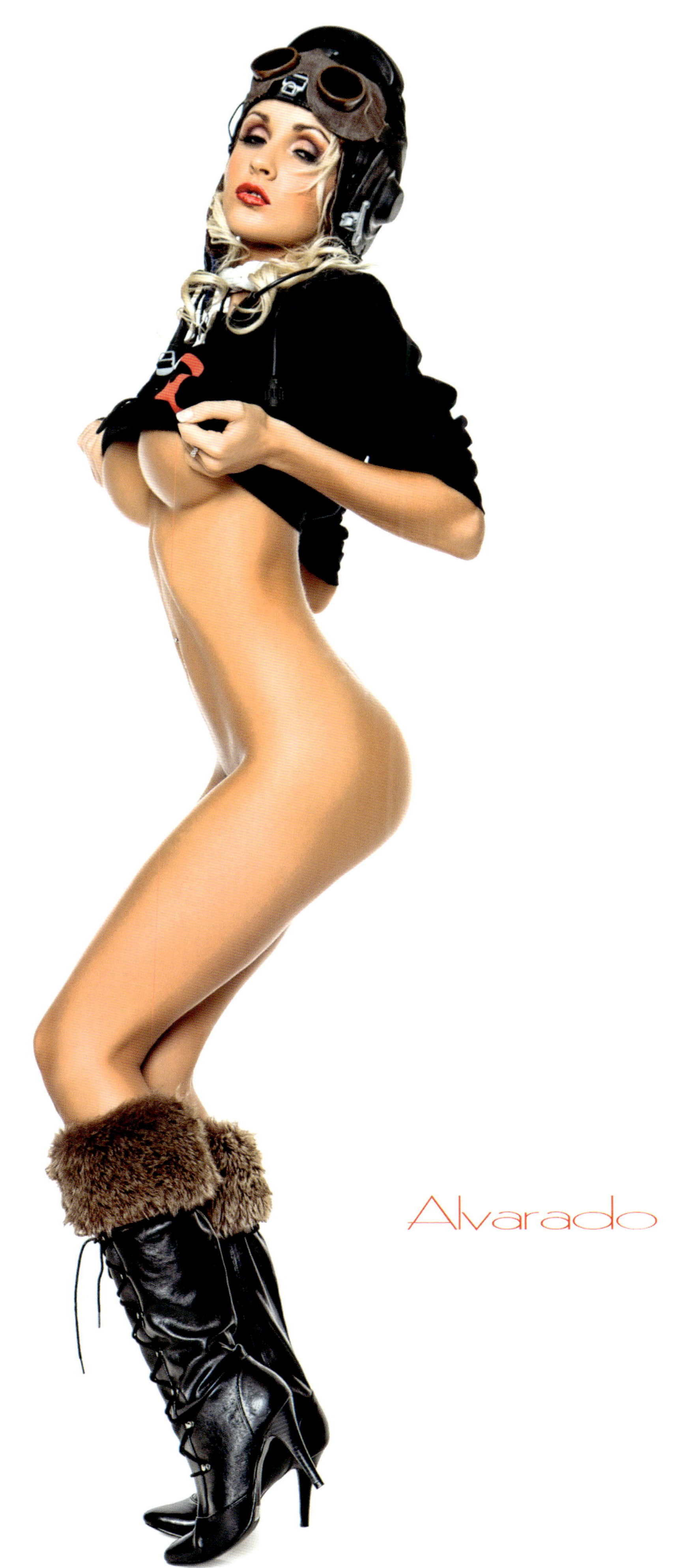

Alvarado

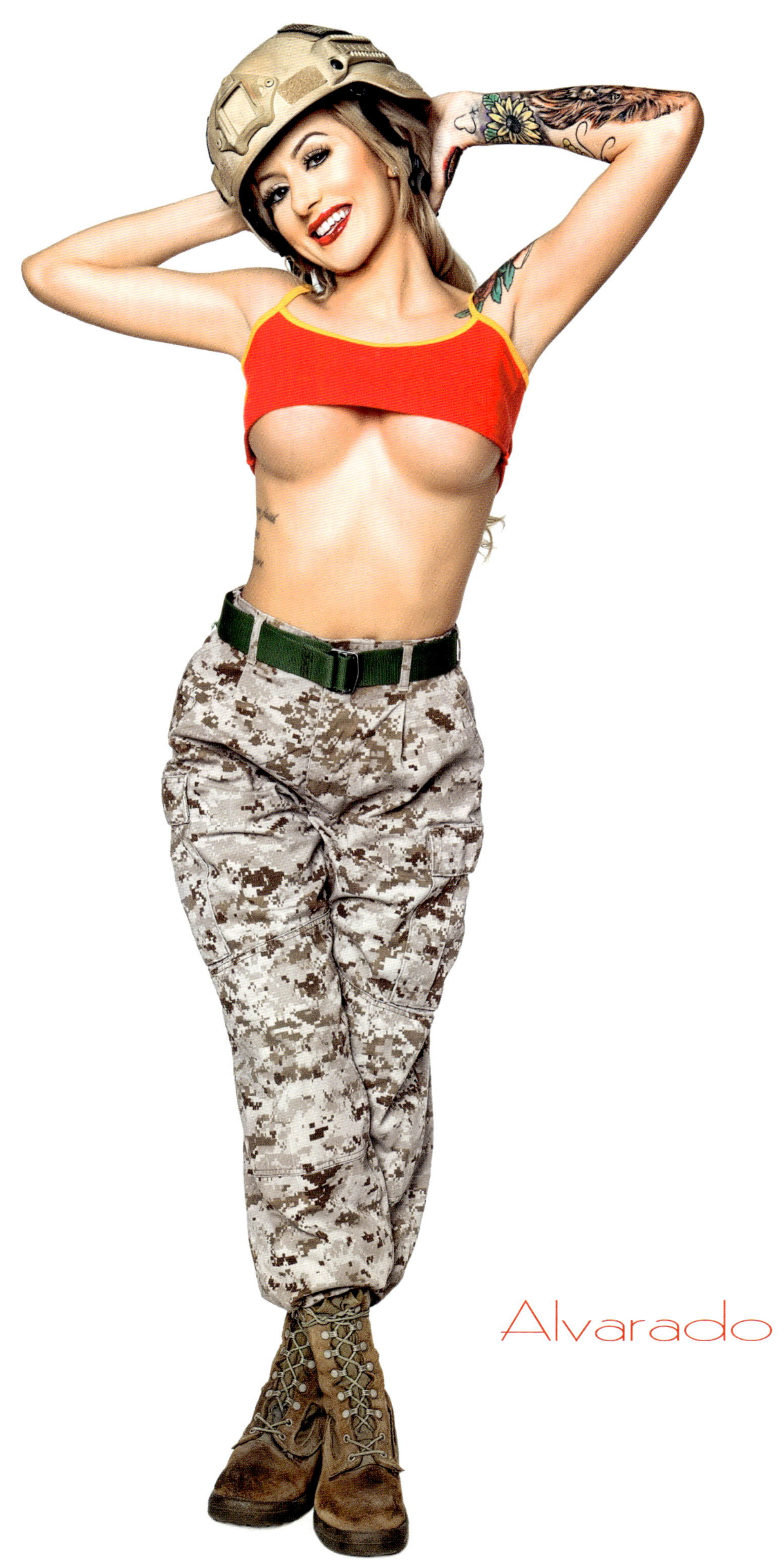

Alvarado

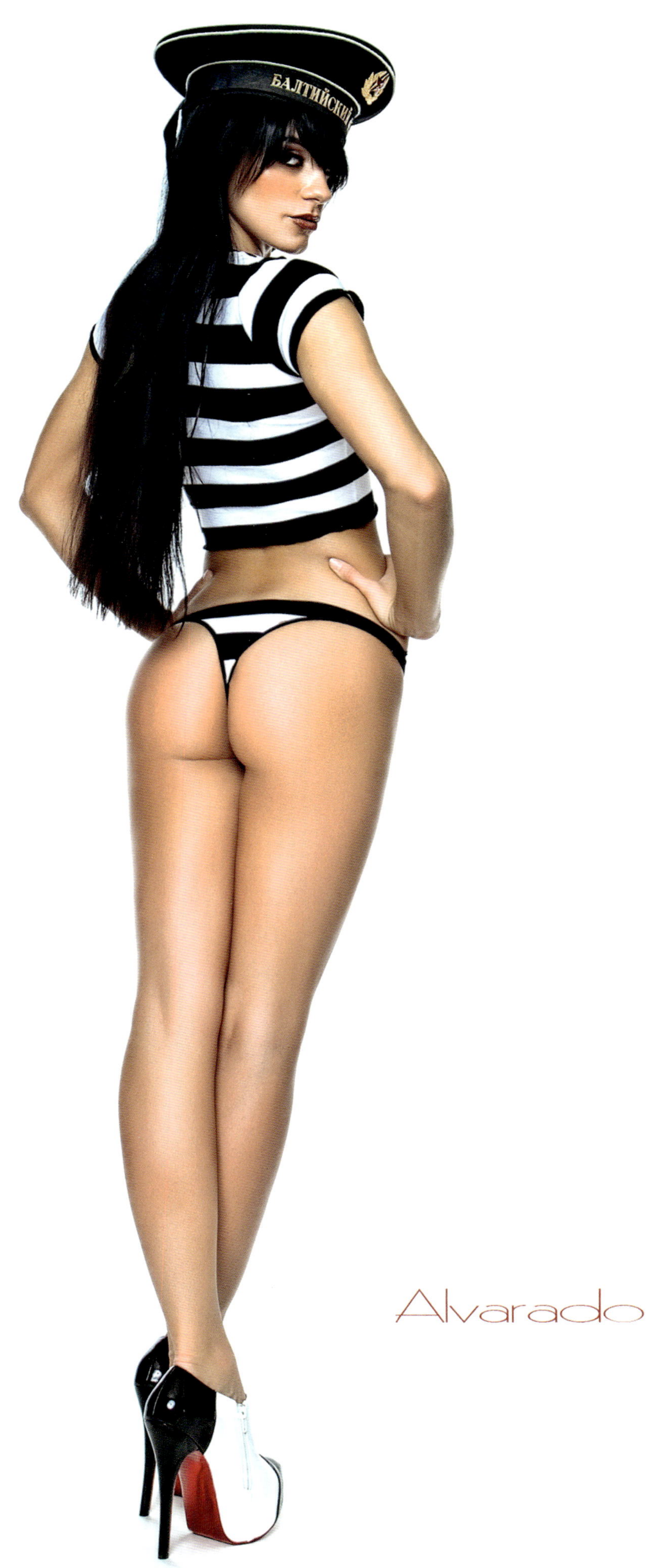

Alvarado

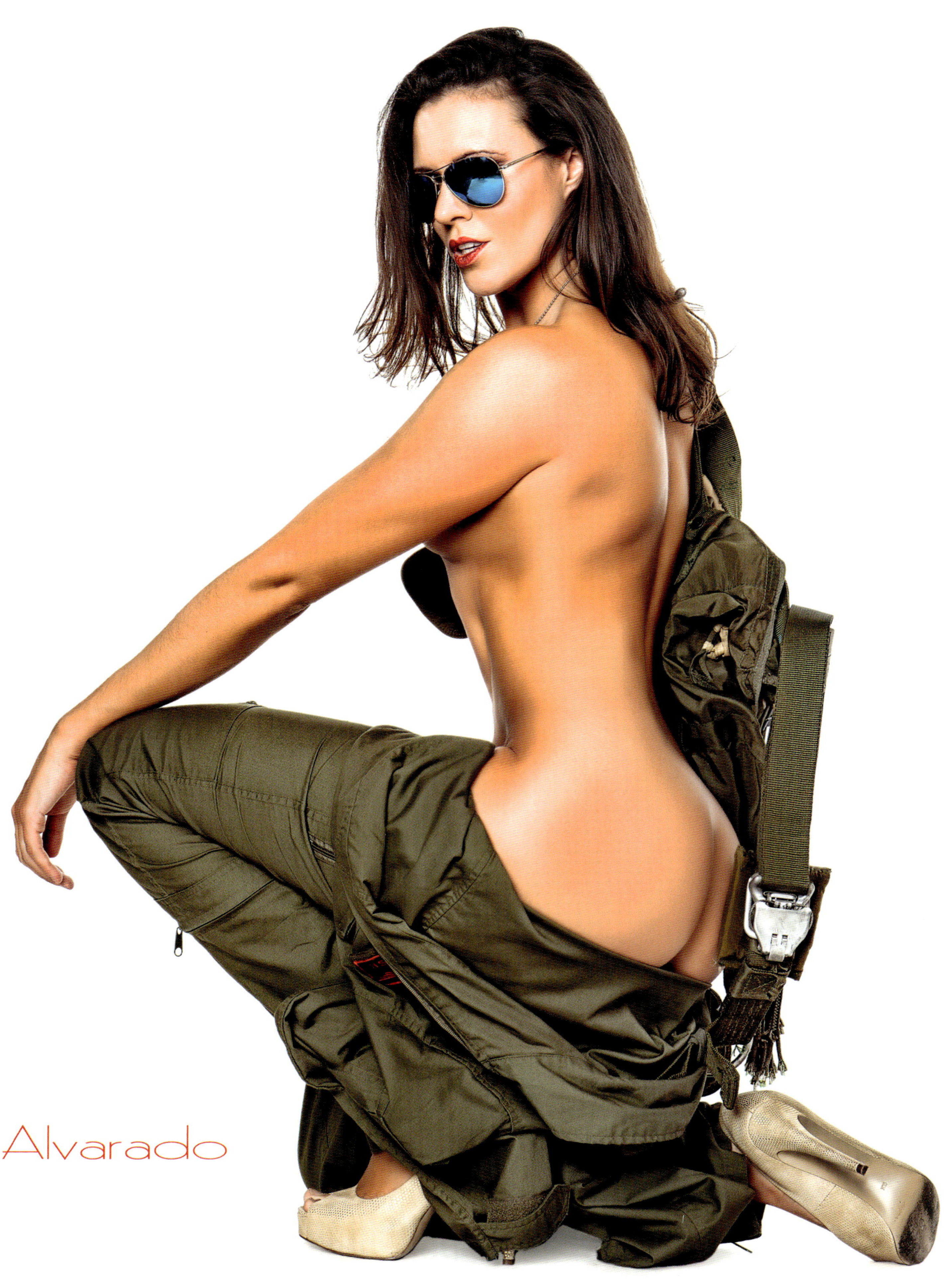

Alvarado

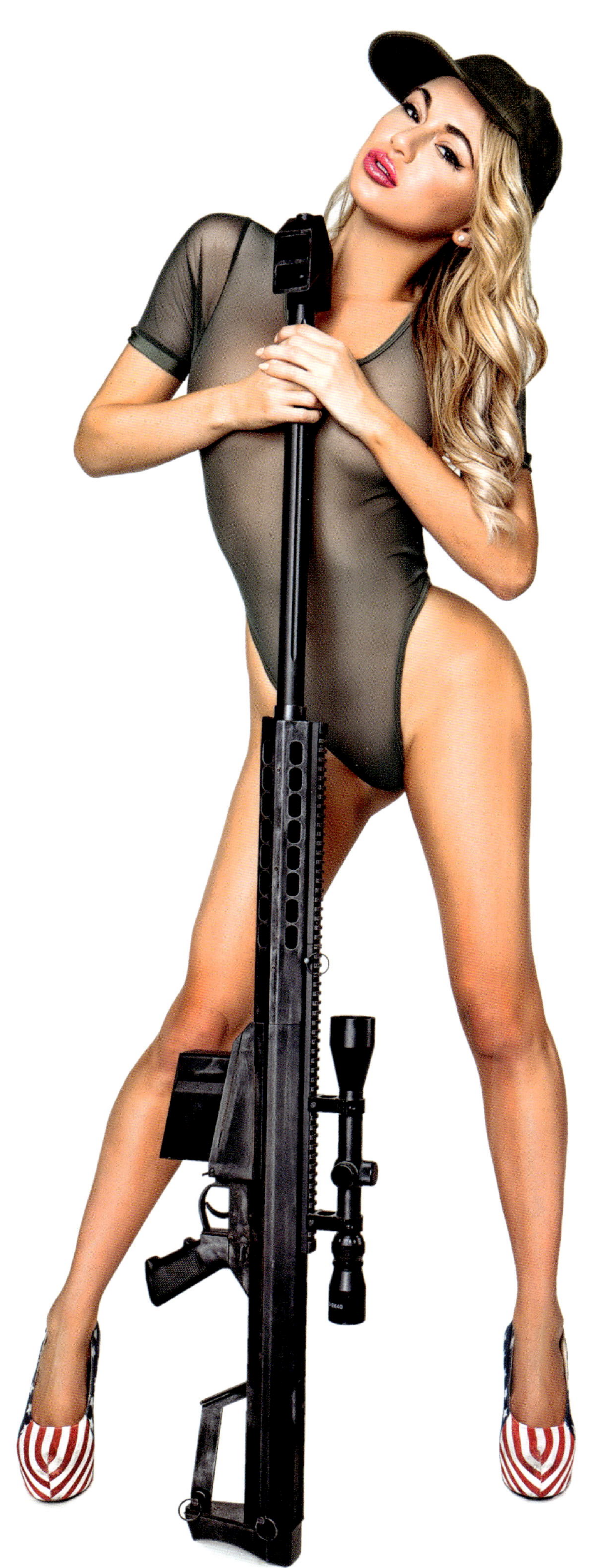

Alvarado

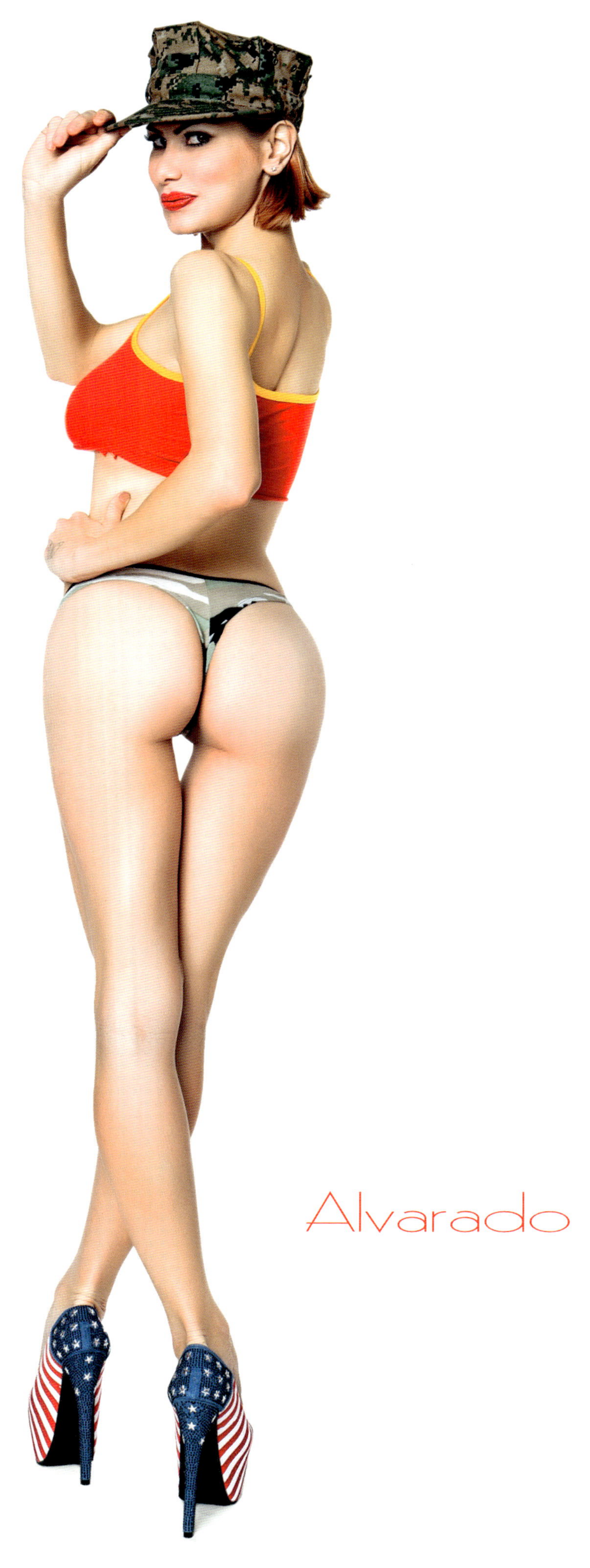

Alvarado

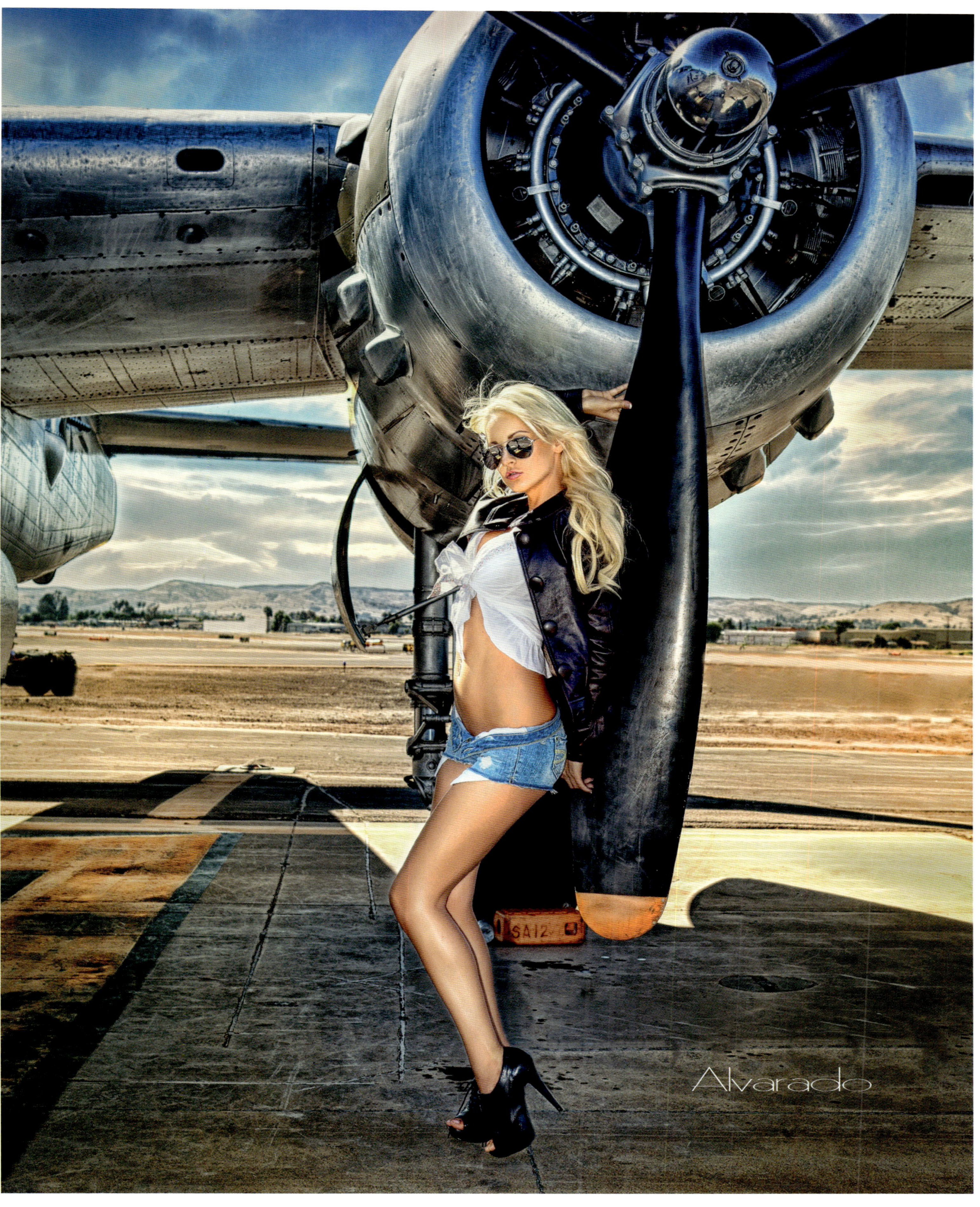
SA12
Alvarado

Alvarado

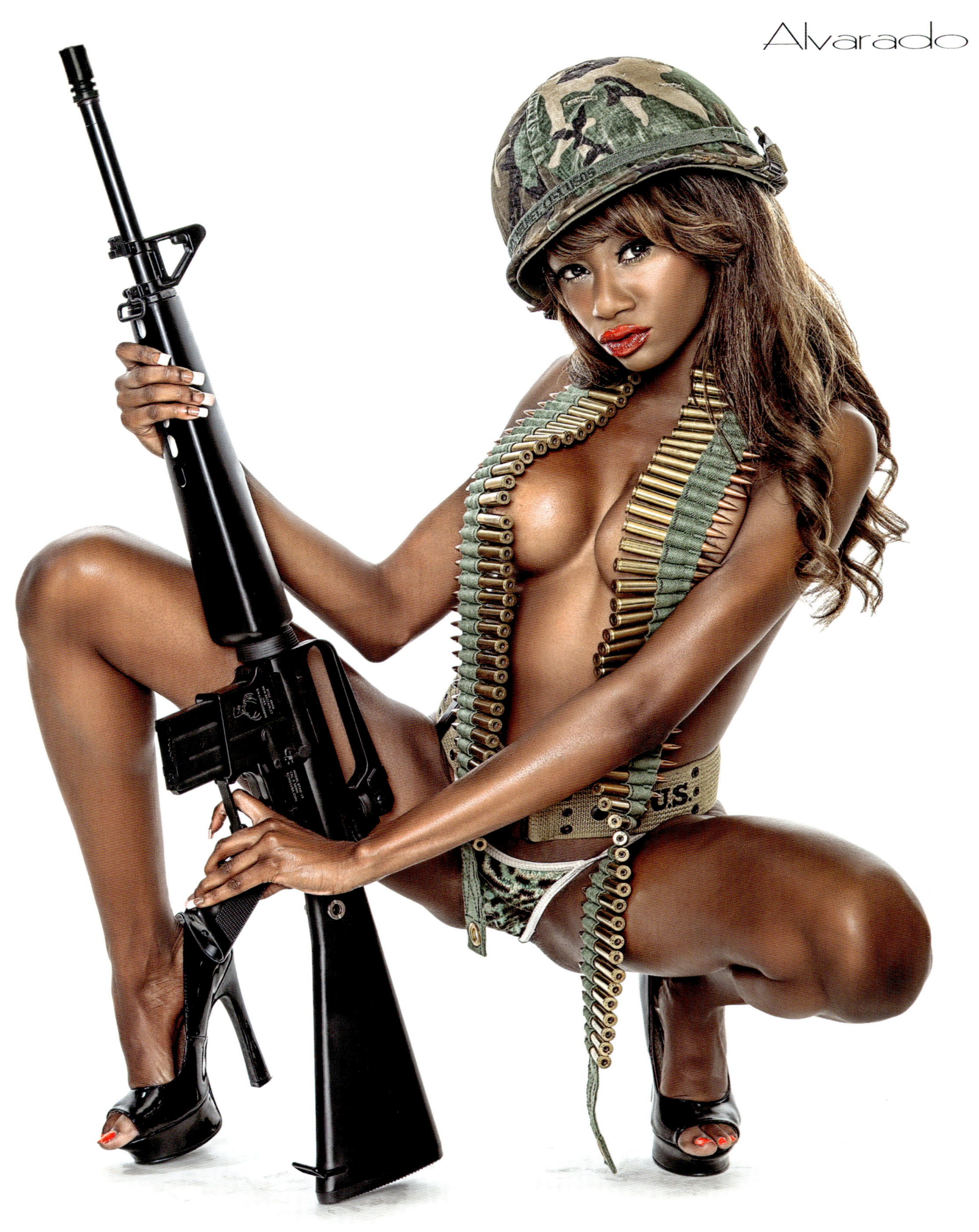

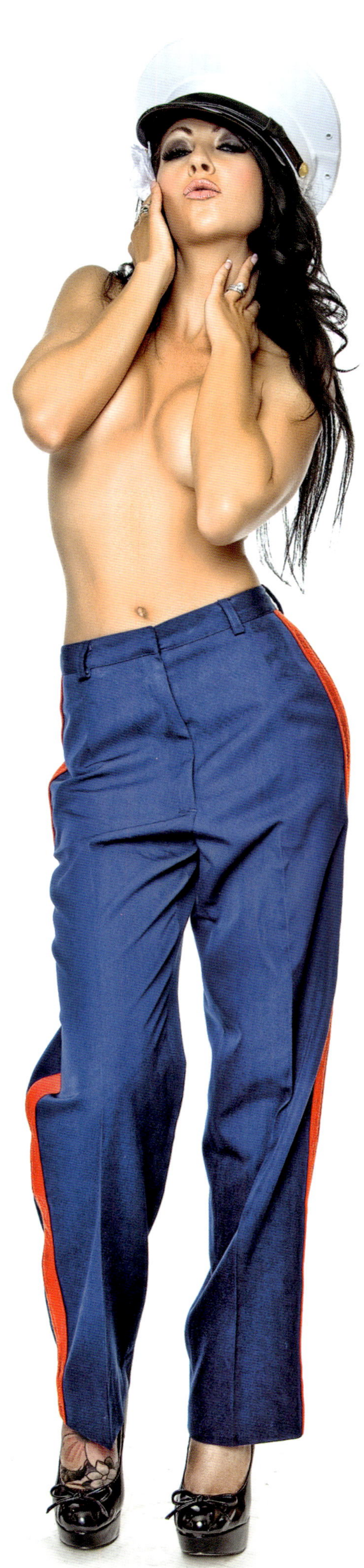

Alvarado

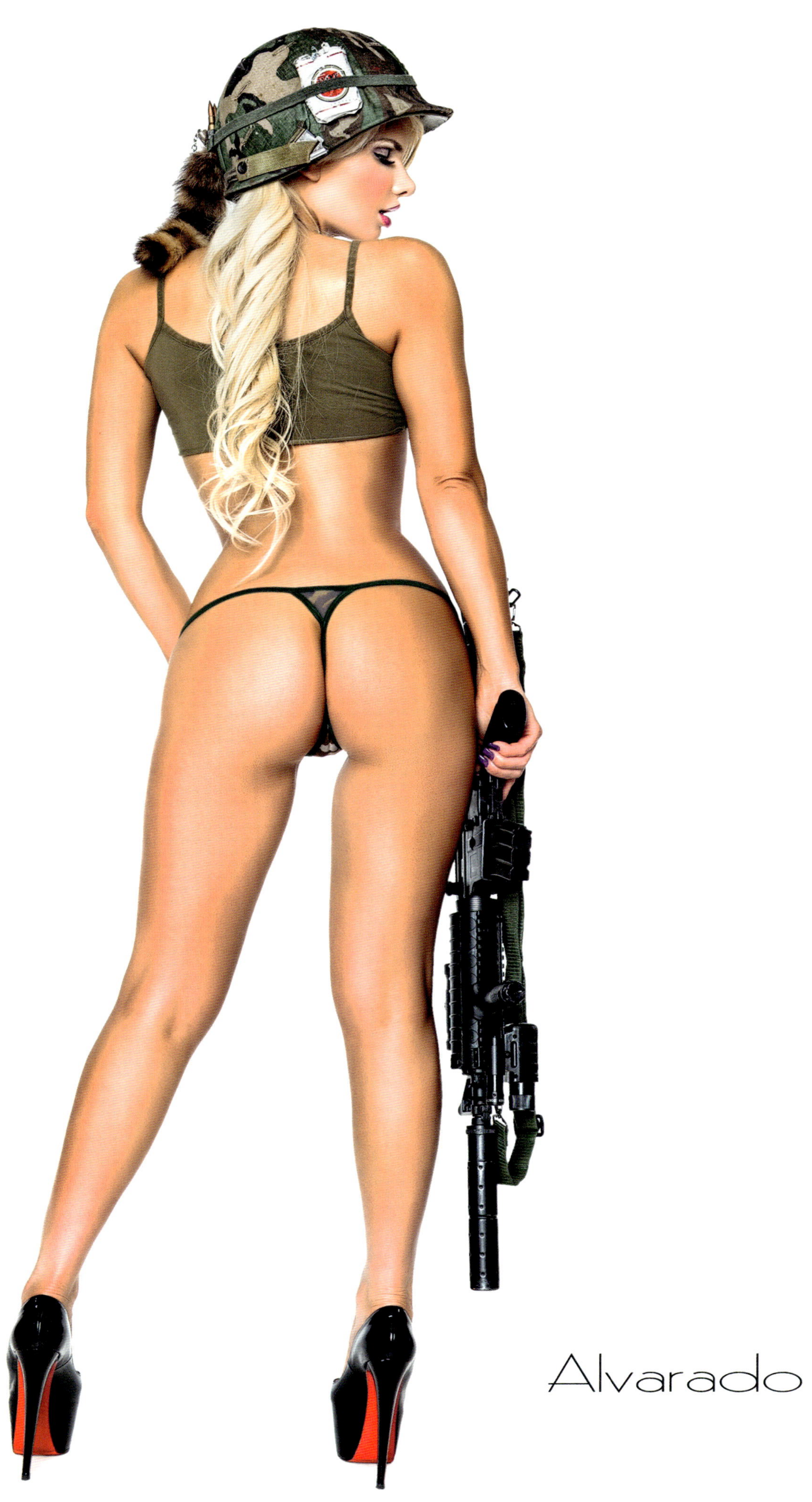

Alvarado

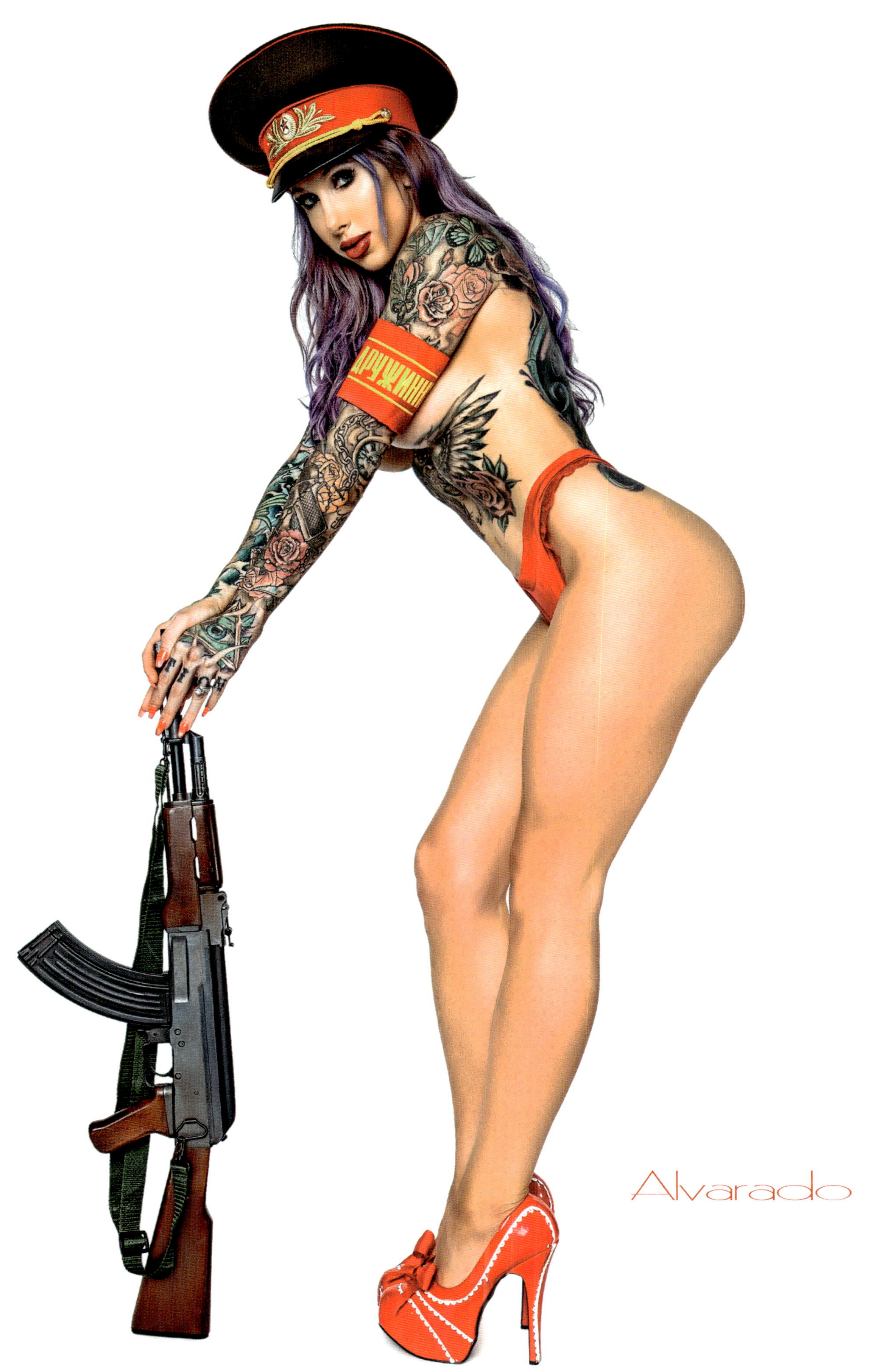
Alvarado

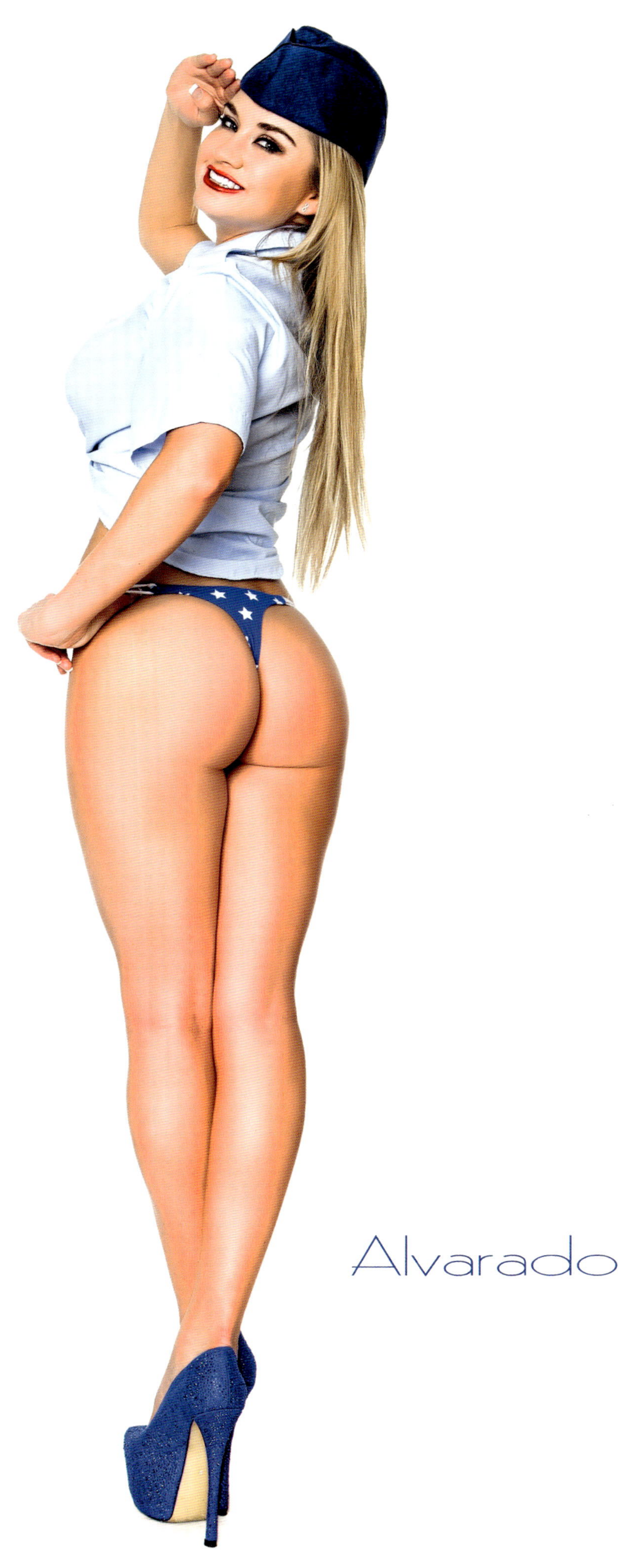

Alvarado

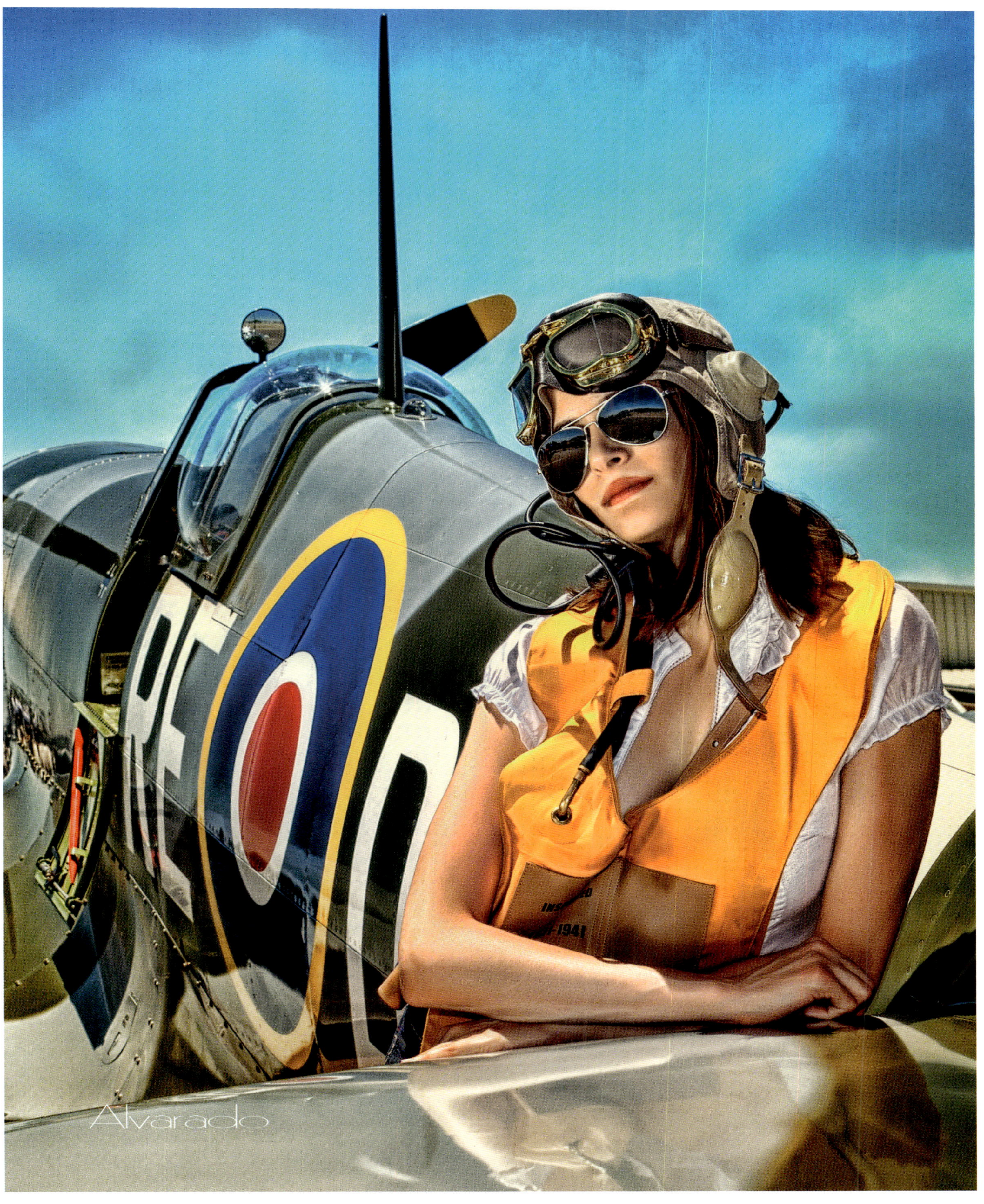
Alvarado

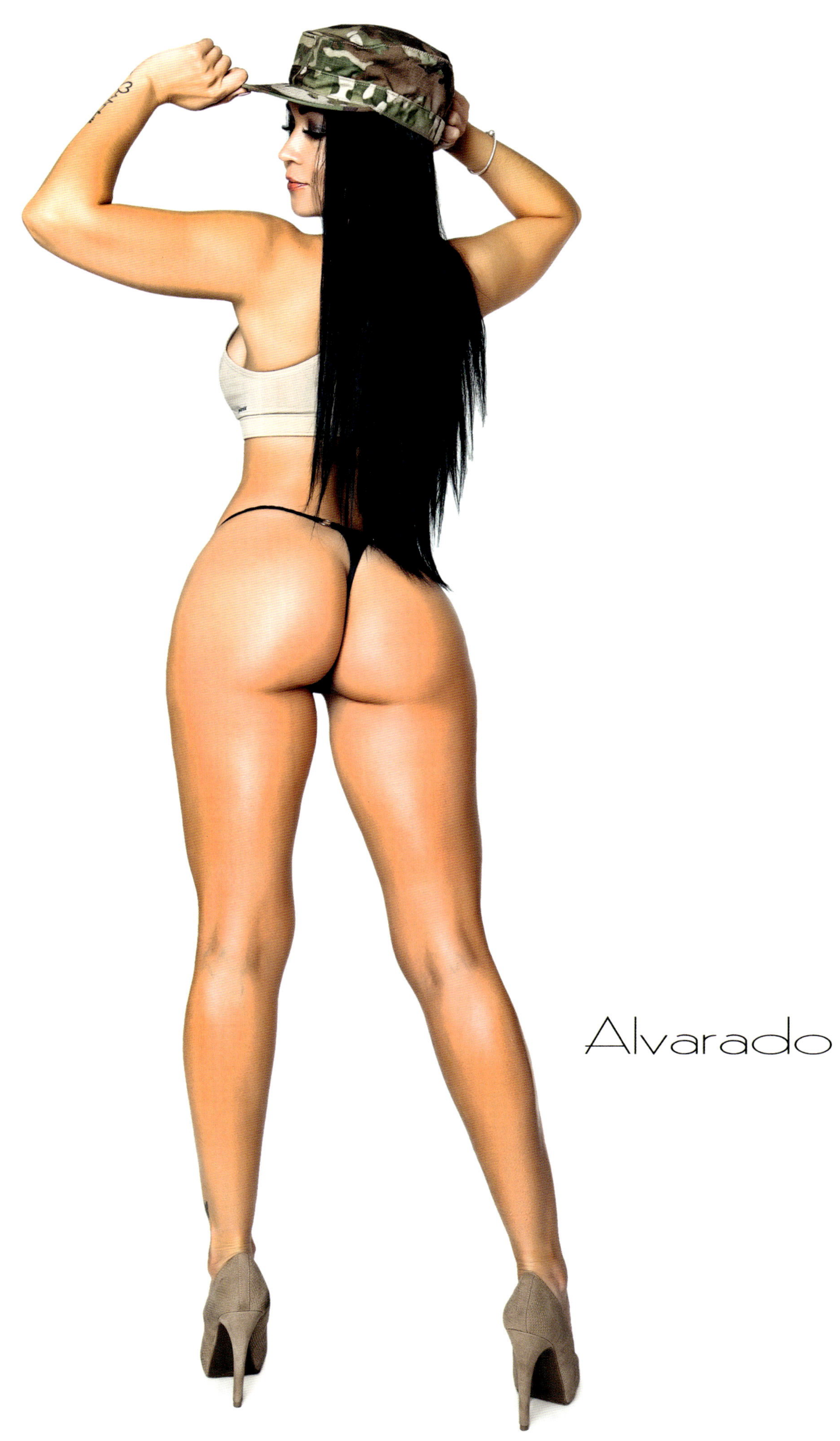

Alvarado

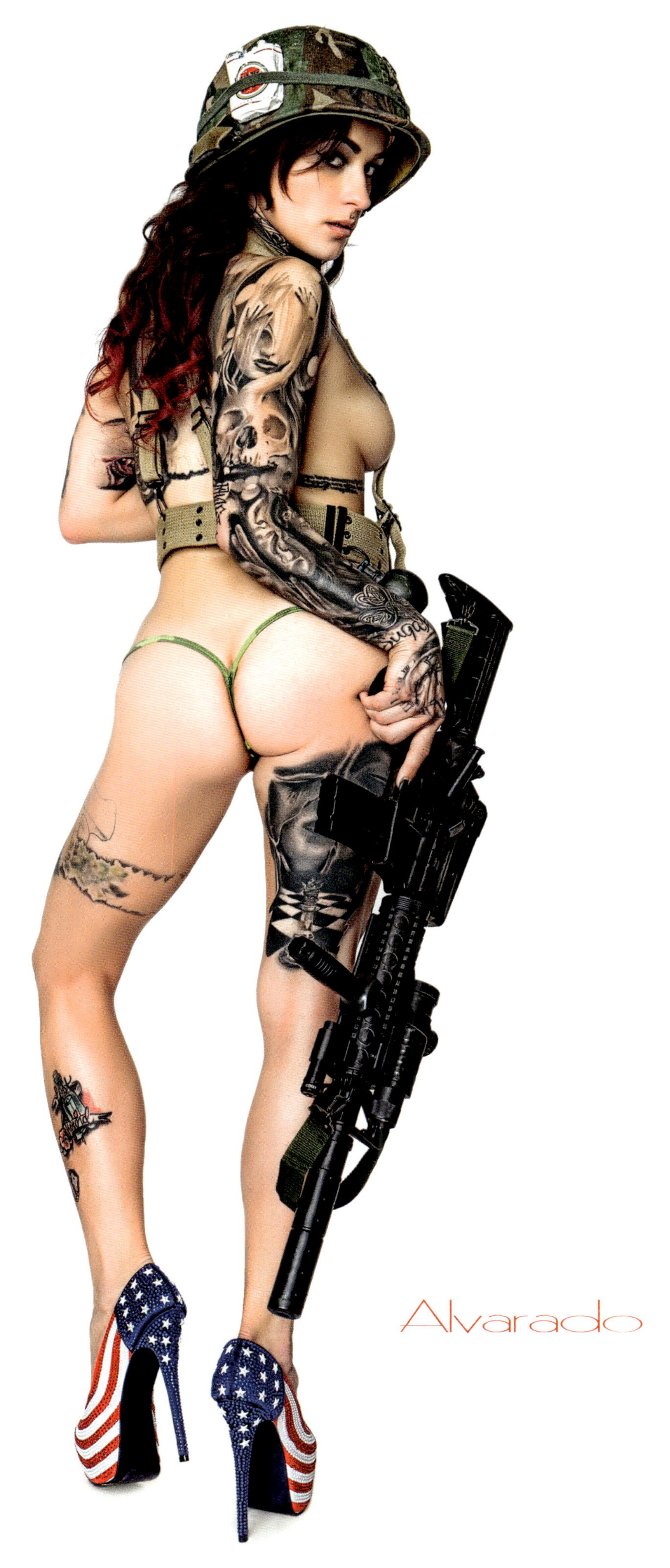

Alvarado

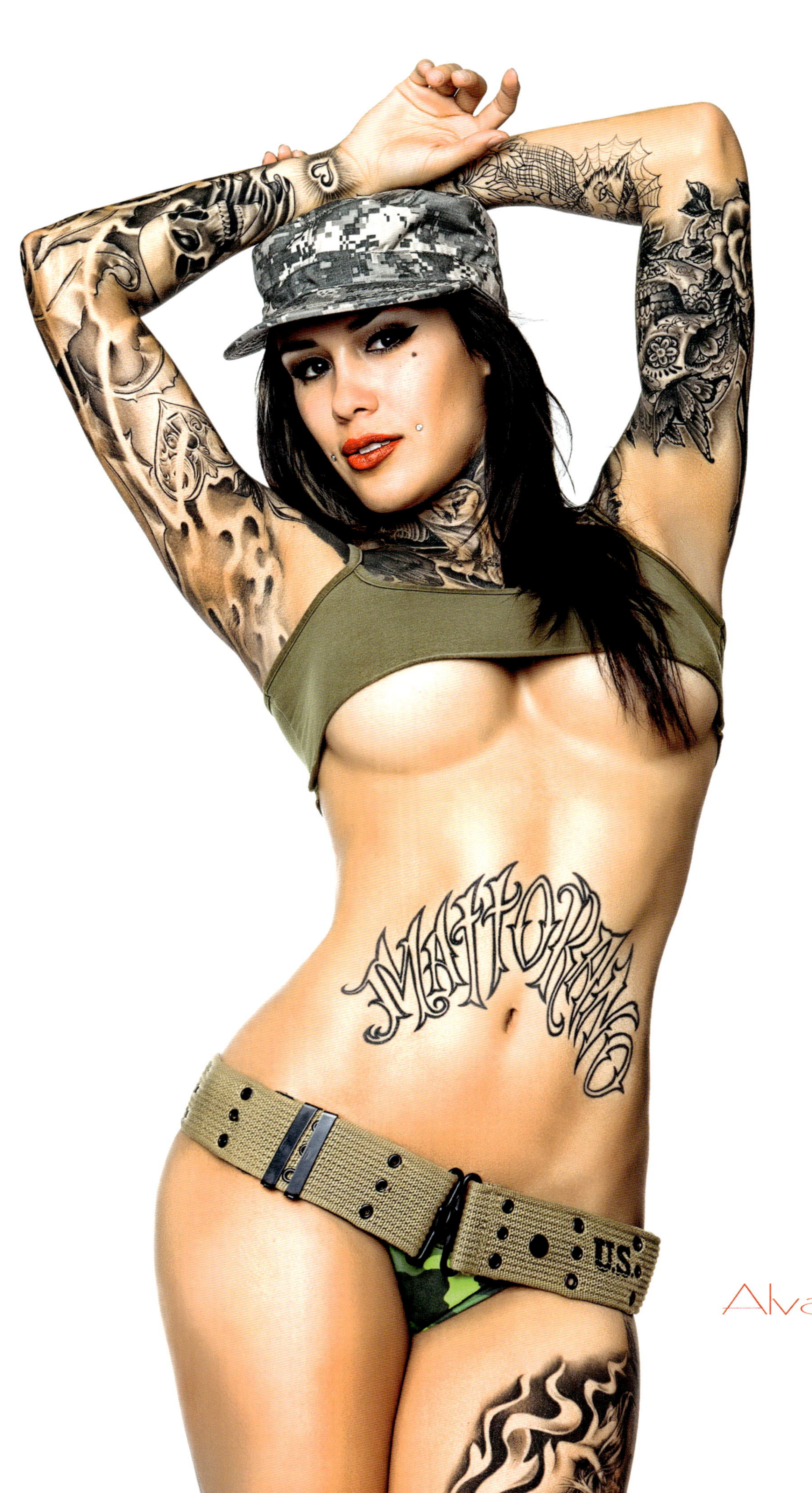

Alvarado

Alvarado

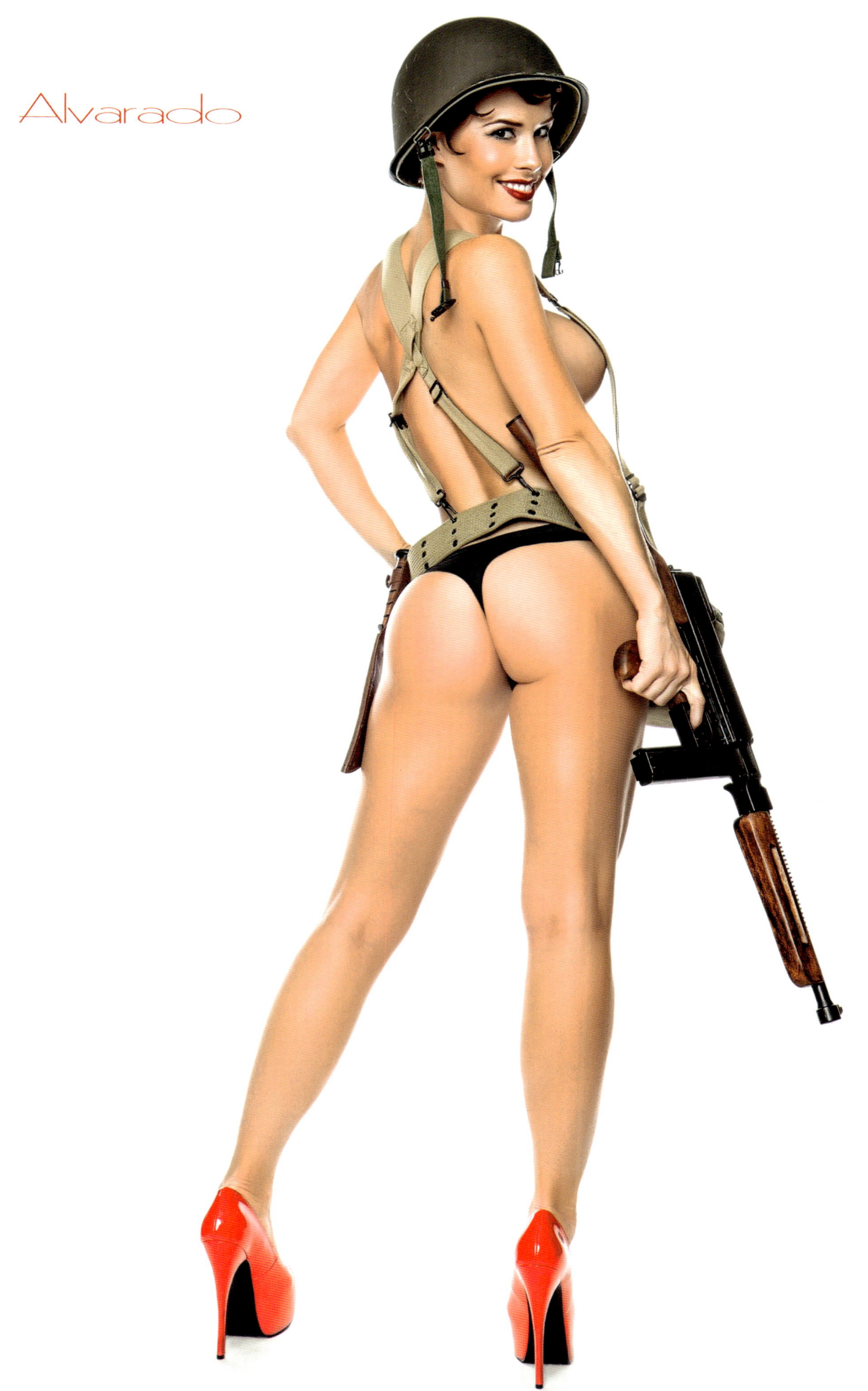

Alvarado

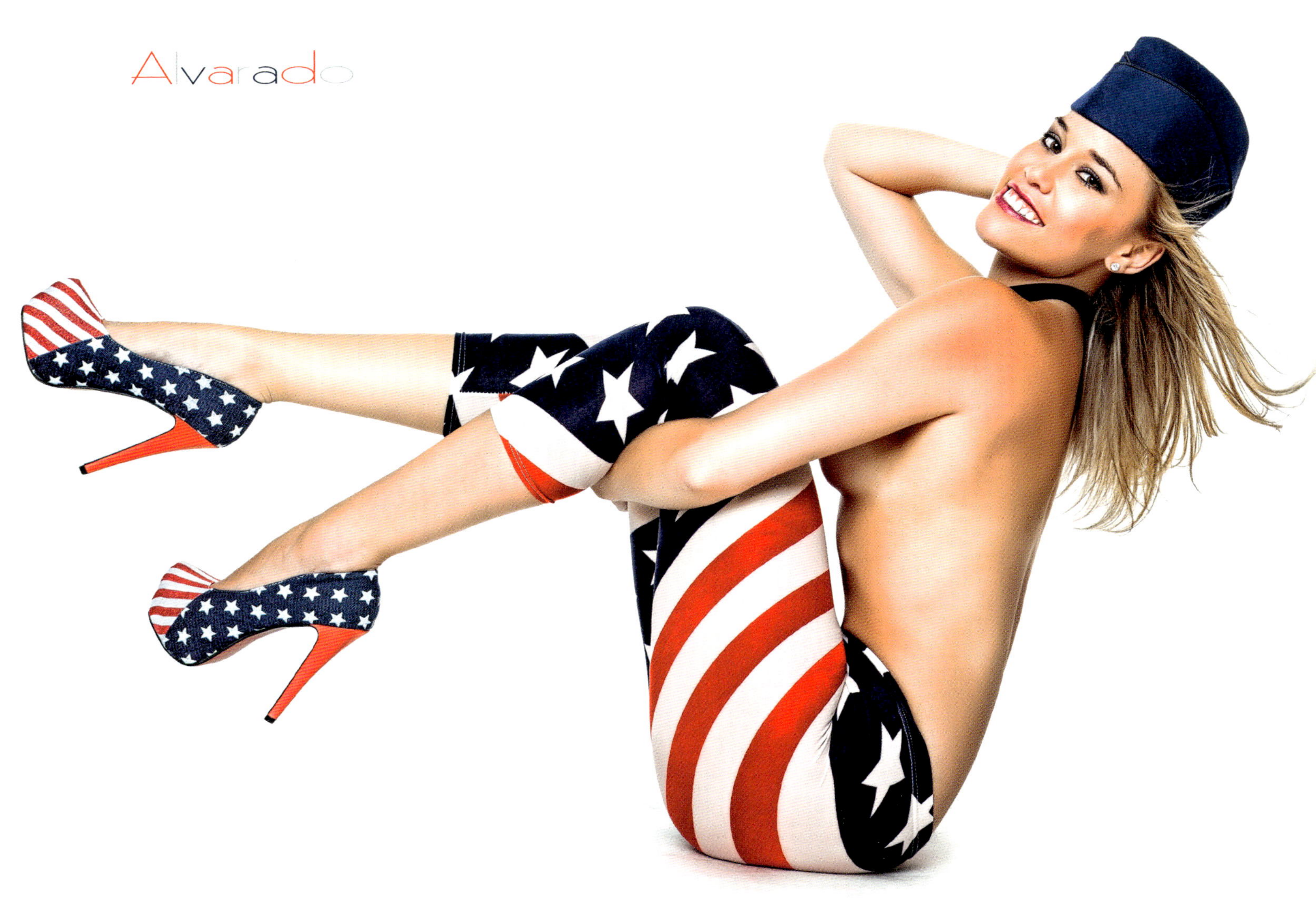

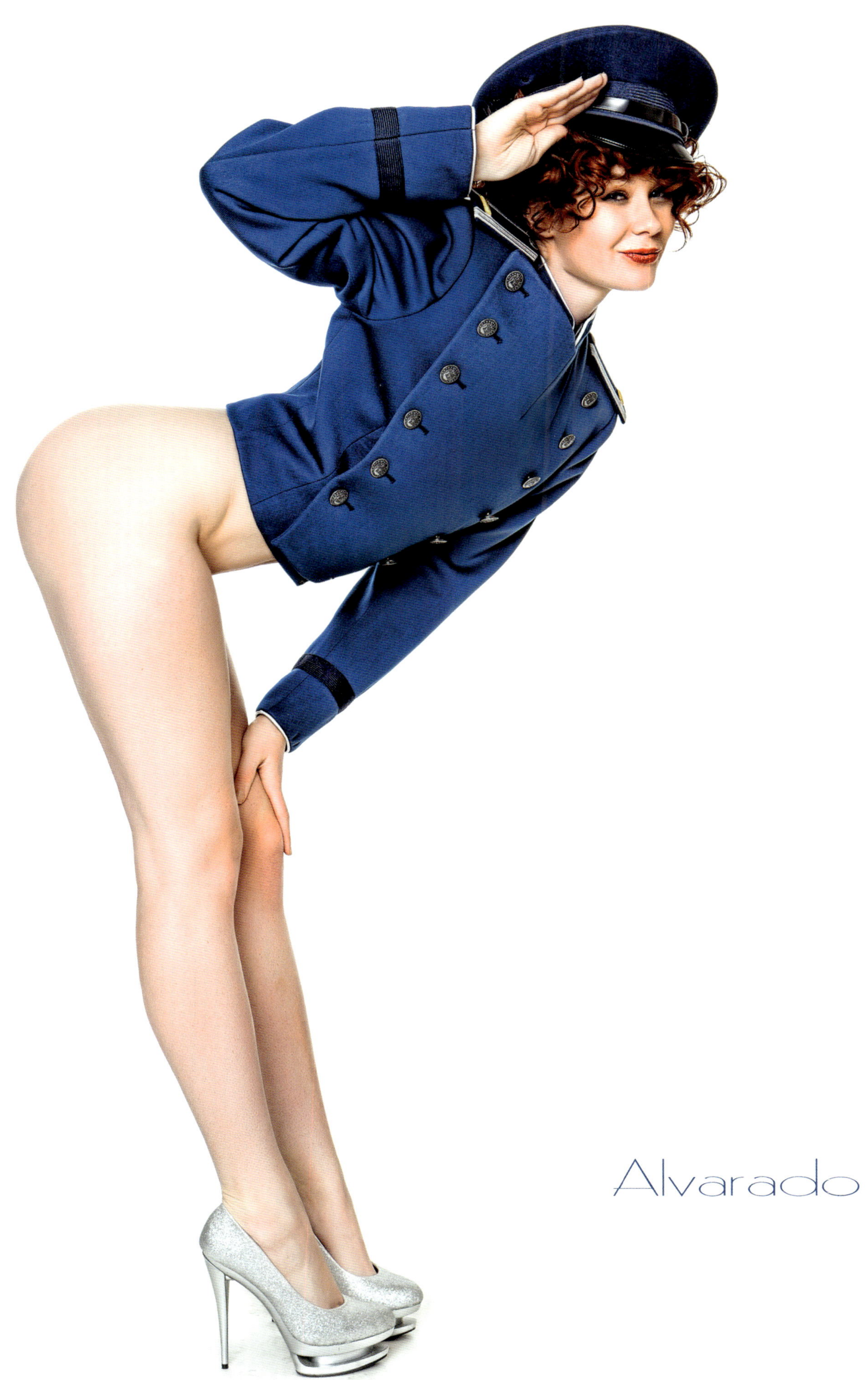

Alvarado

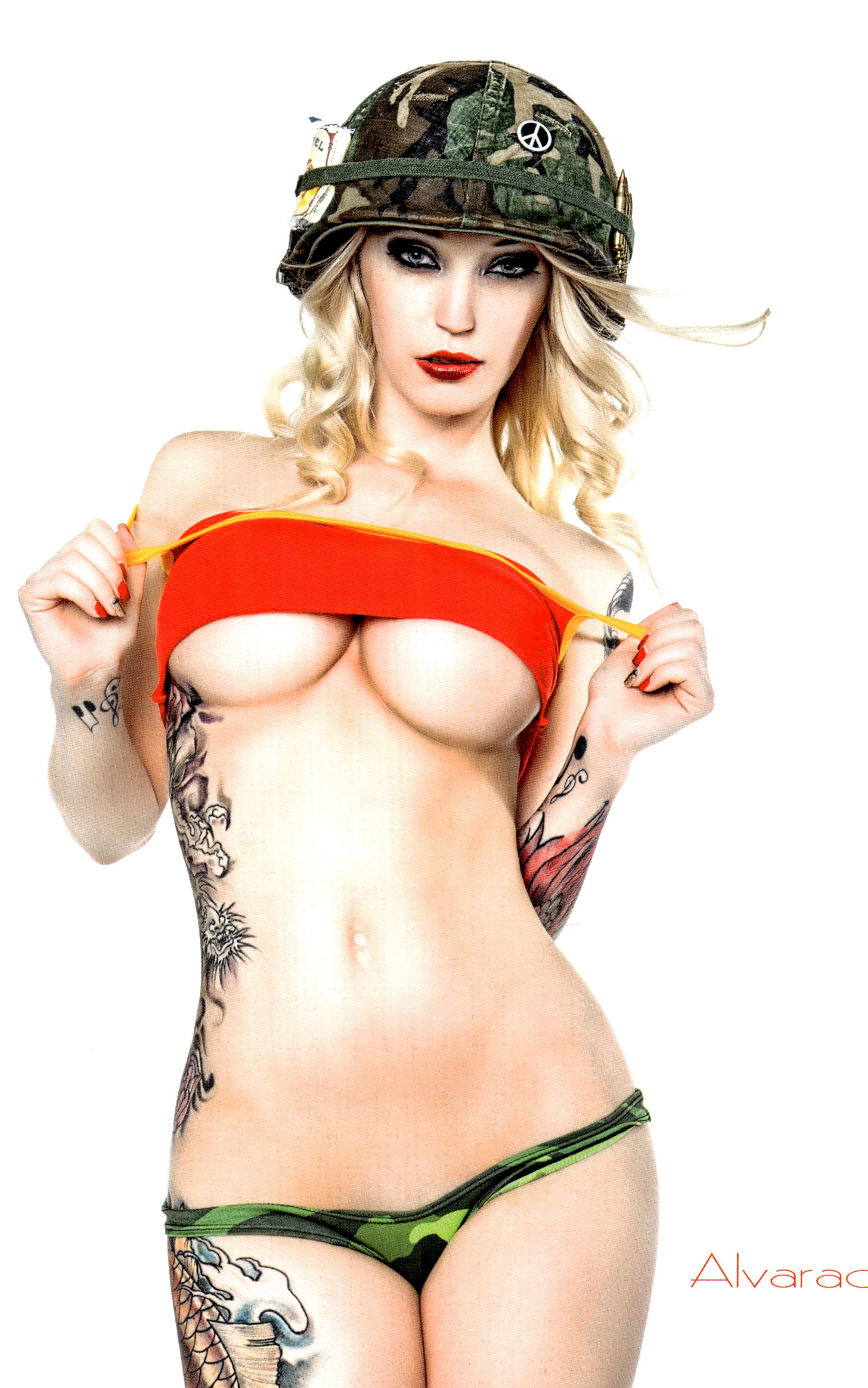

Alvarado

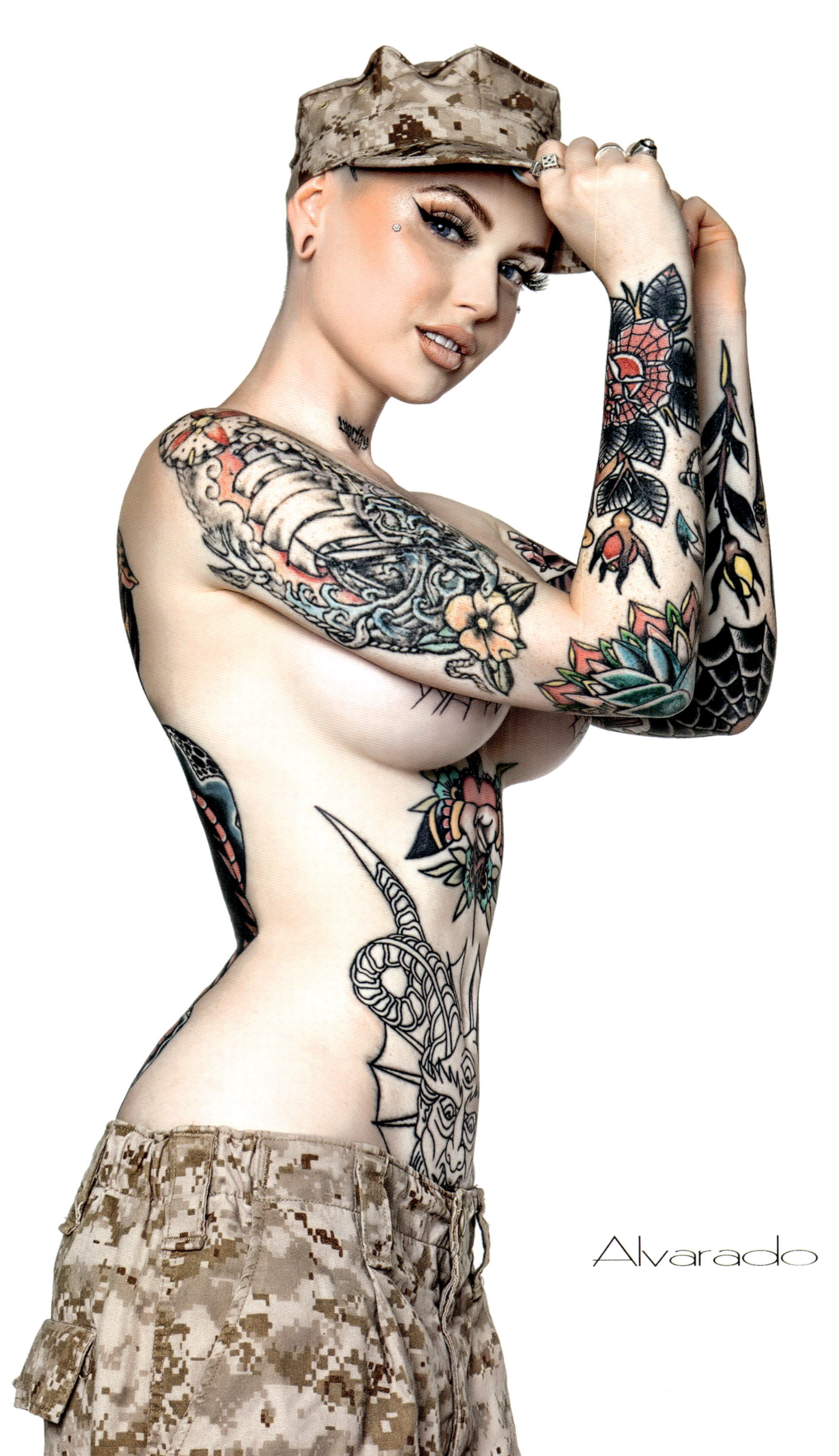

Alvarado

Alvarado

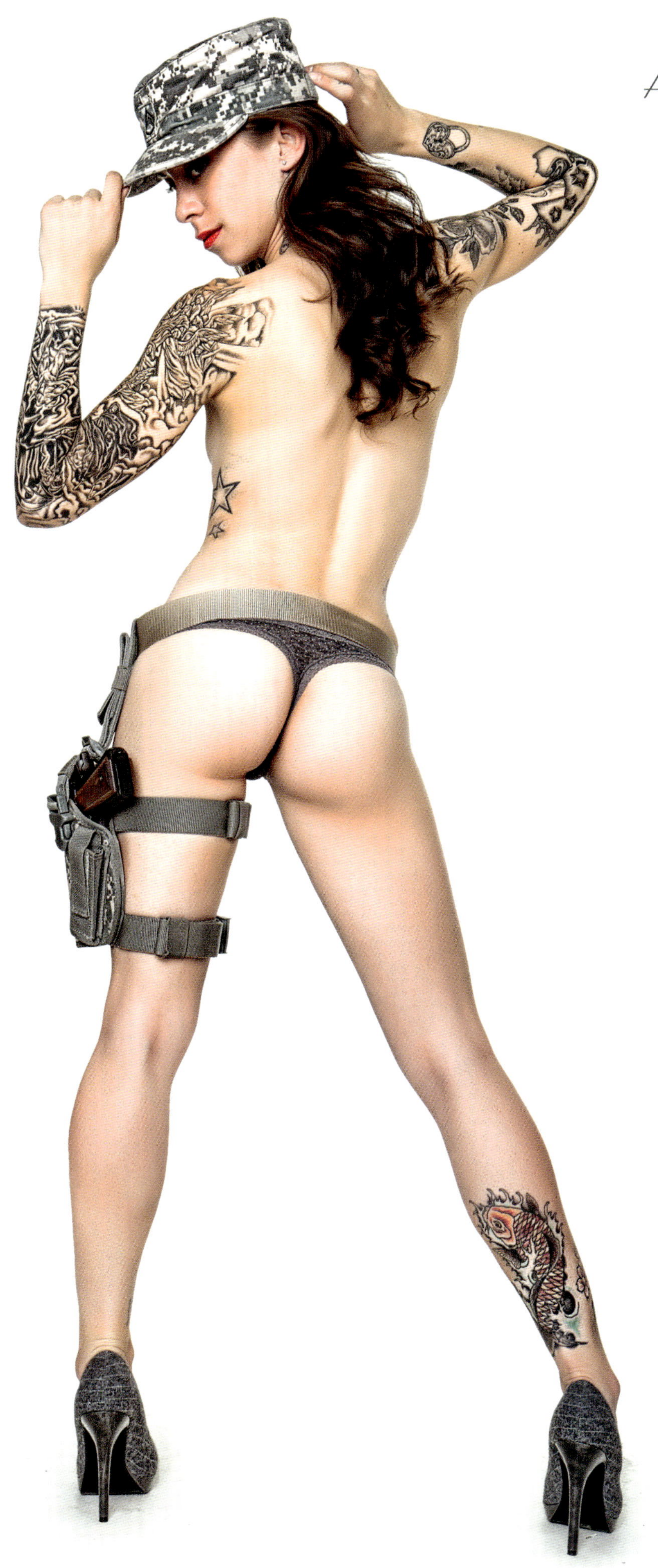

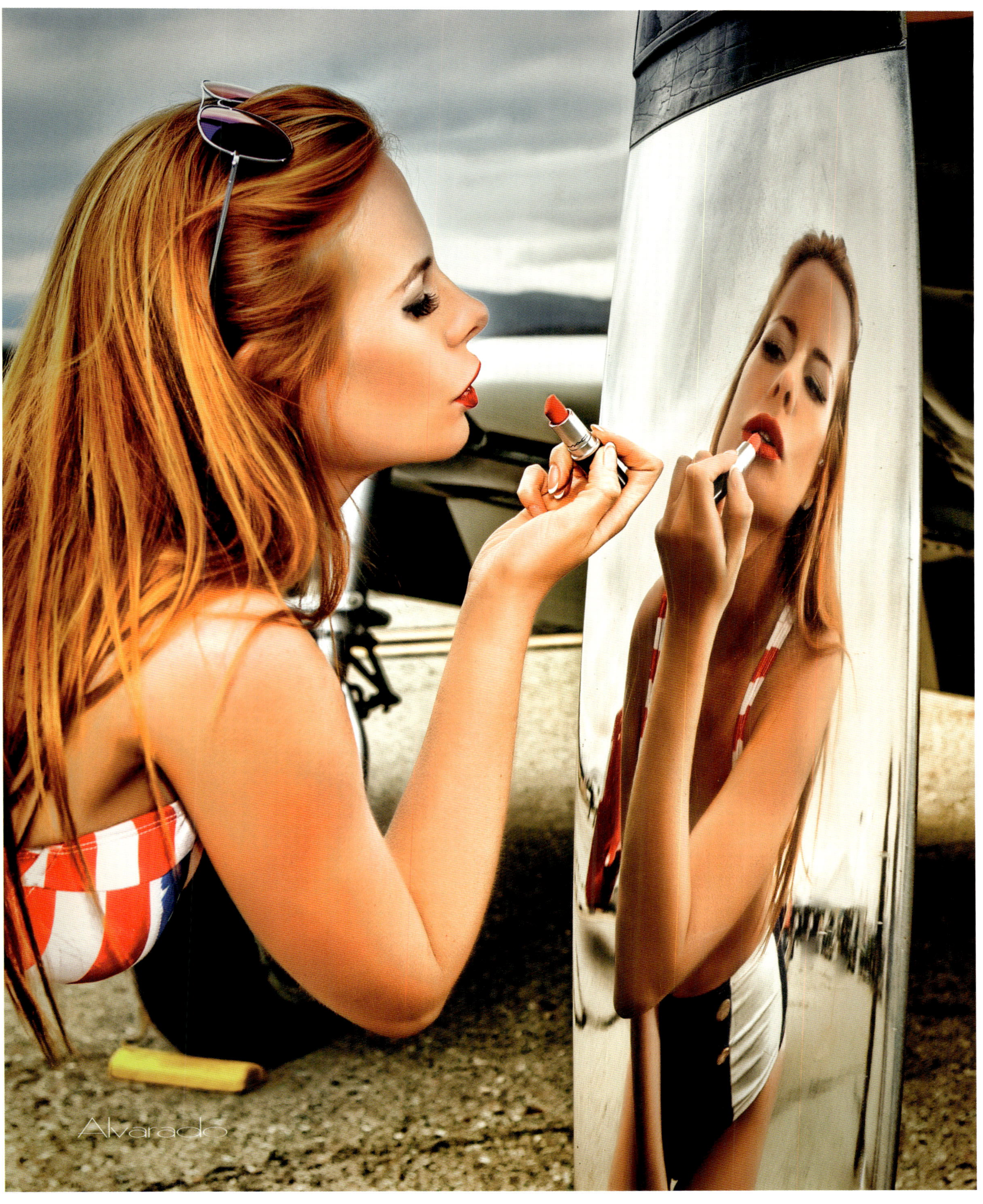
Alvarado

Alvarado

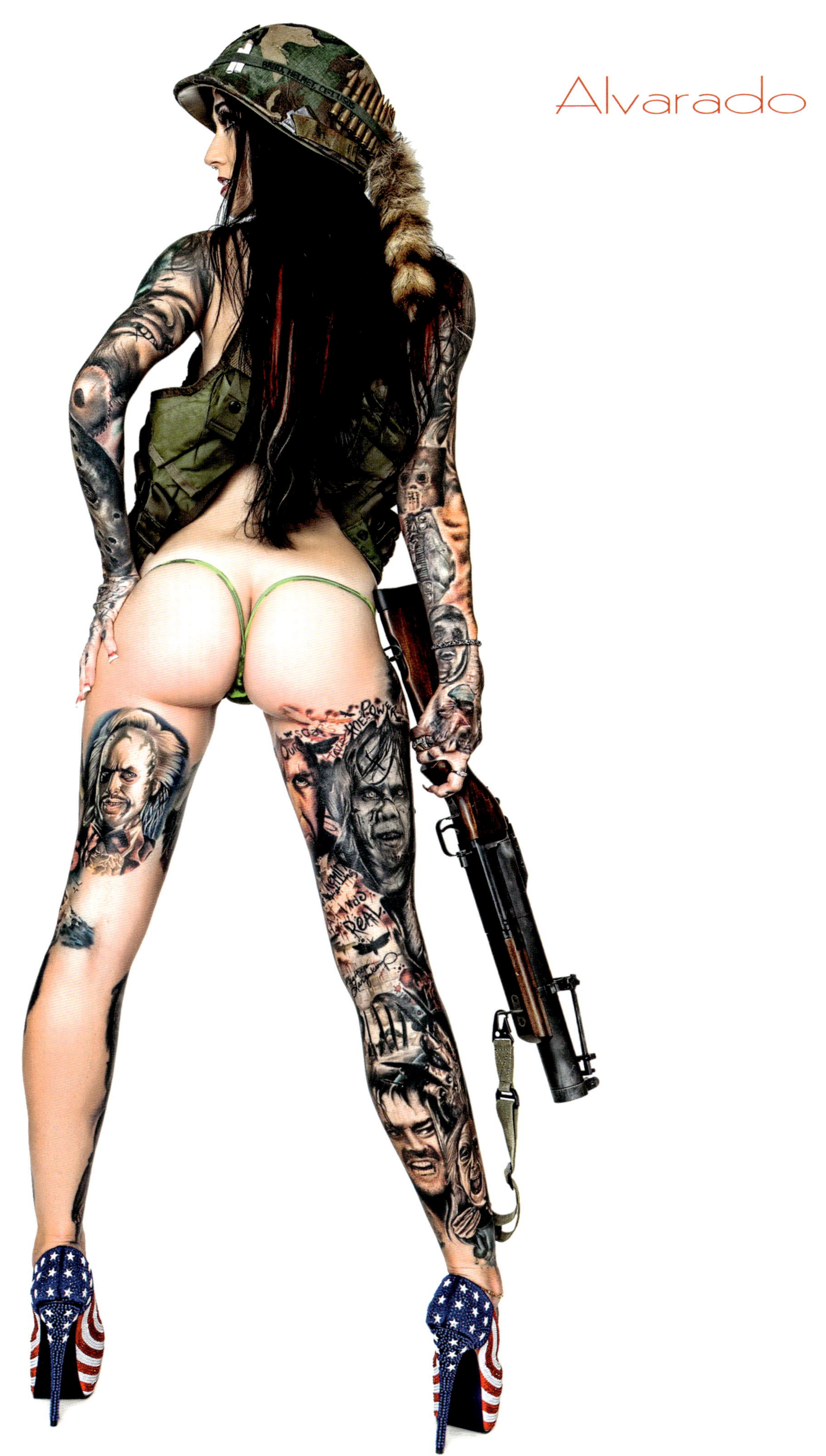

Alvarado

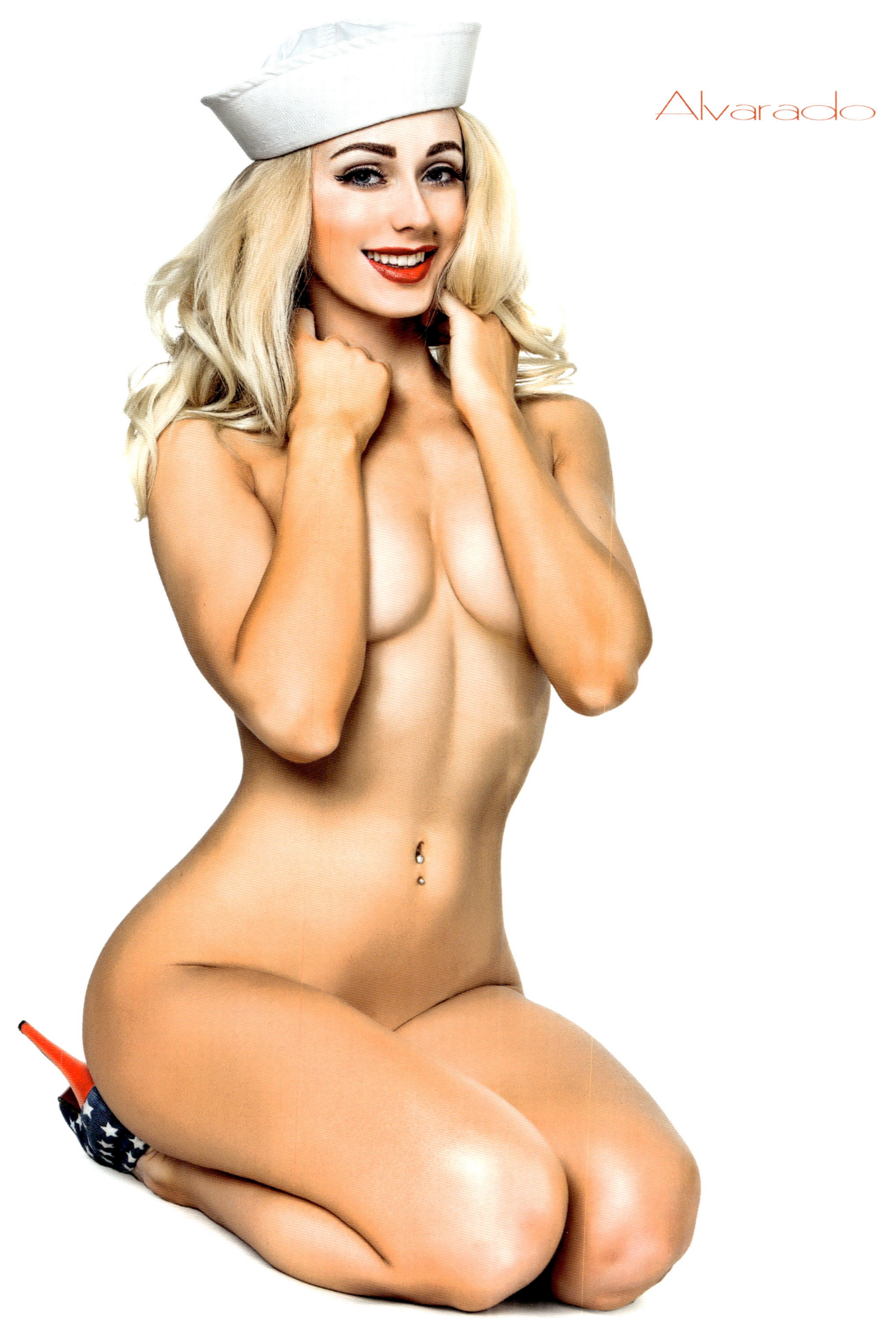

Alvarado

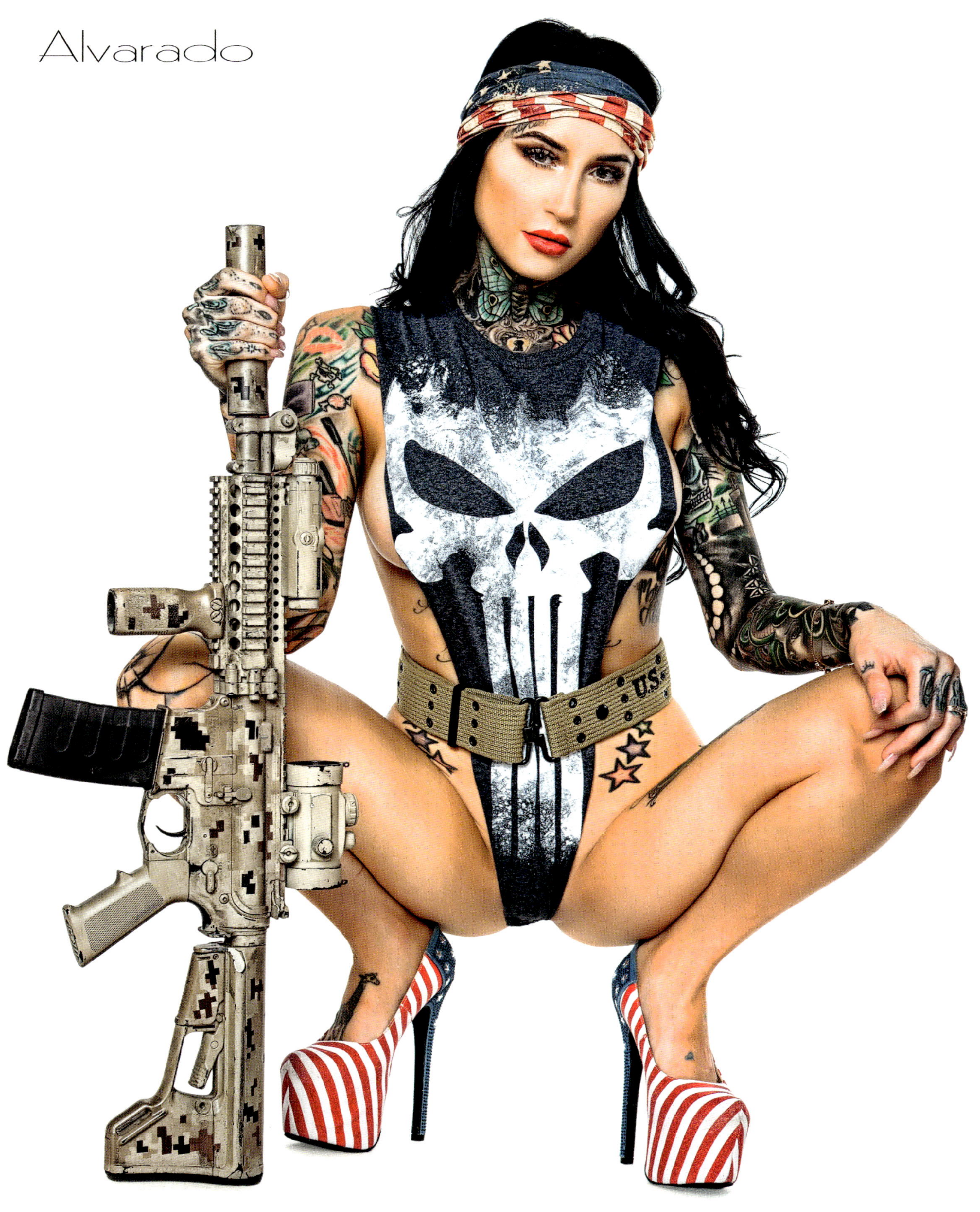

Alvarado

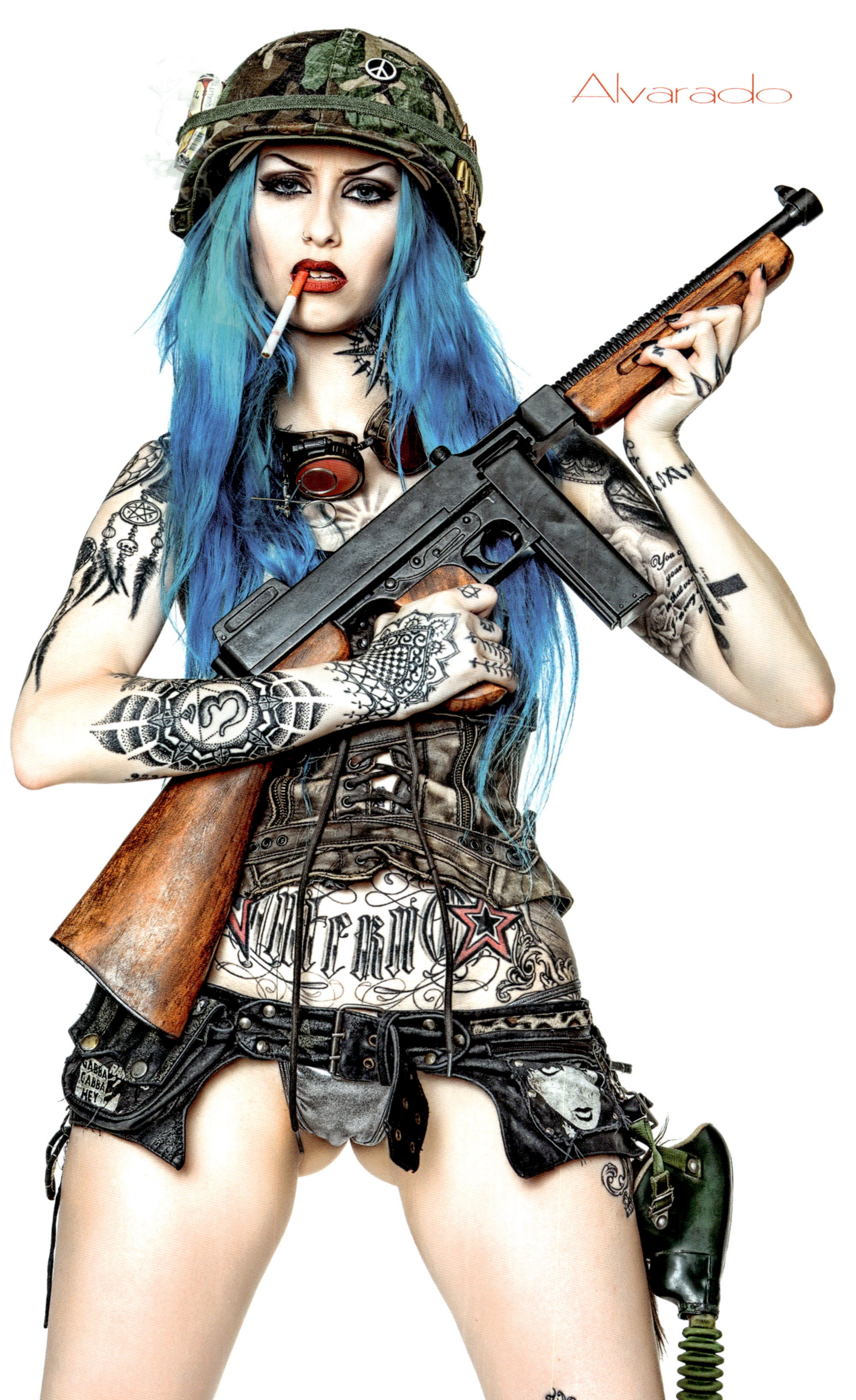

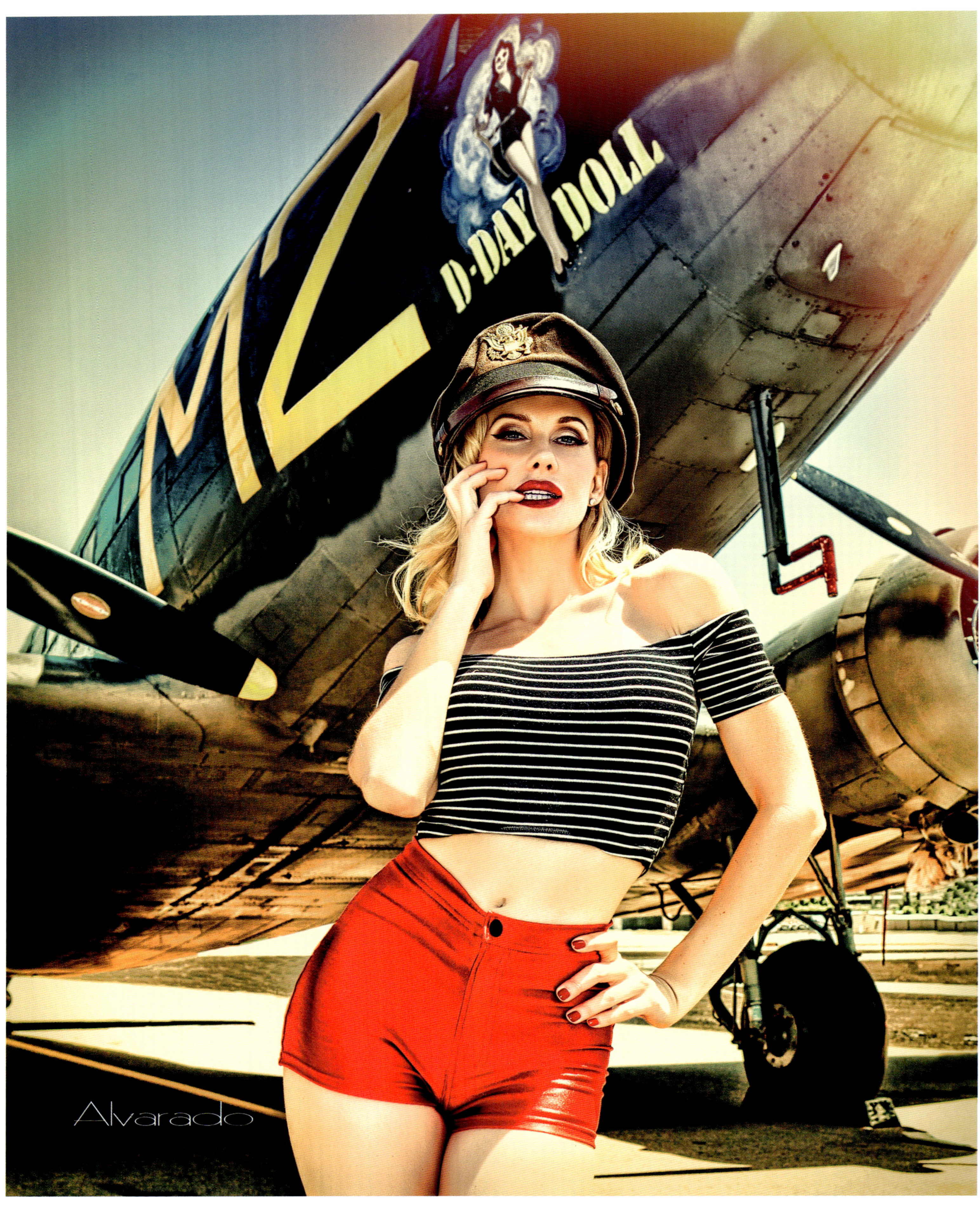
D-DAY DOLL
Alvarado

Alvarado

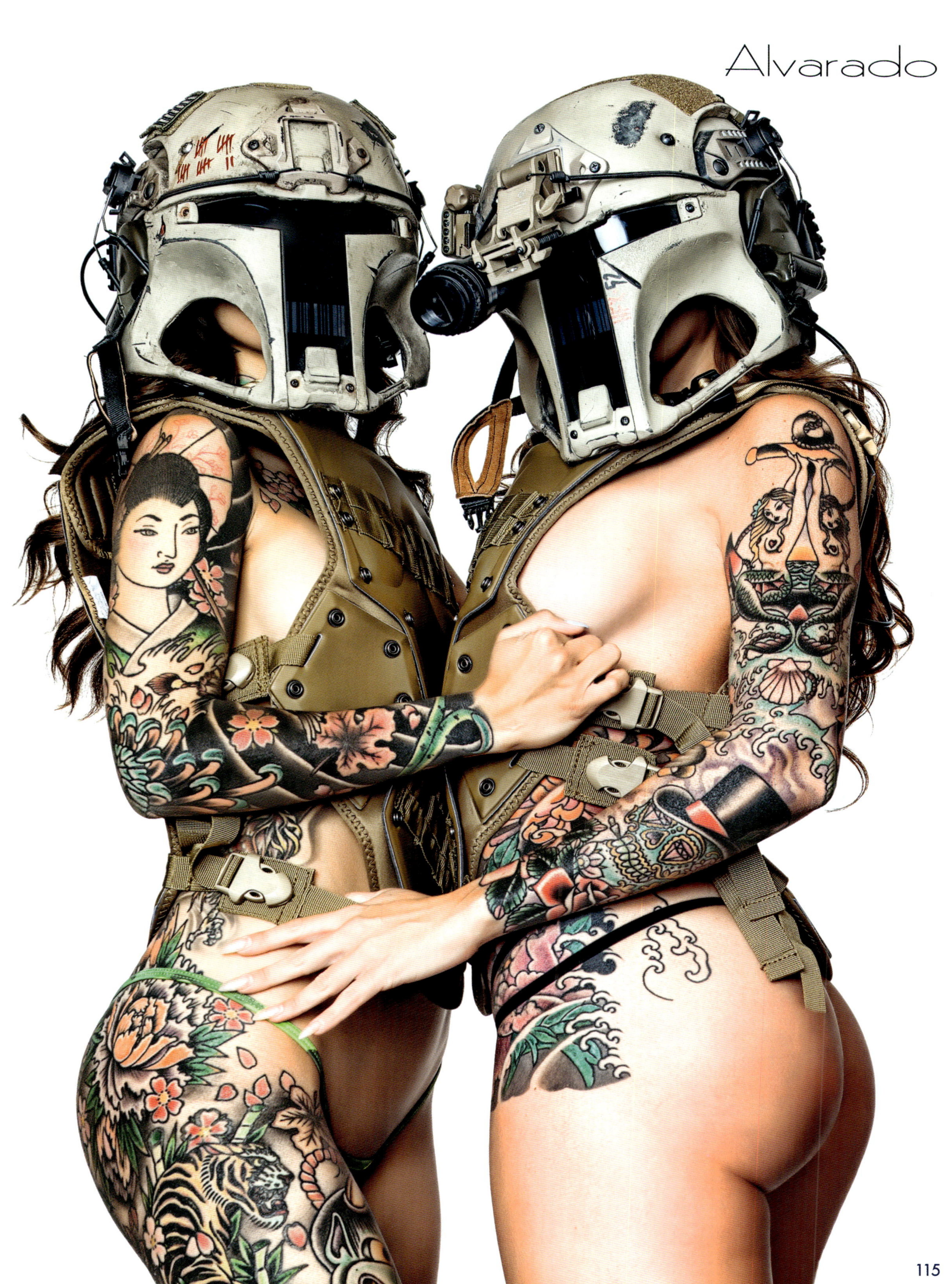

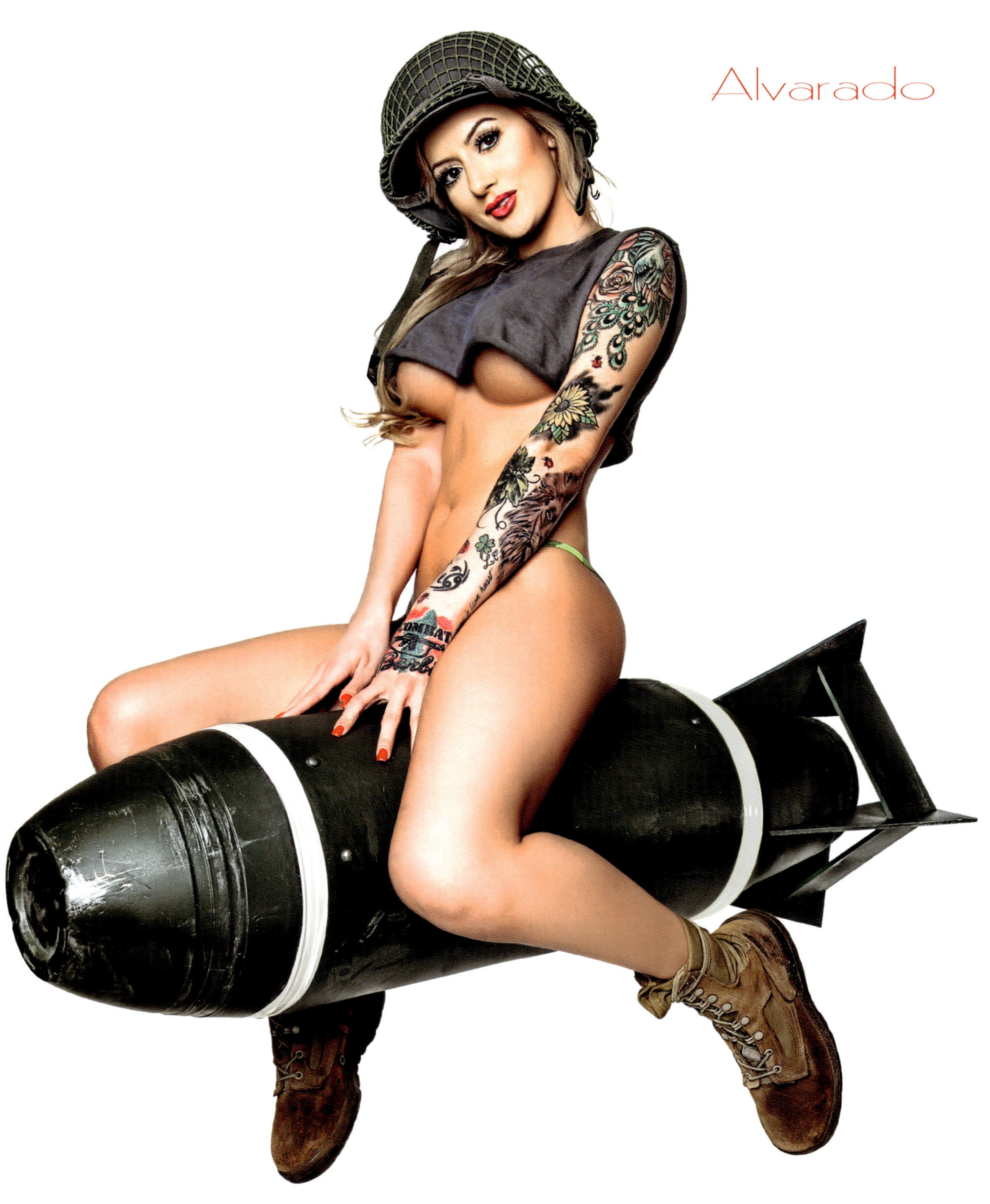

Alvarado

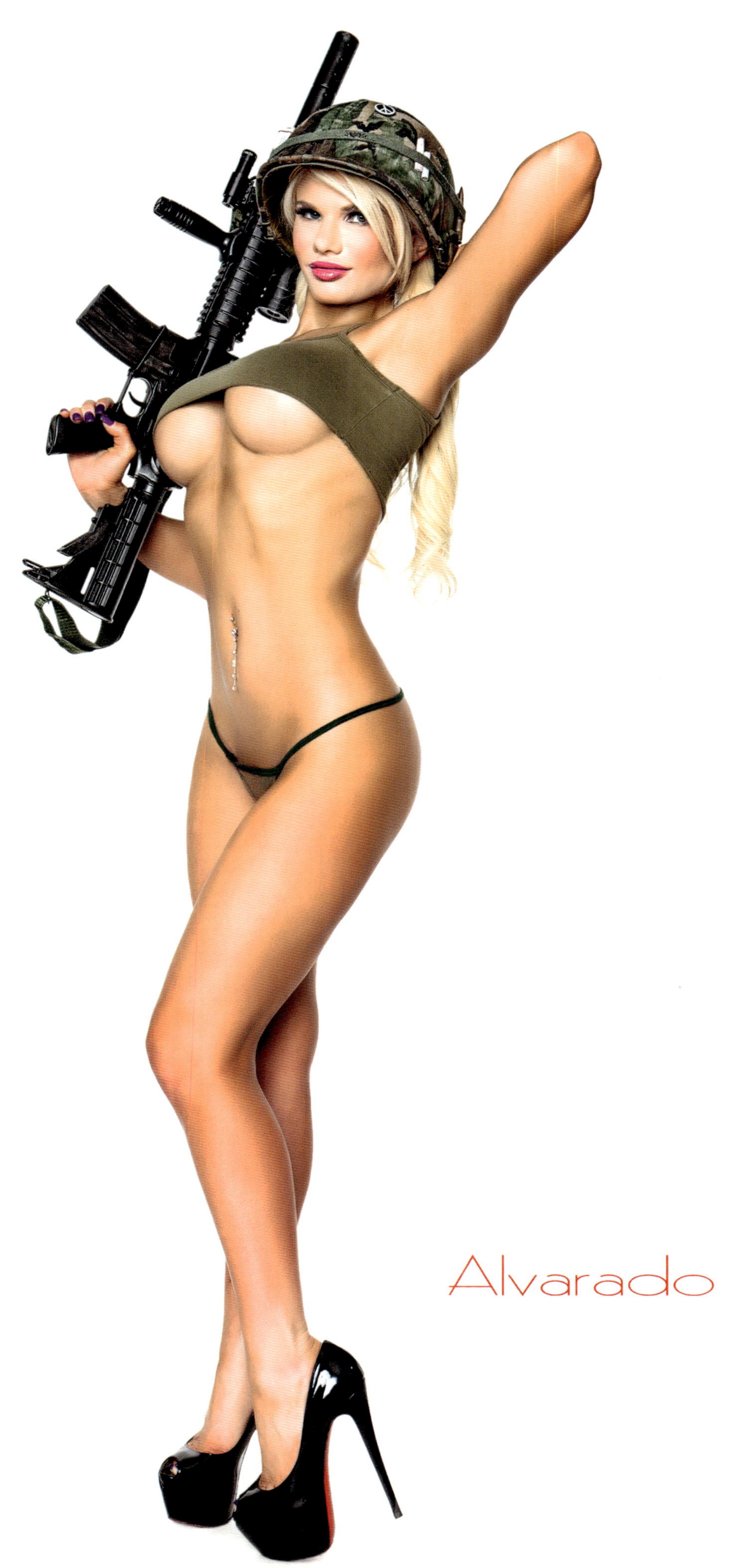

Alvarado

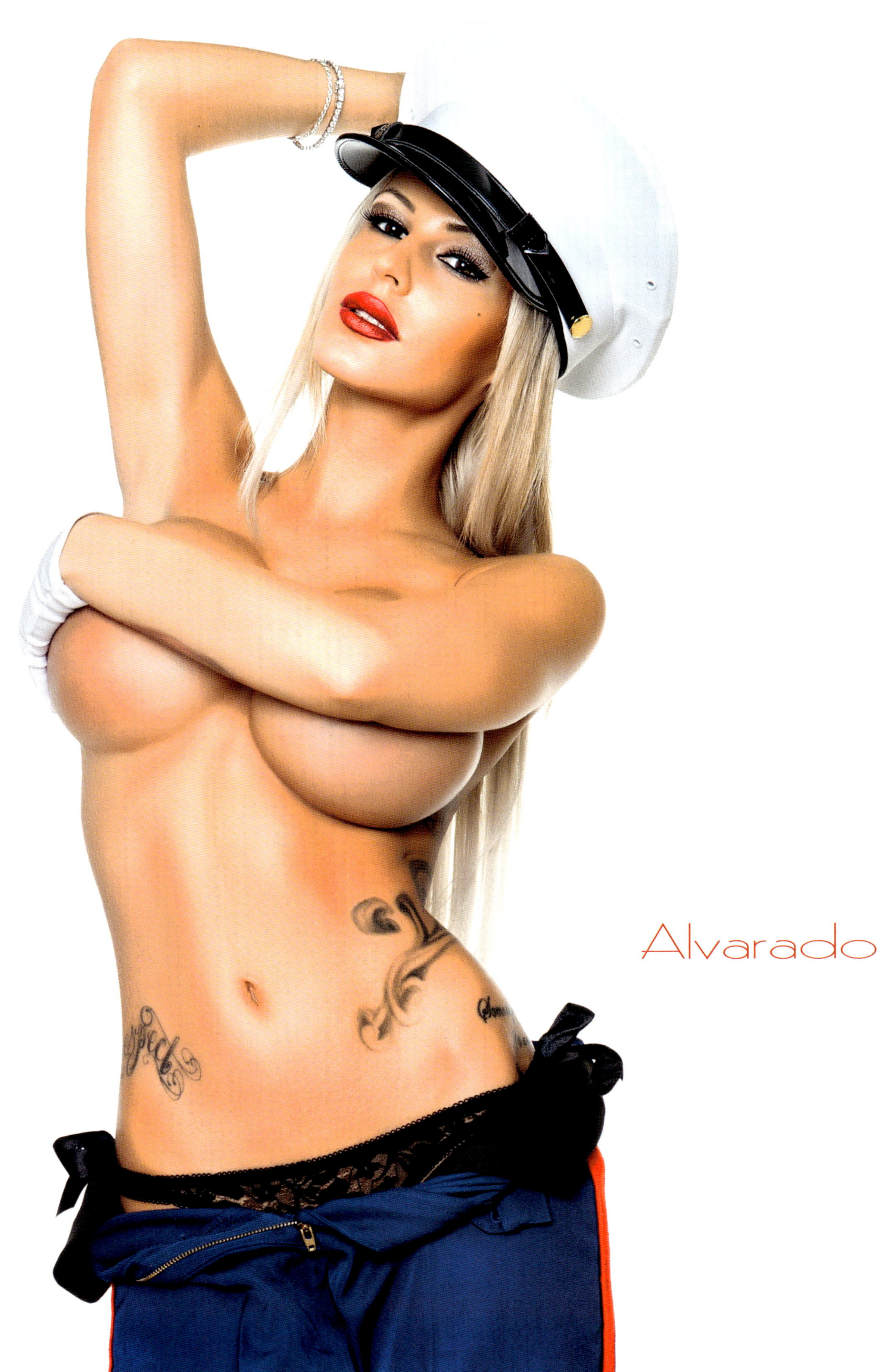
Alvarado

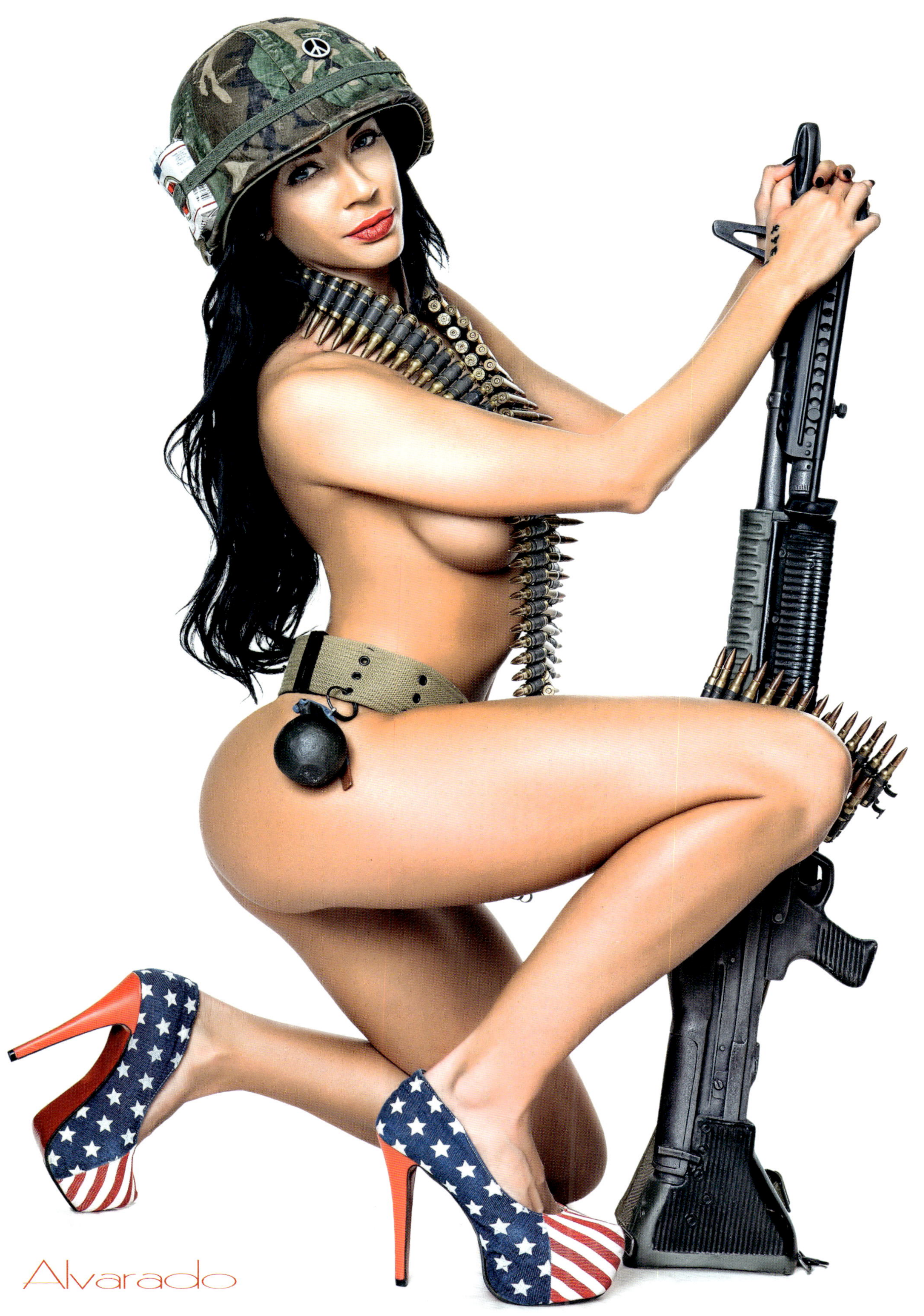
Alvarado

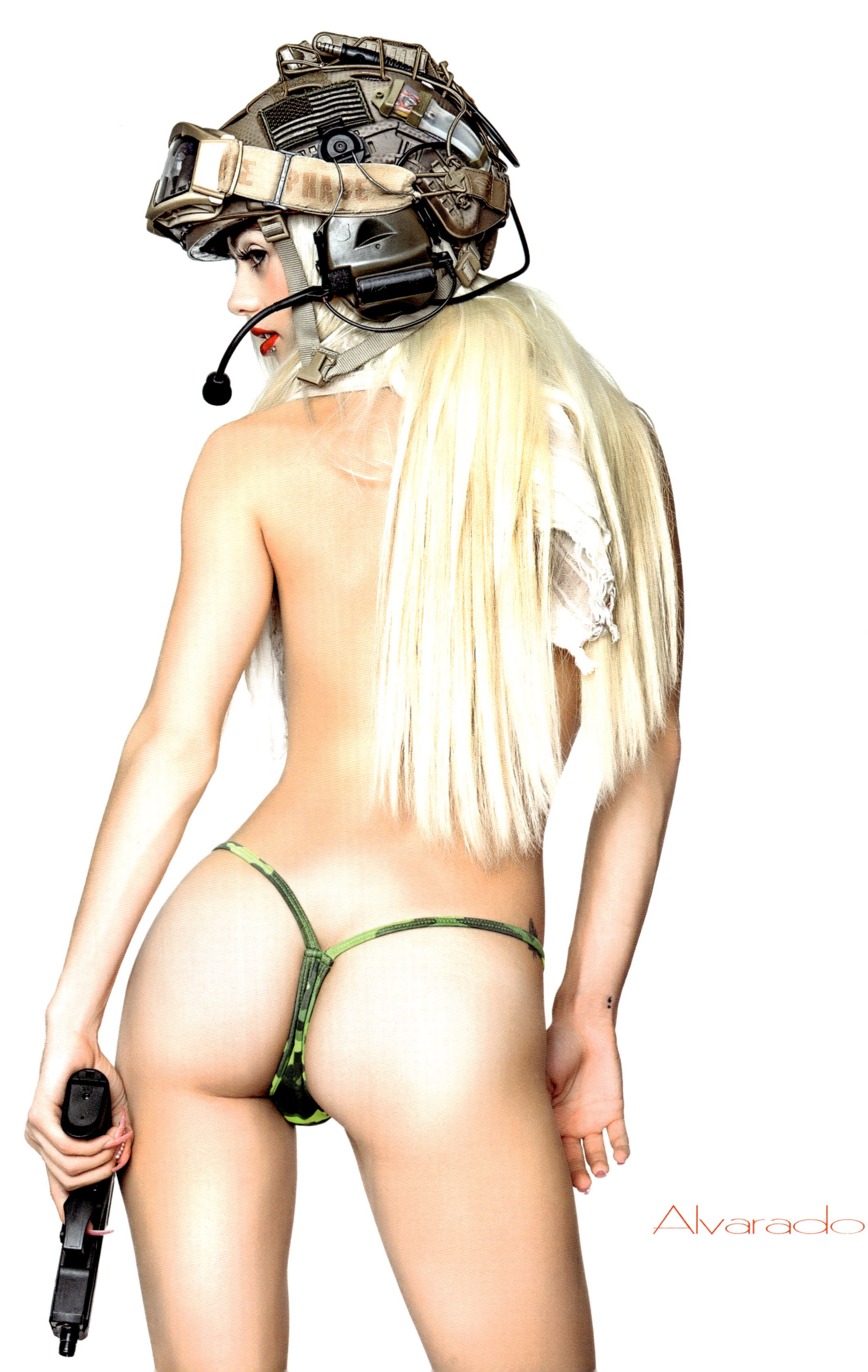

Alvarado

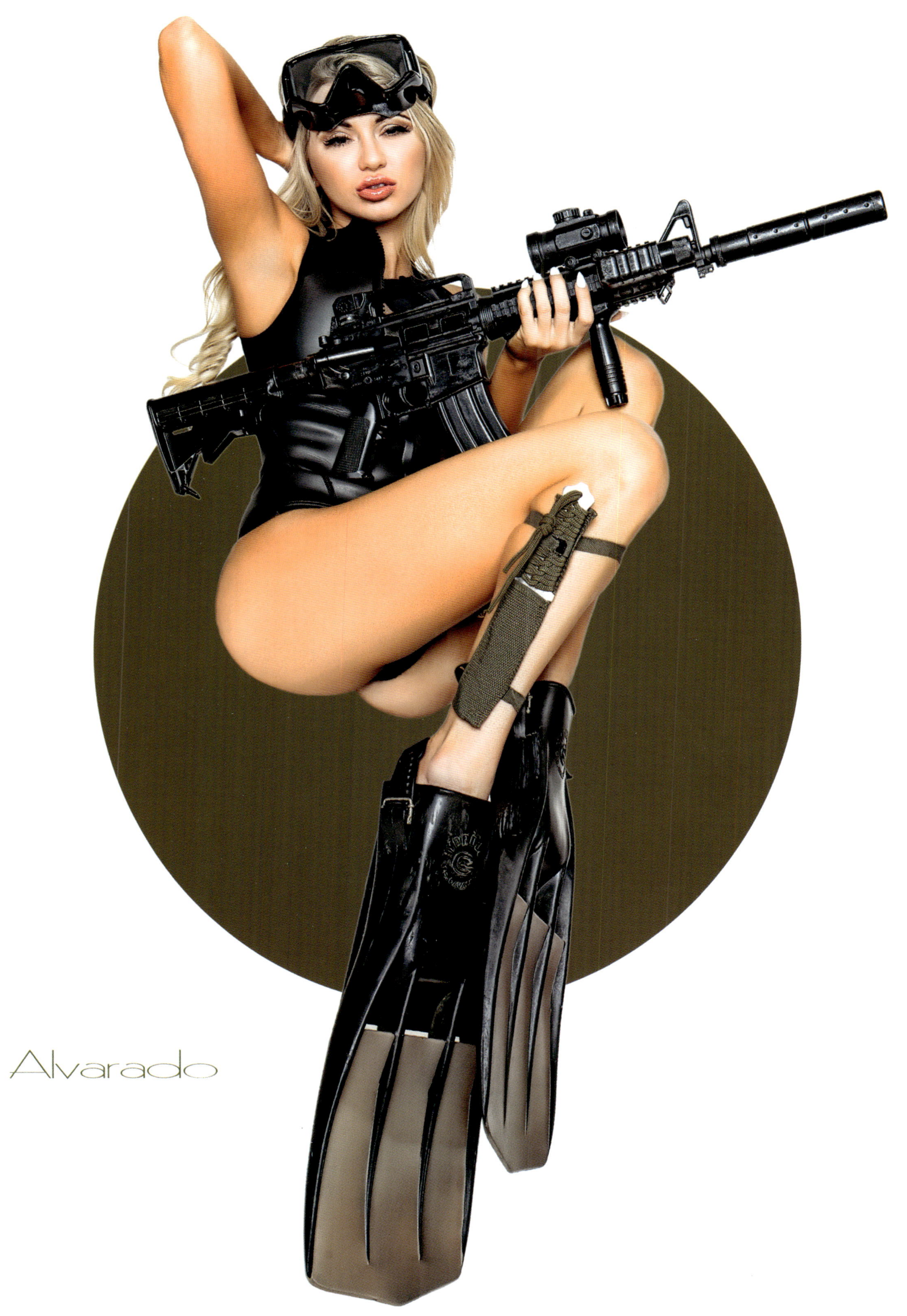

Alvarado

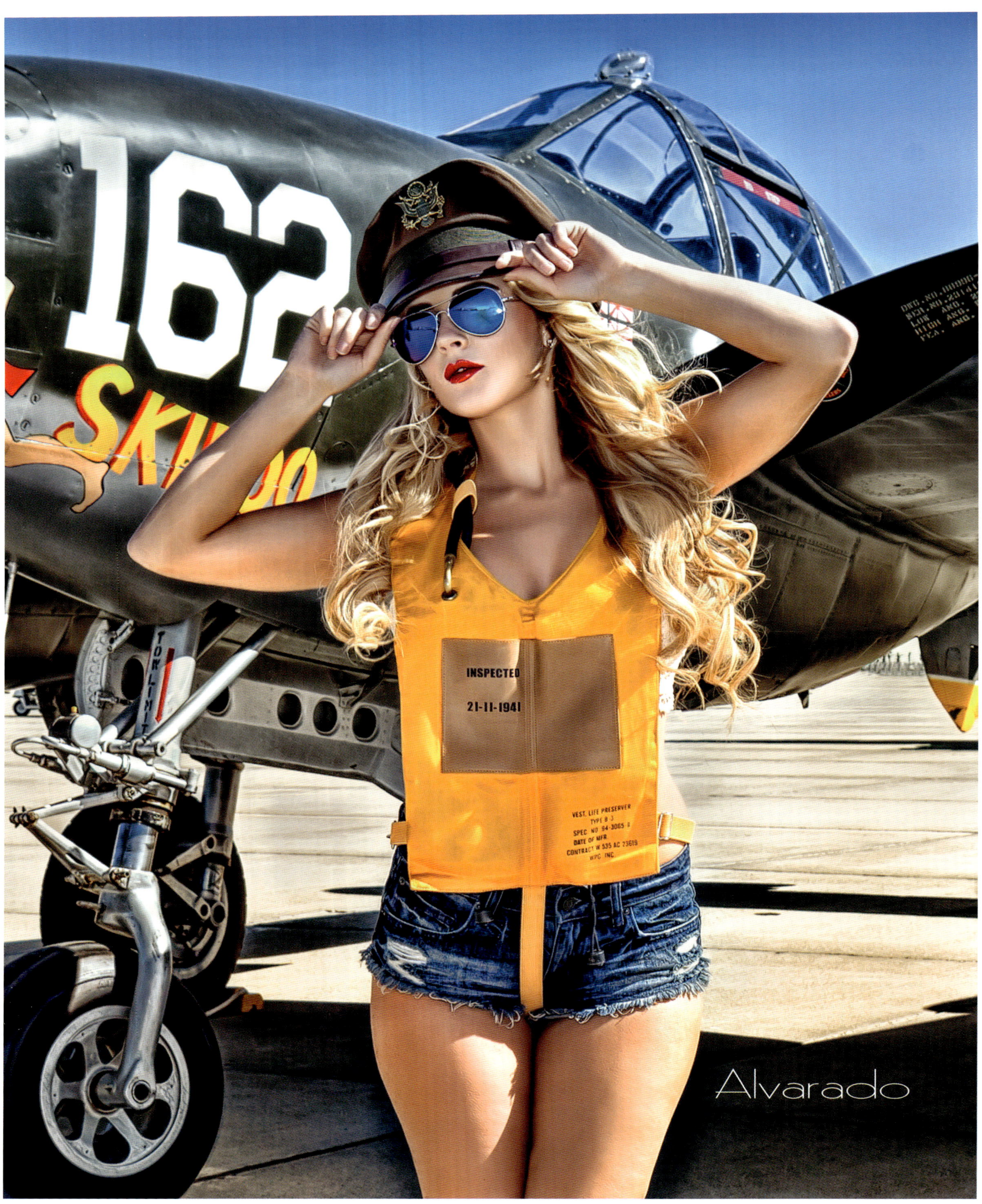
162
INSPECTED
21-11-1941
Alvarado

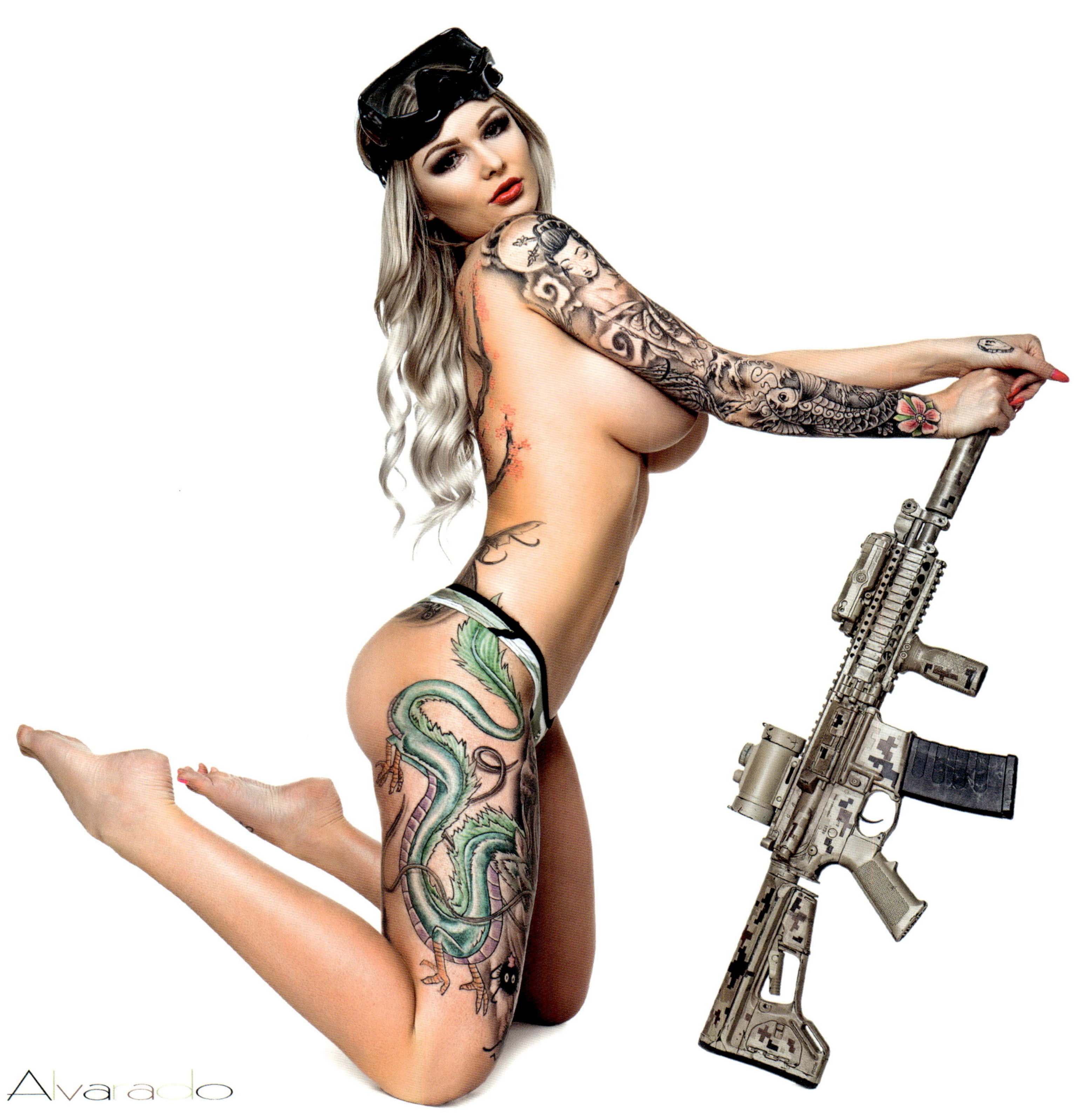
Alvarado

Alvarado

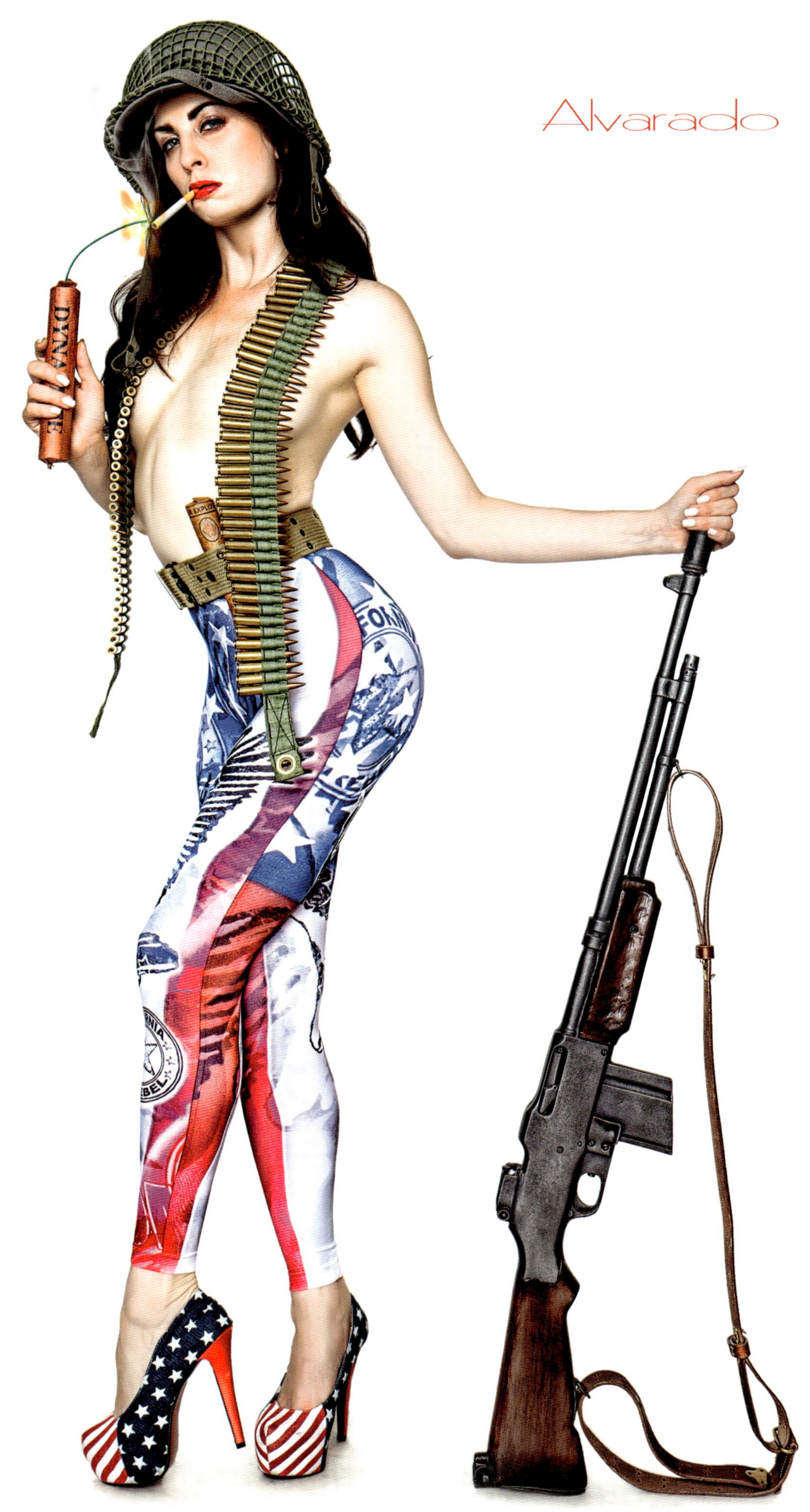

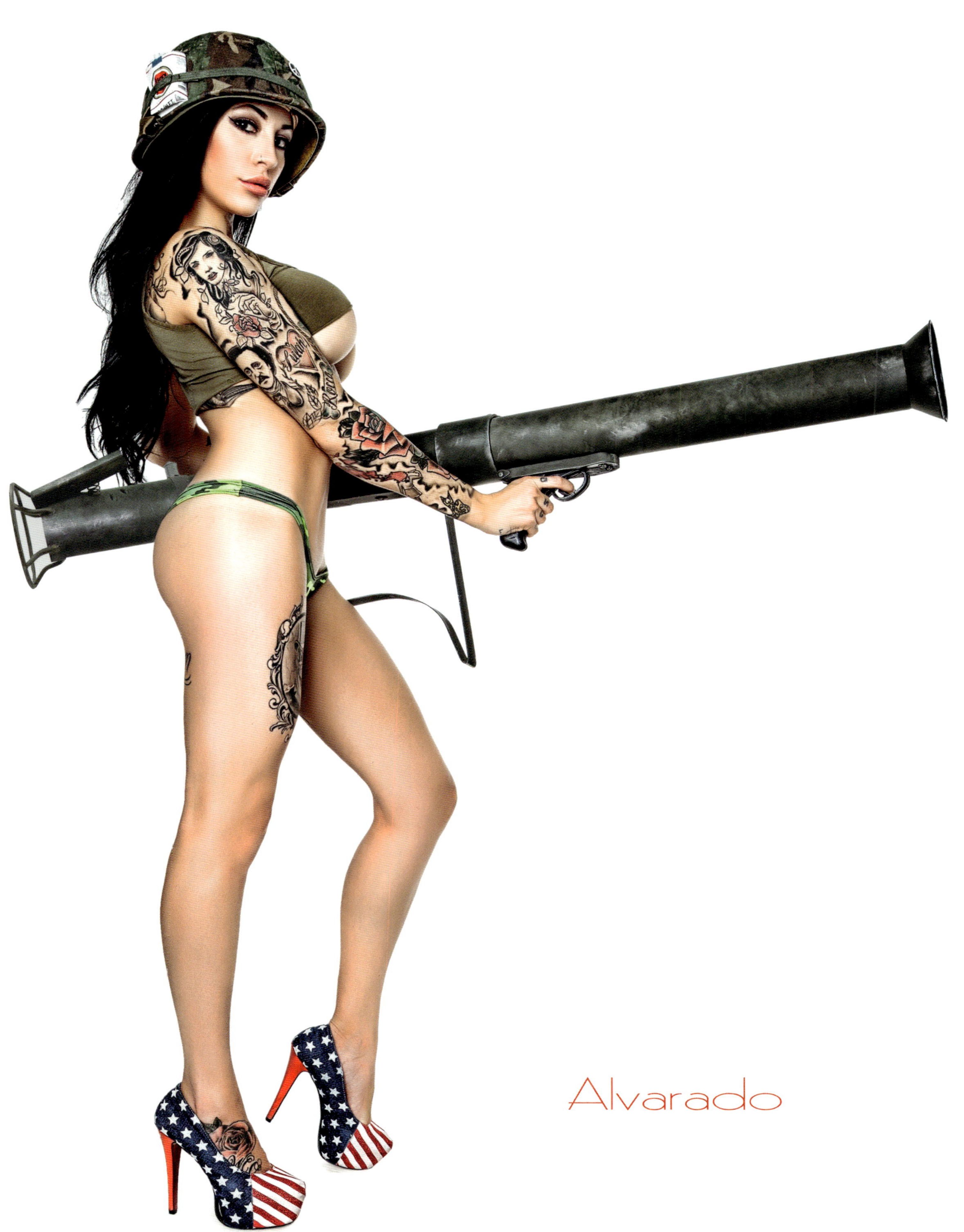

Alvarado

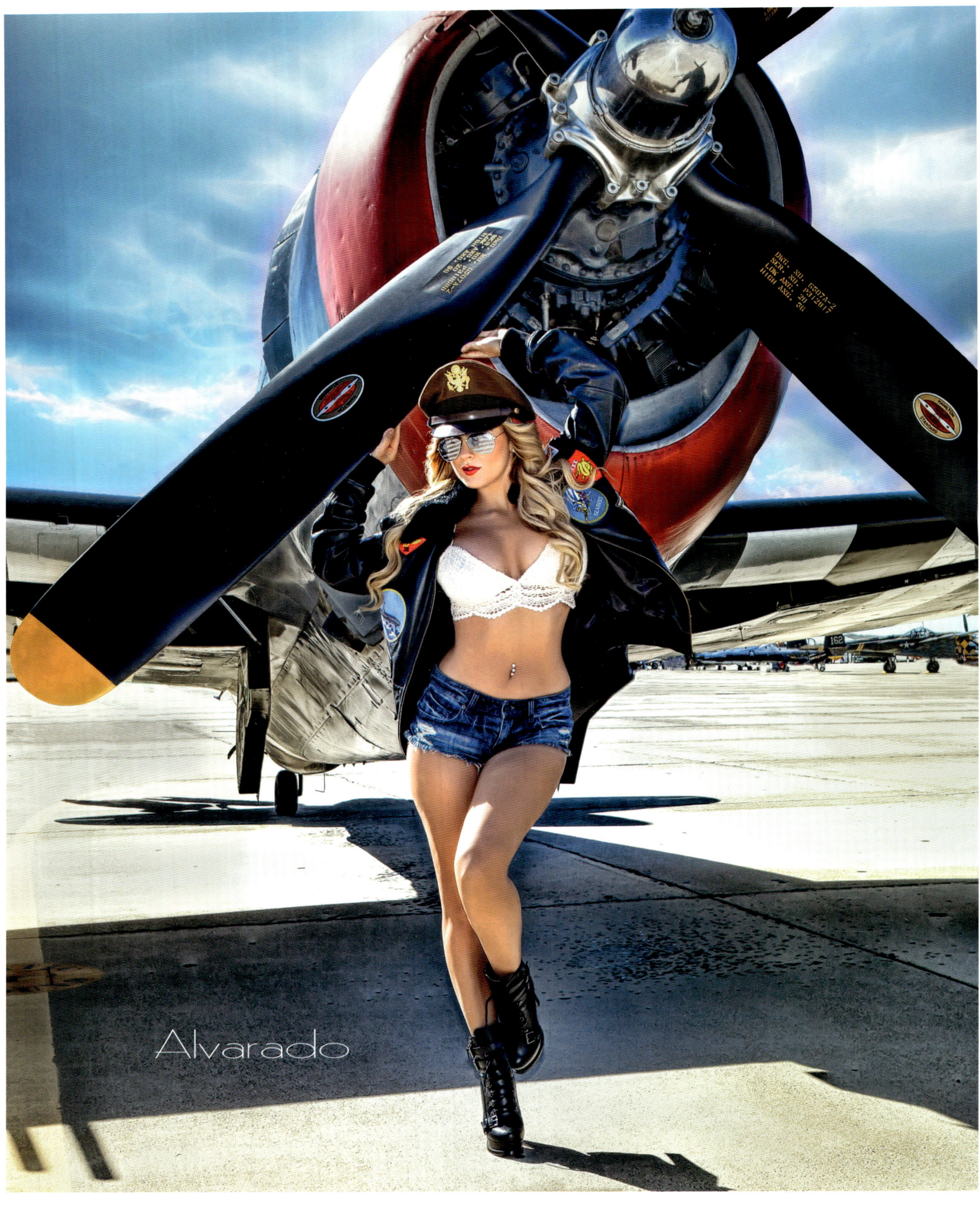
Alvarado

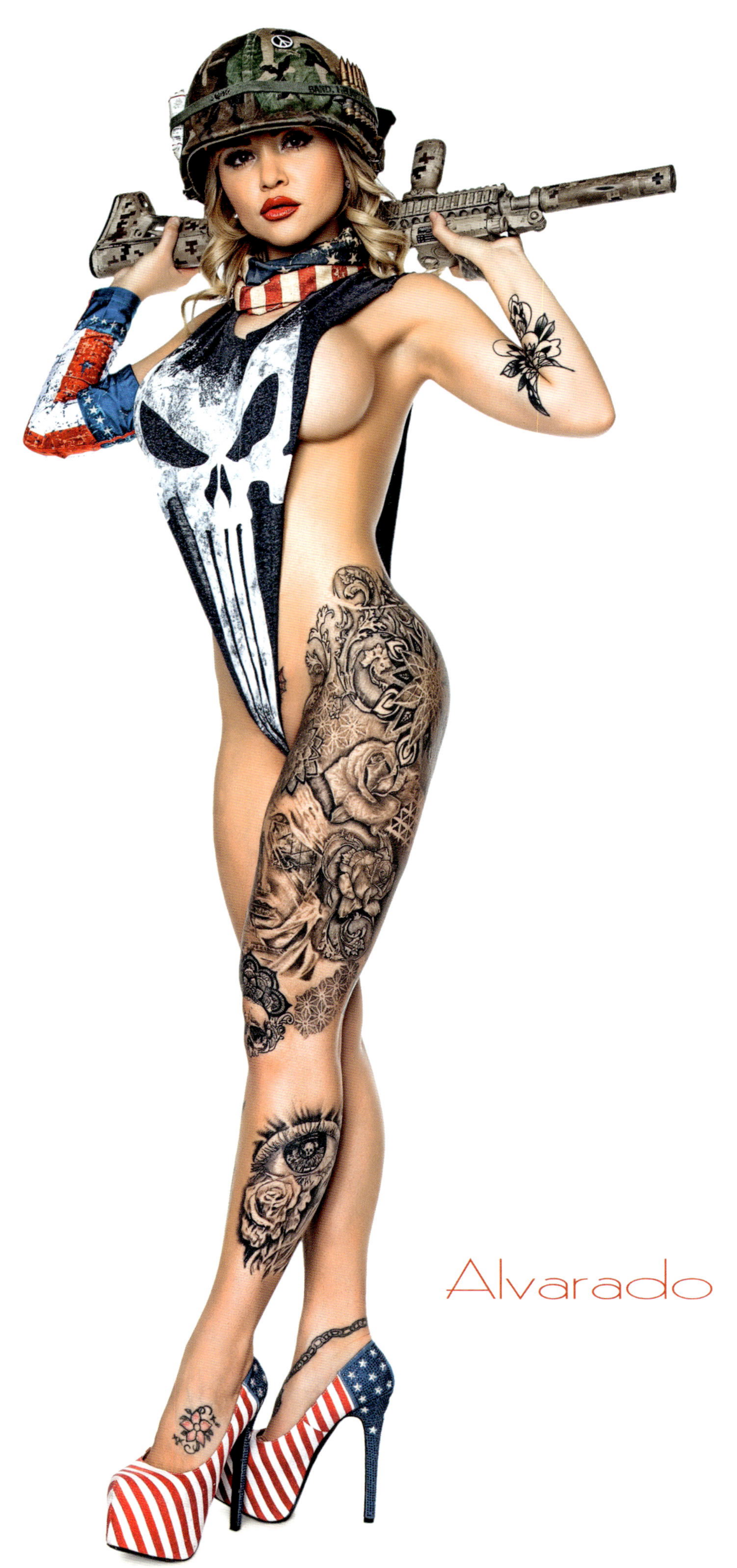

Alvarado

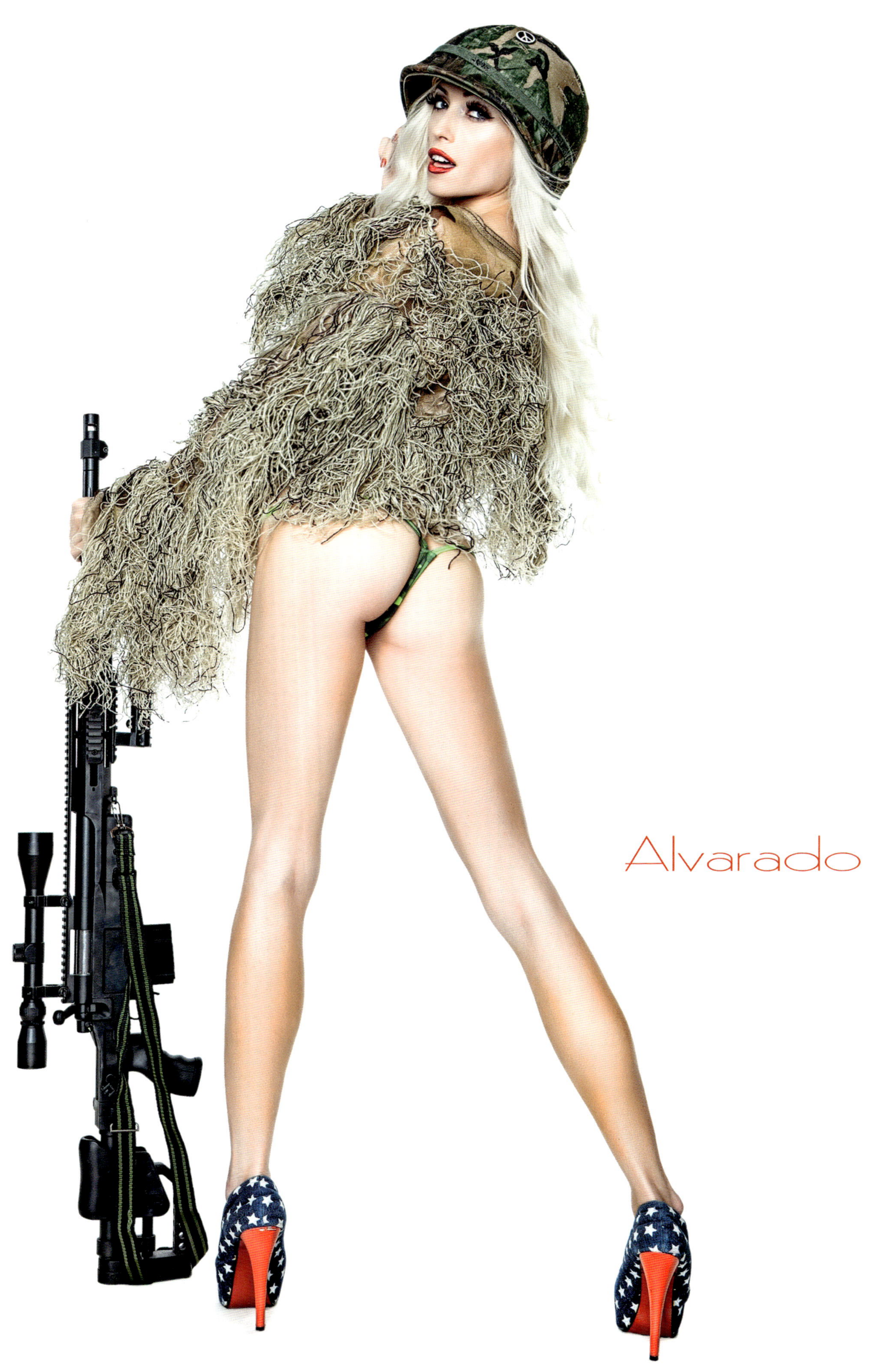

Alvarado

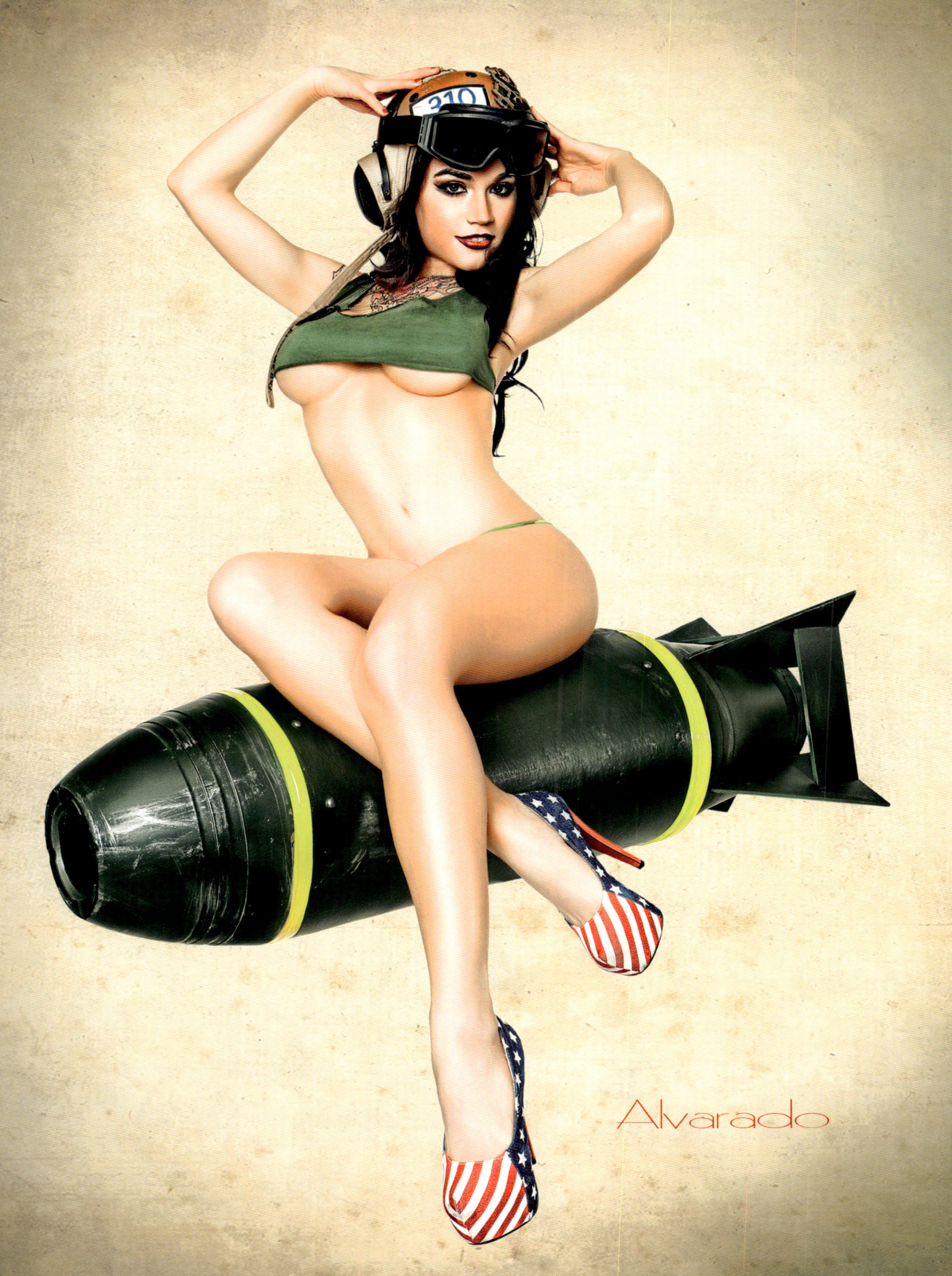
310
Alvarado

Alvarado

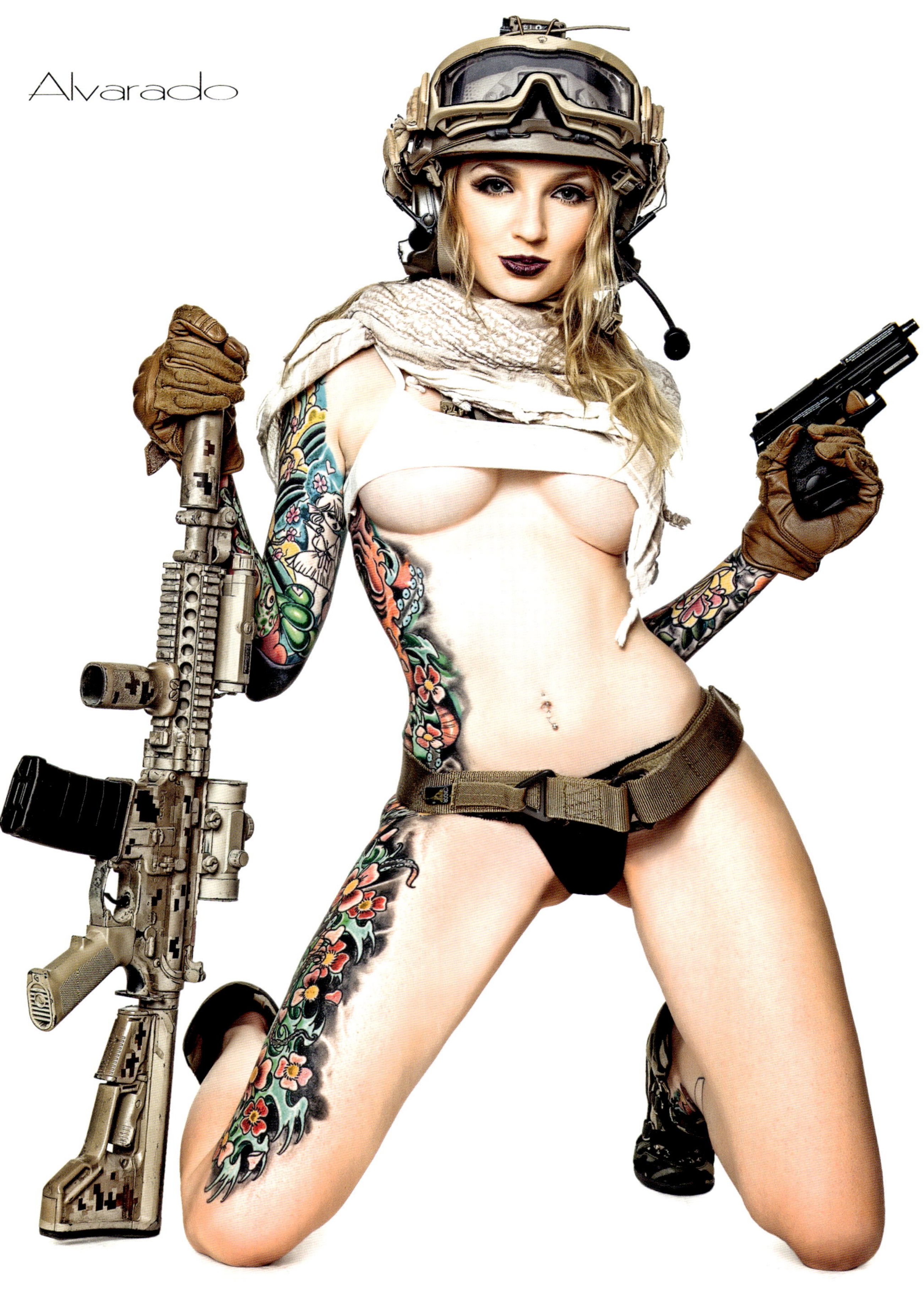

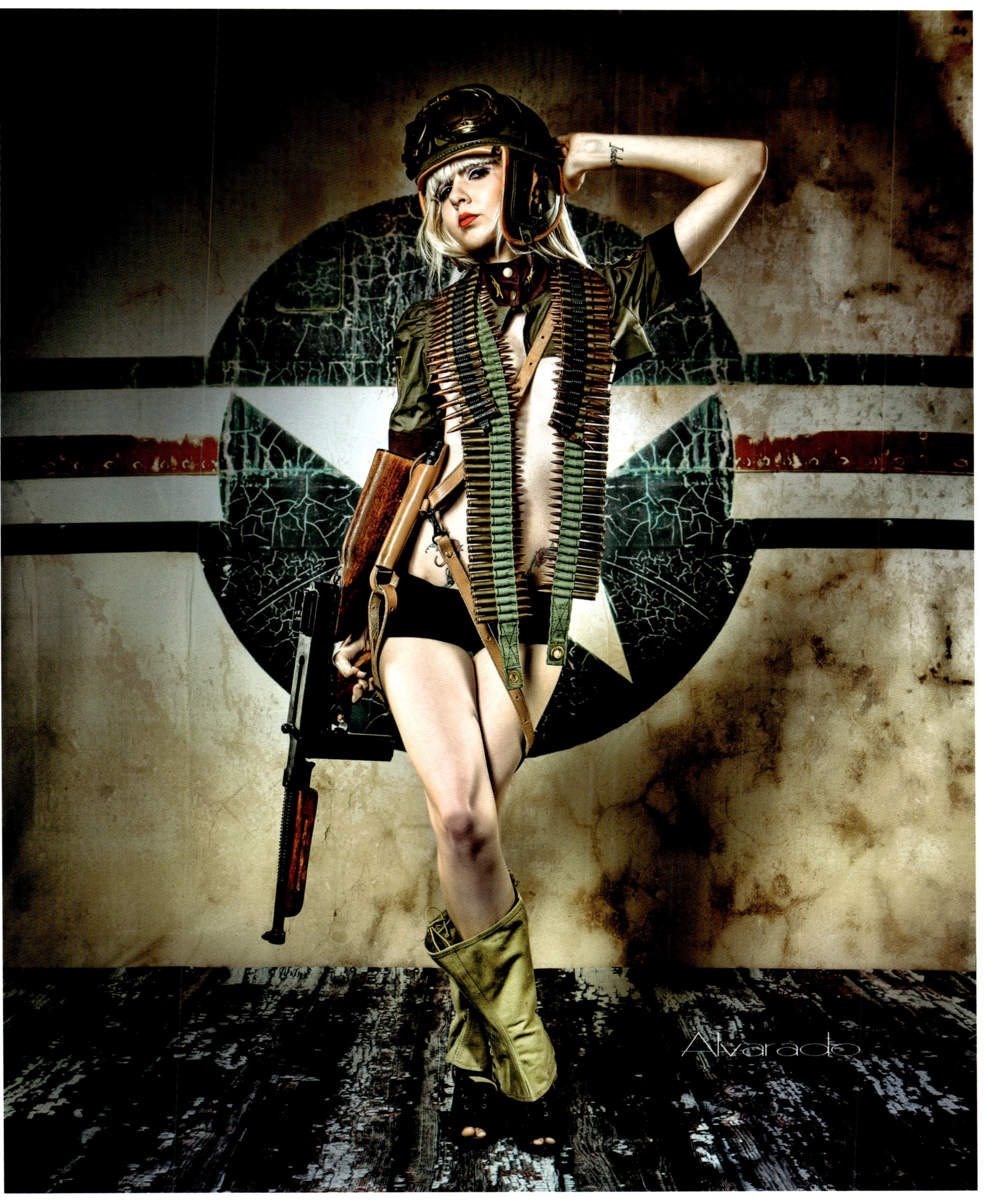
Alvarado

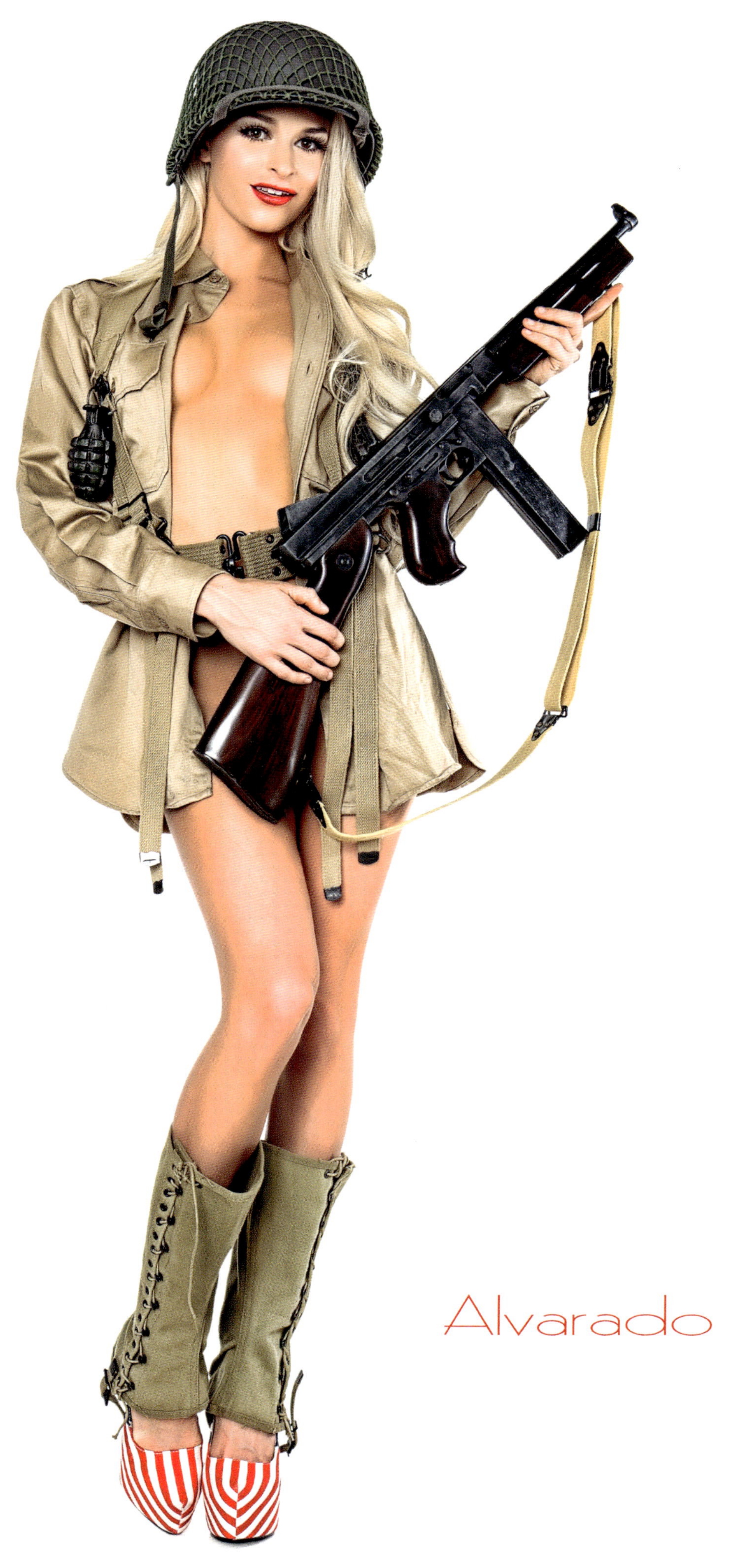

Alvarado

Alvarado

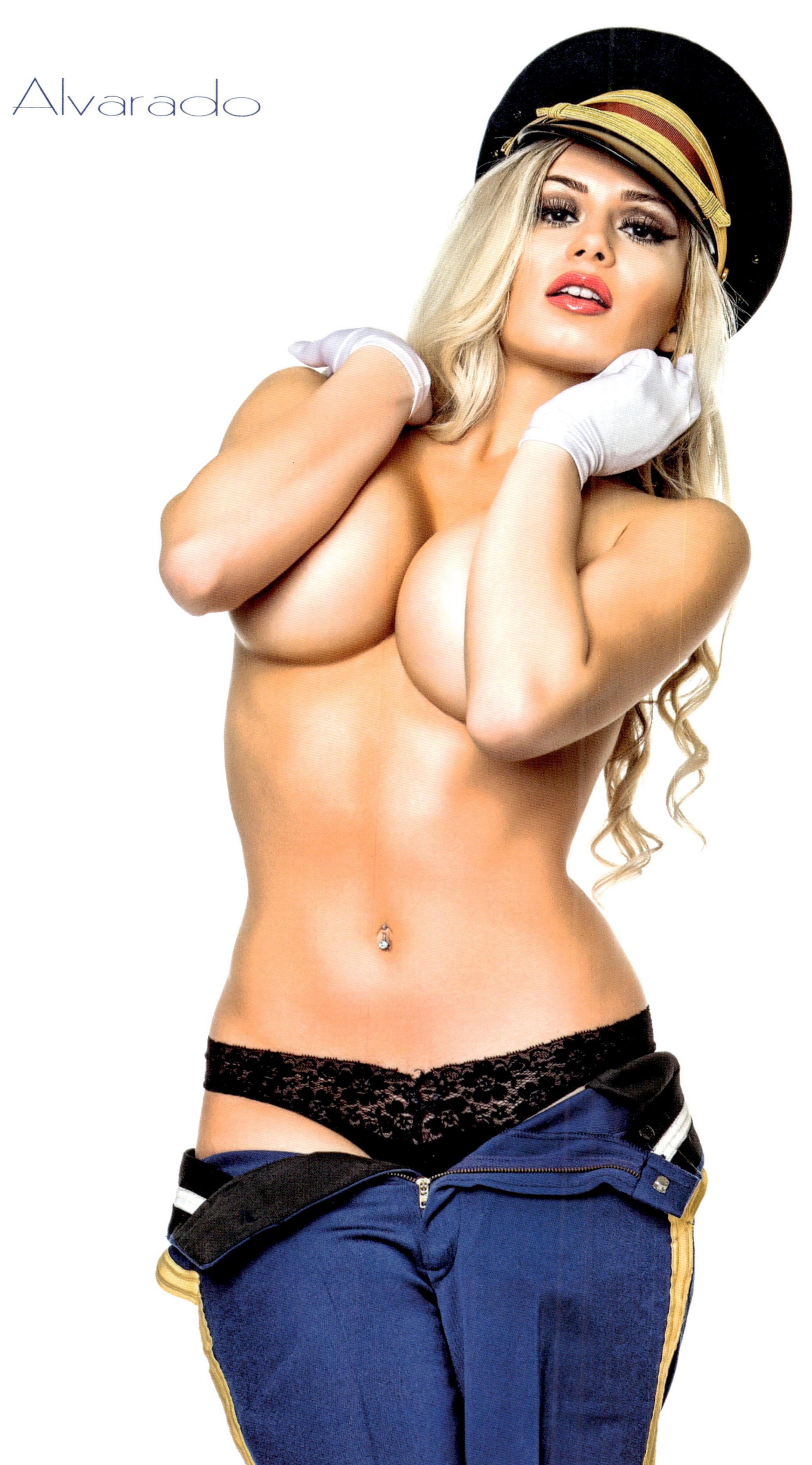

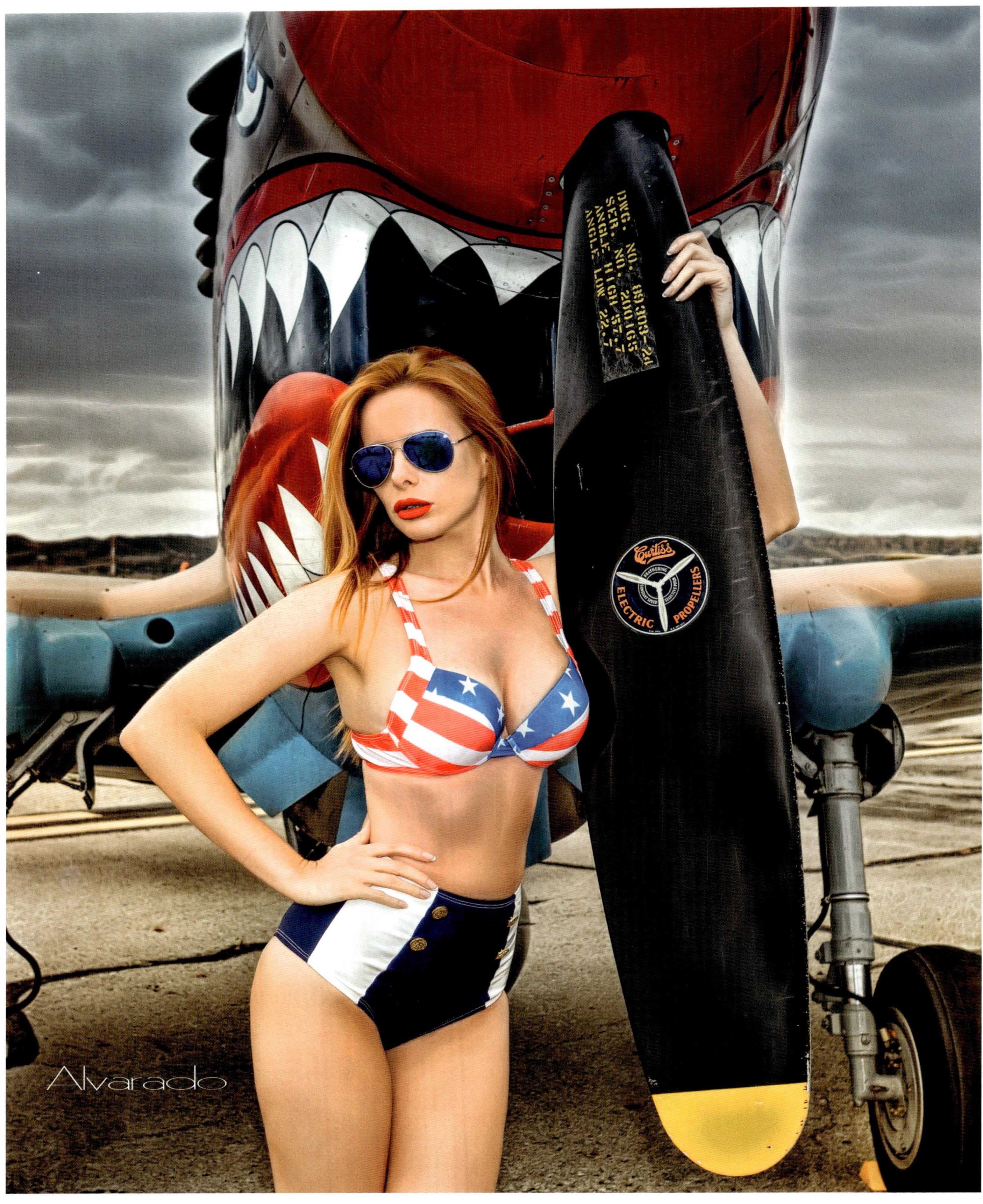
DWG. NO. 89303-24
SER. NO. 200165
ANGLE HIGH 37.7
ANGLE LOW 22.7
Curtiss
ELECTRIC PROPELLERS
Alvarado

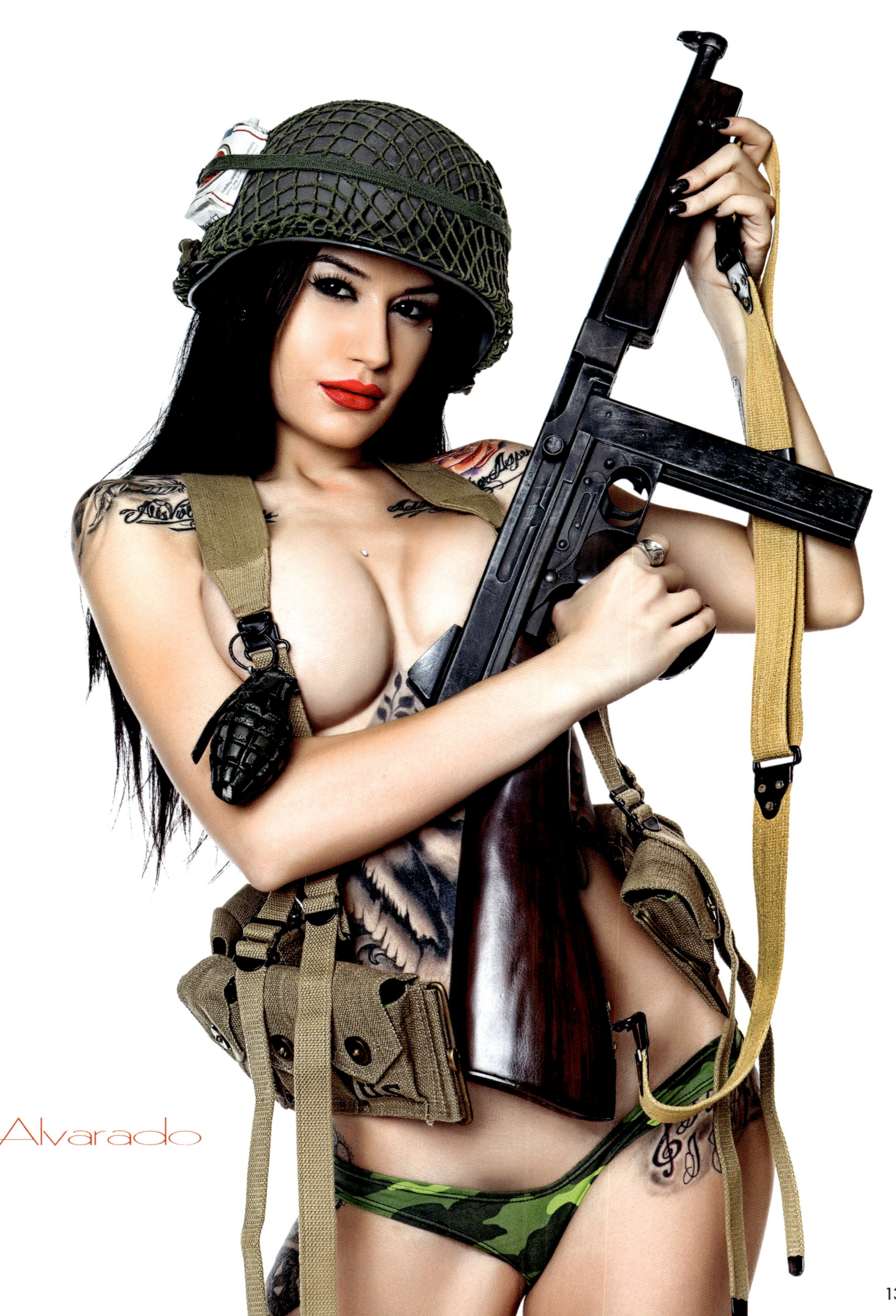

Alvarado

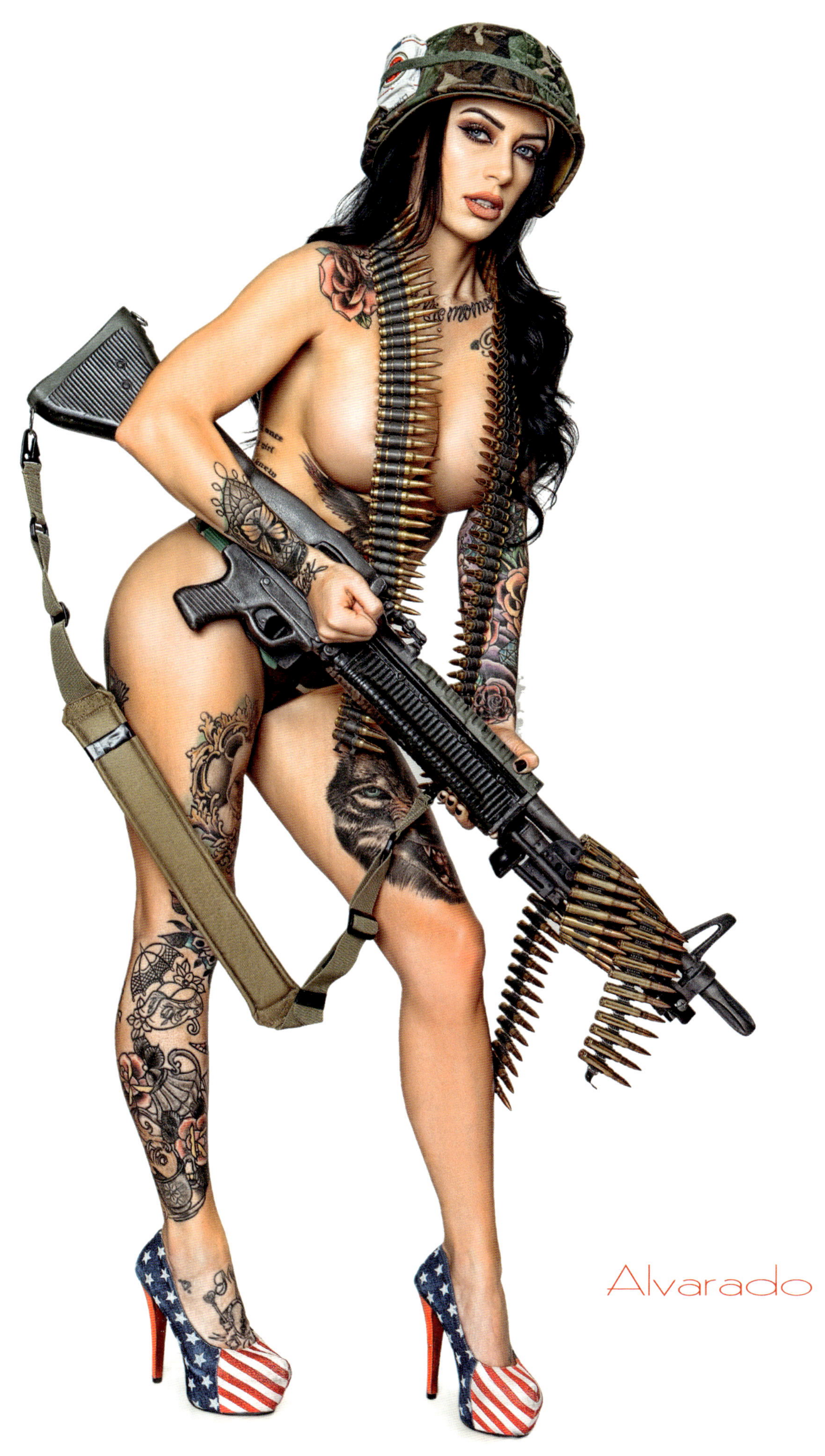

Alvarado

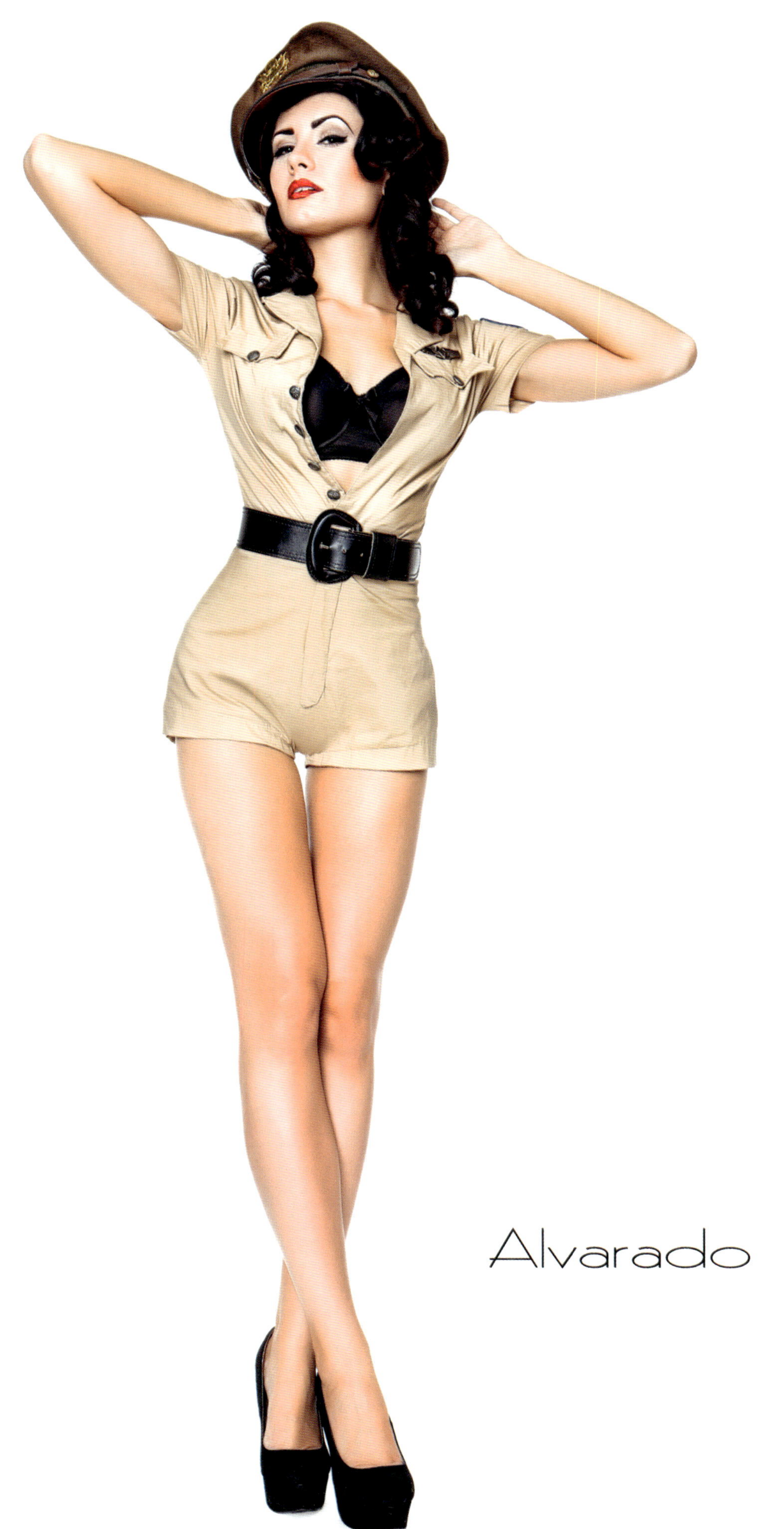

Alvarado

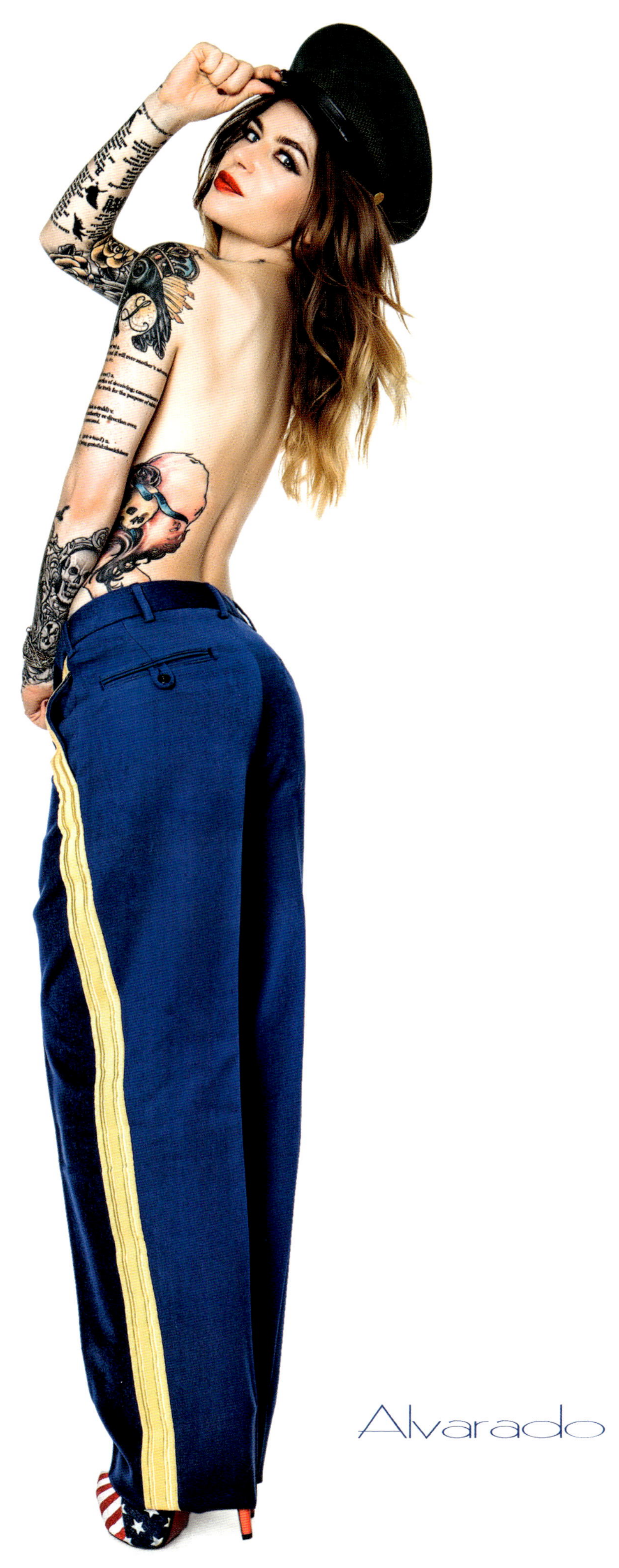

Alvarado

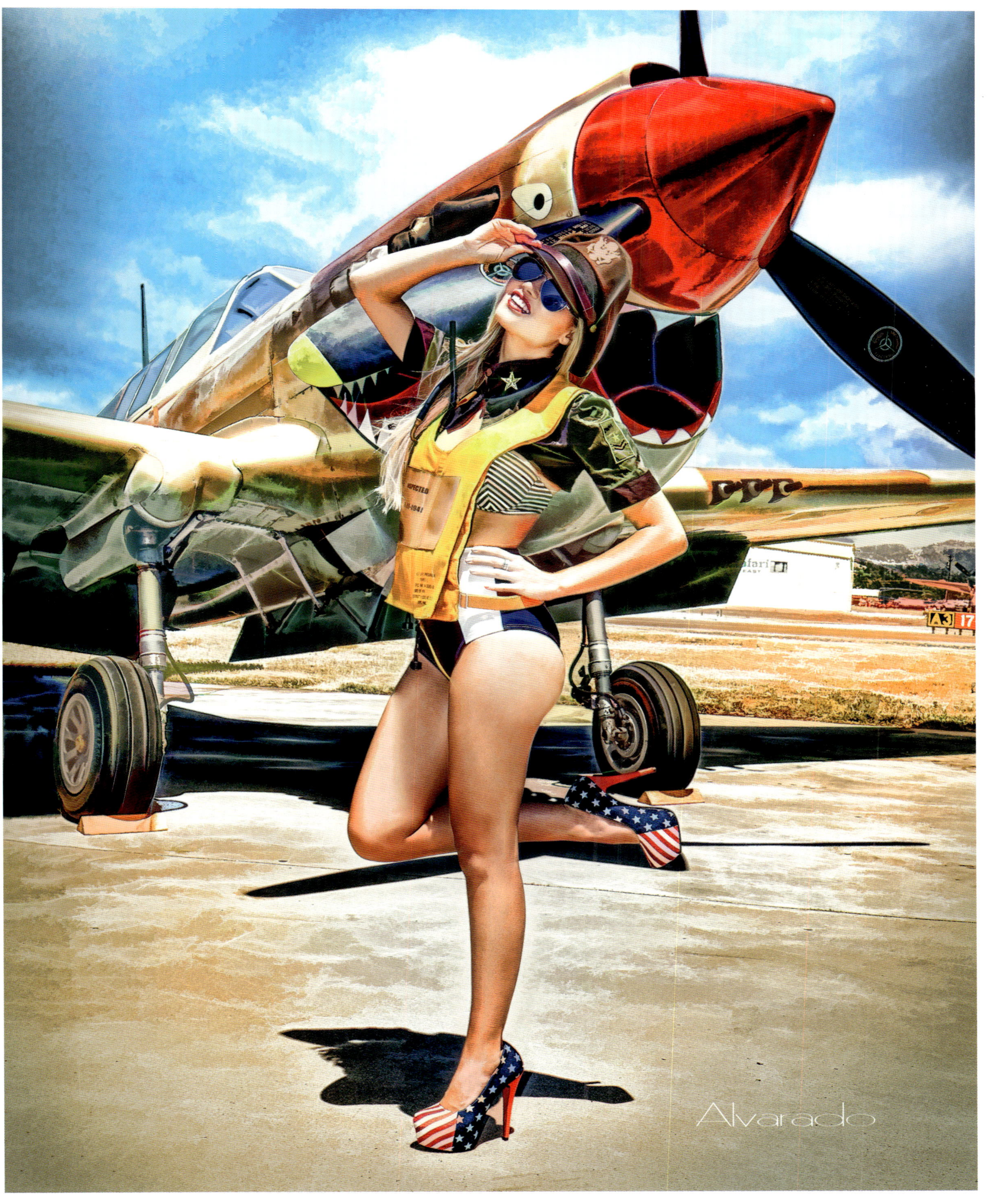
A3
17
Alvarado

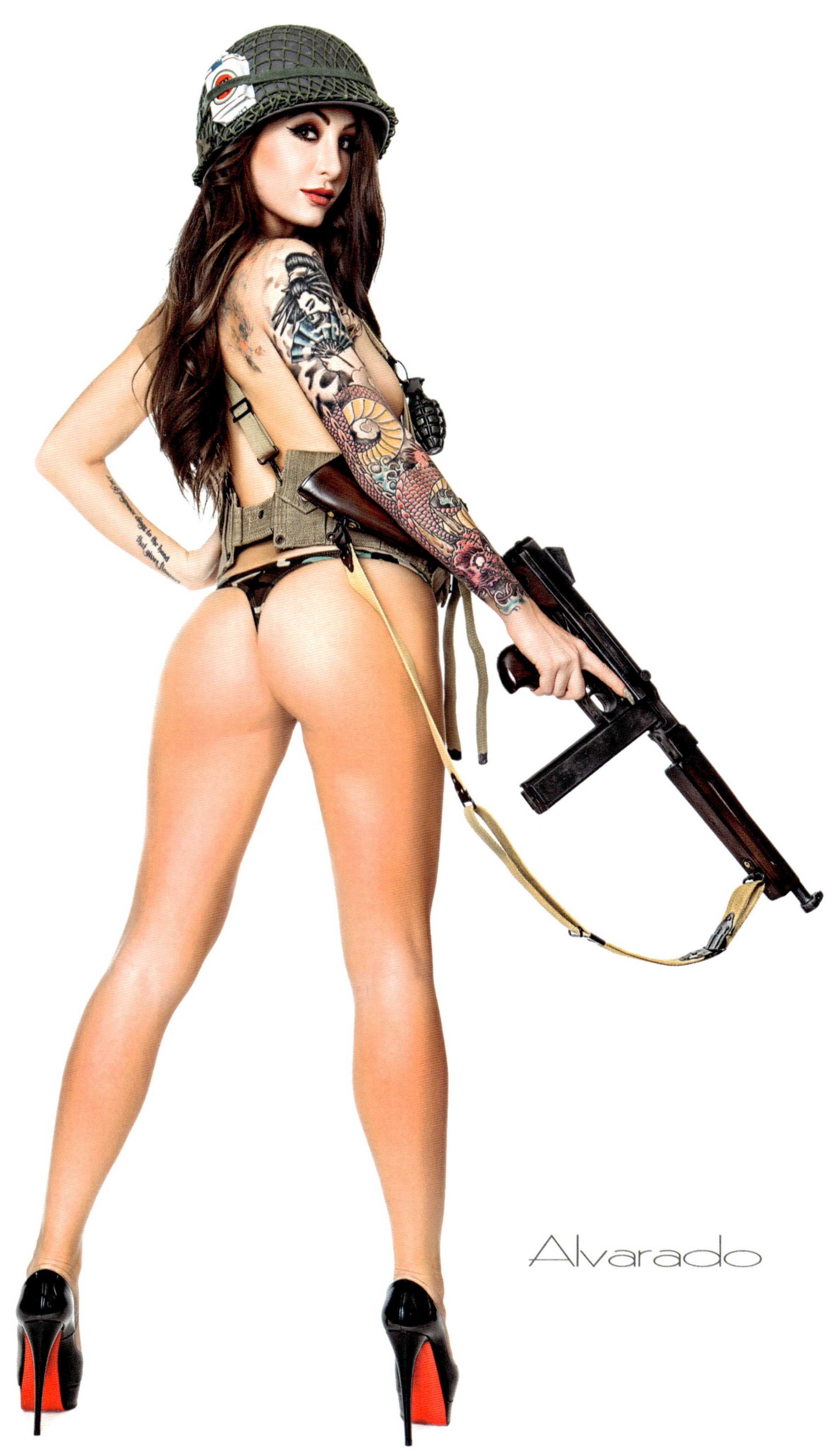
Alvarado

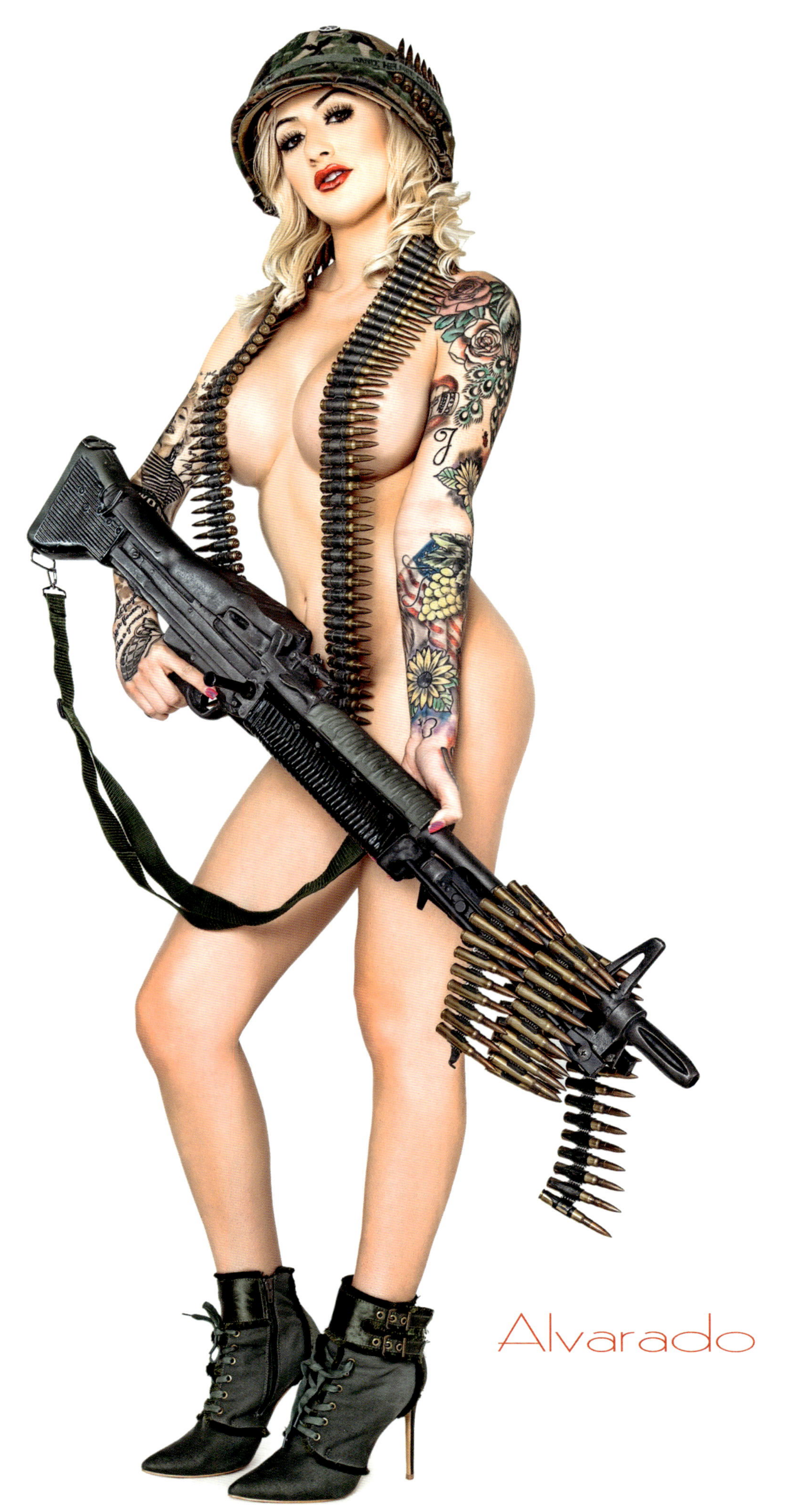

Alvarado

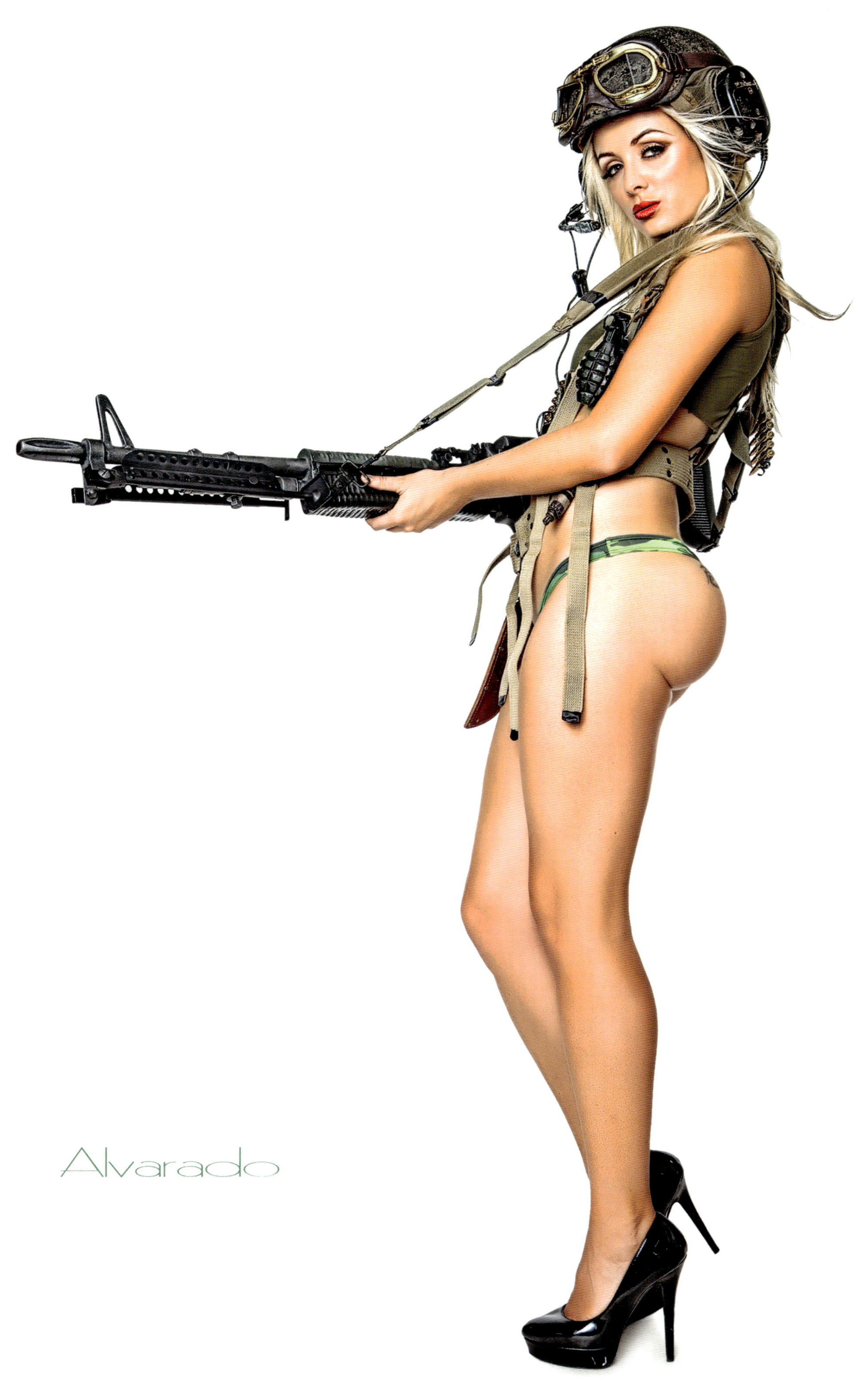

Alvarado

Alvarado

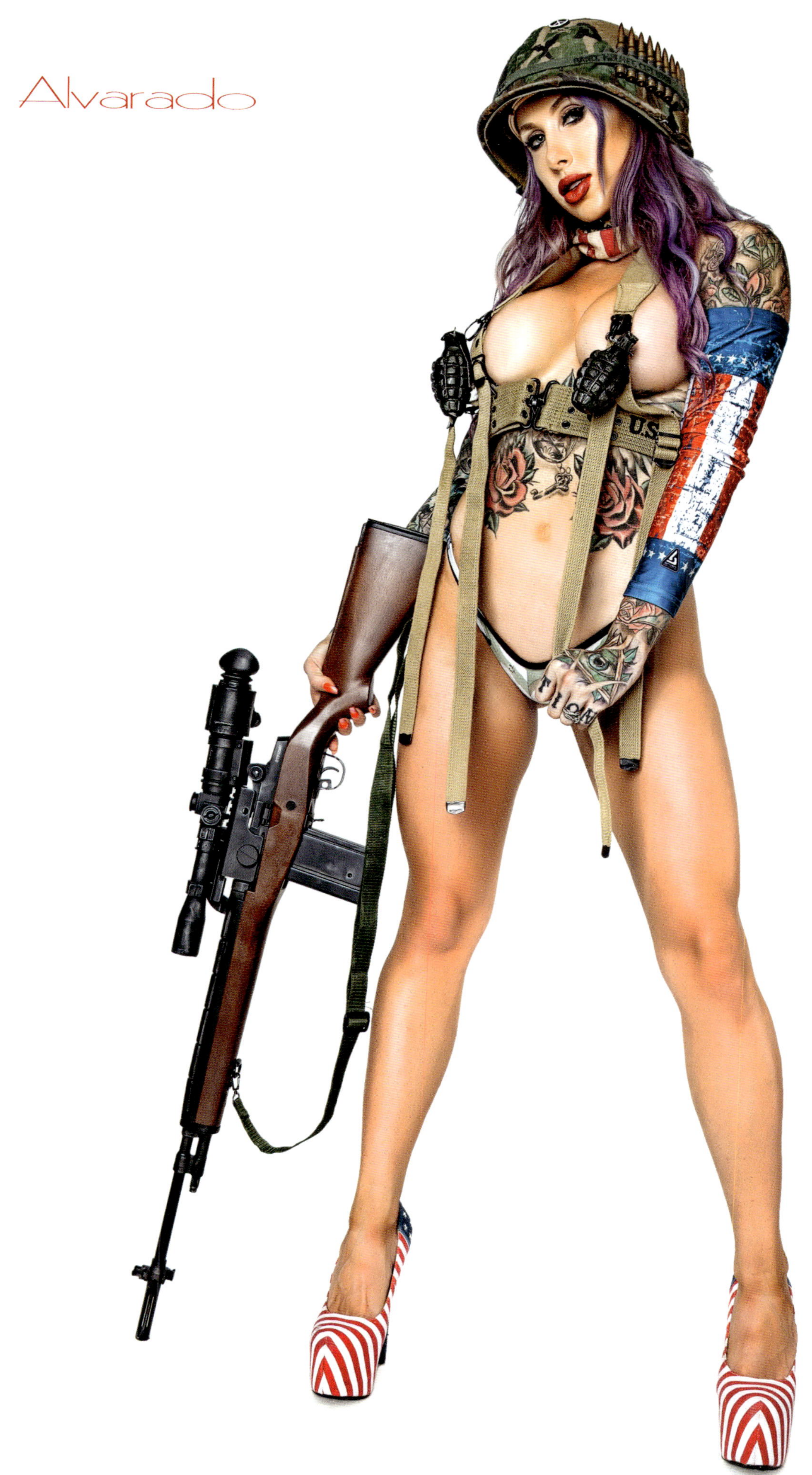

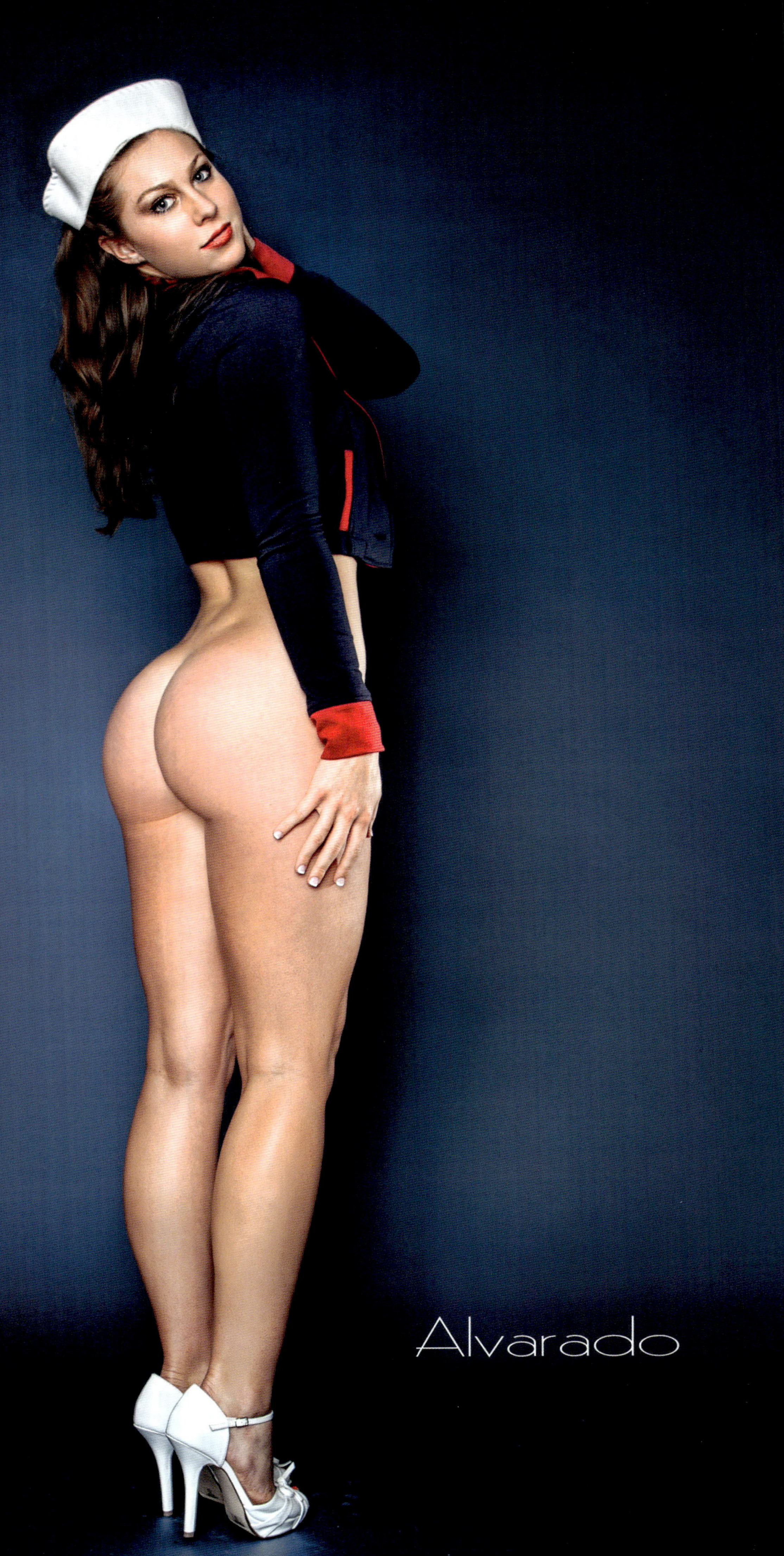
Alvarado

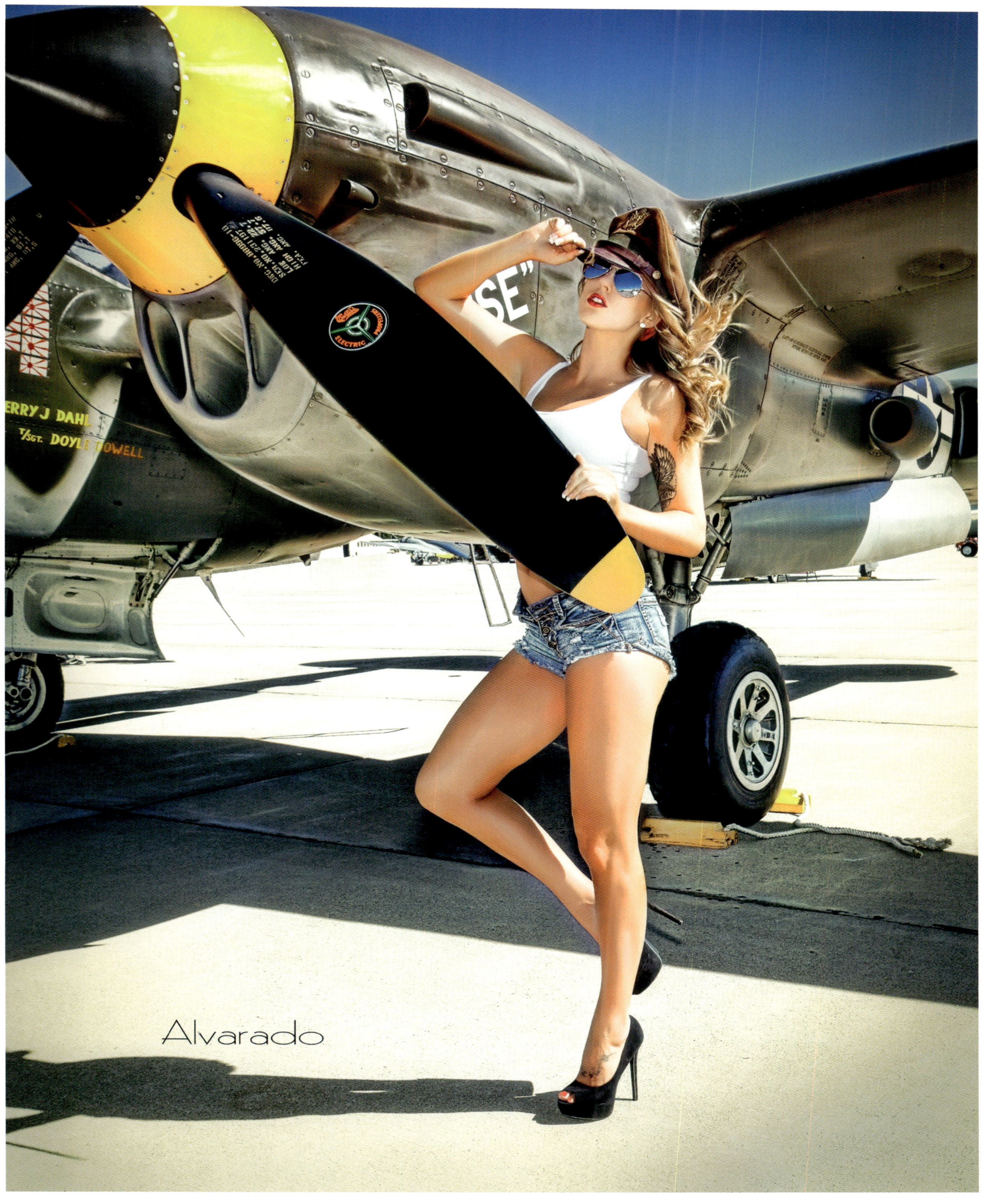

Alvarado

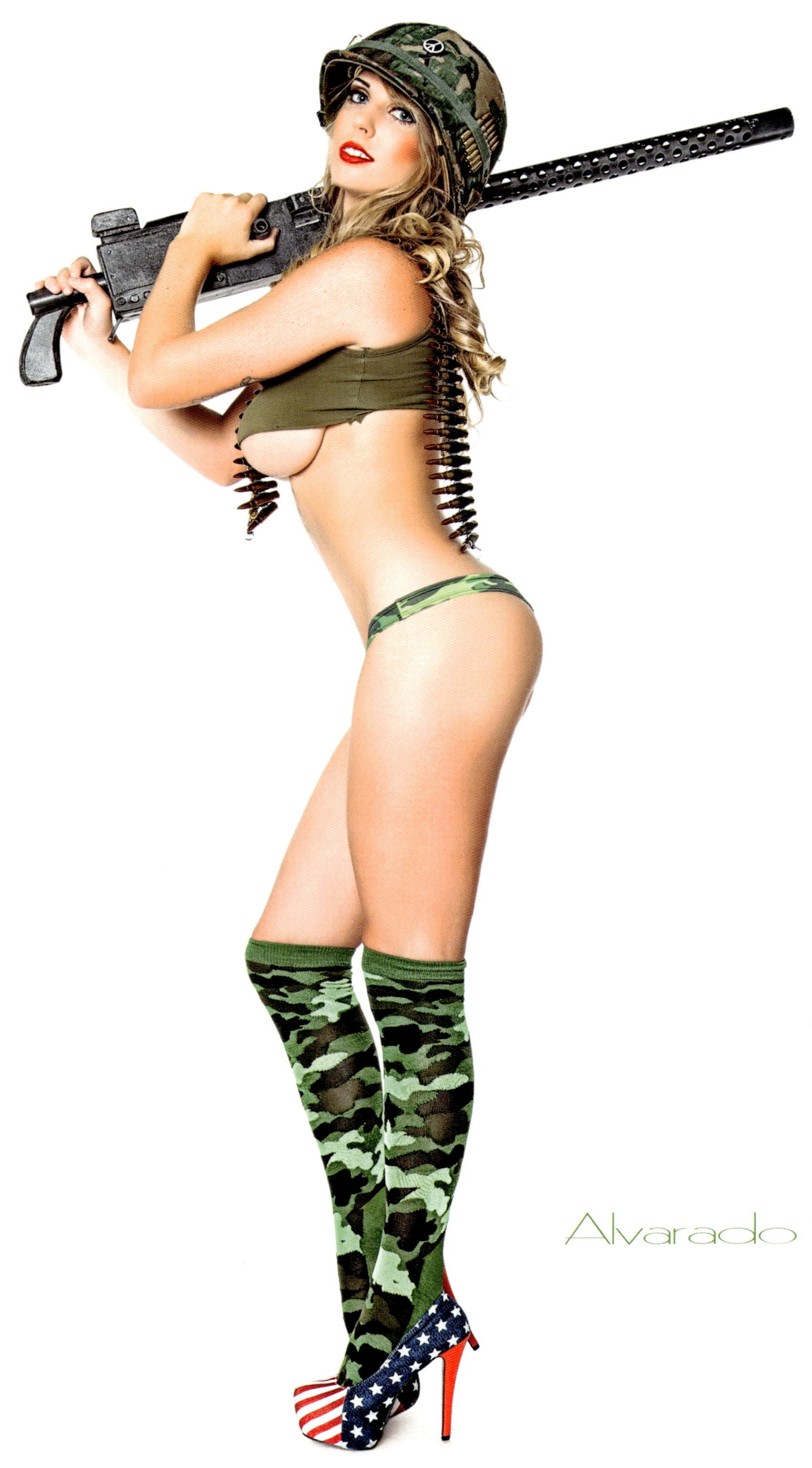

Alvarado

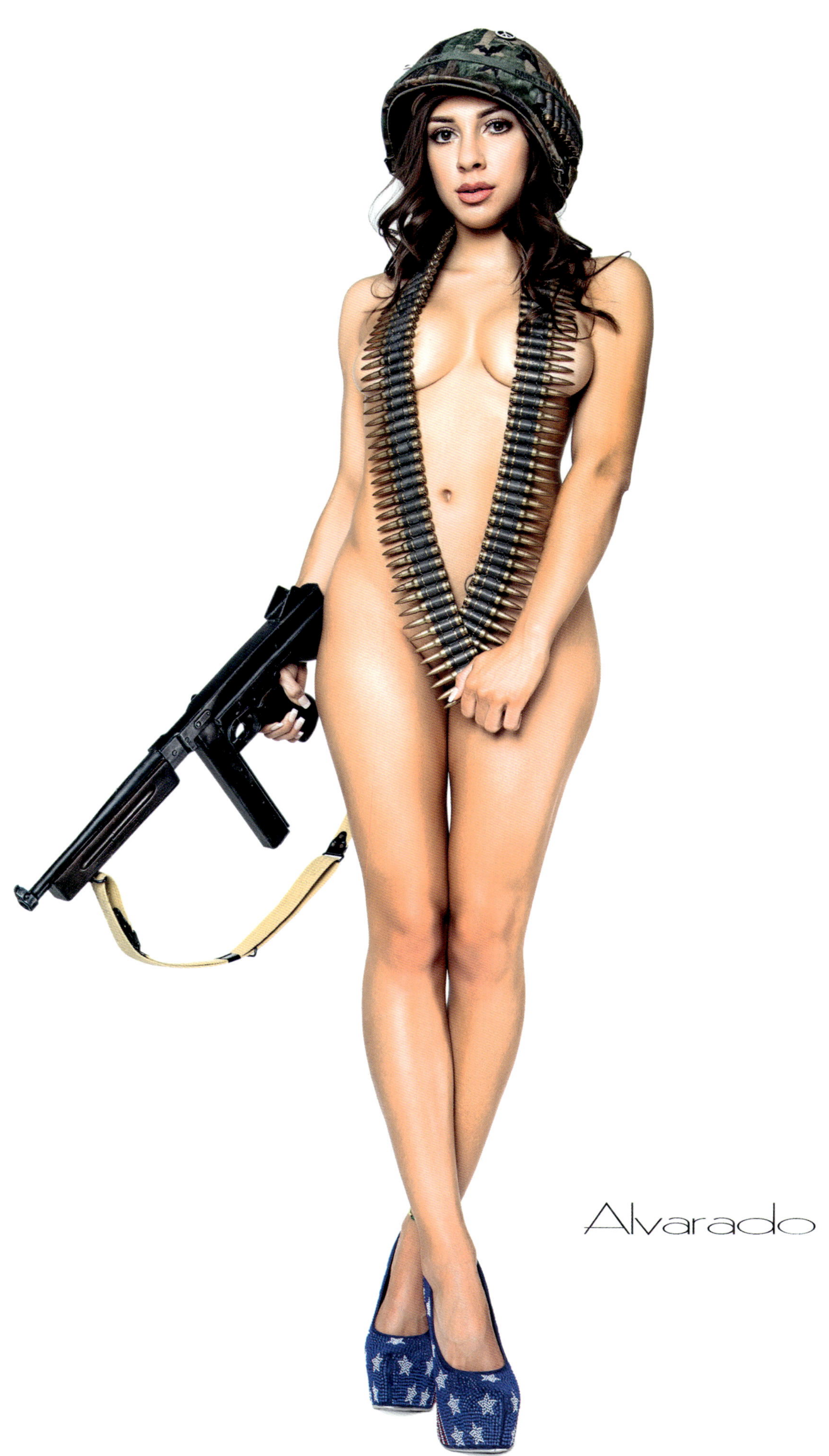
Alvarado

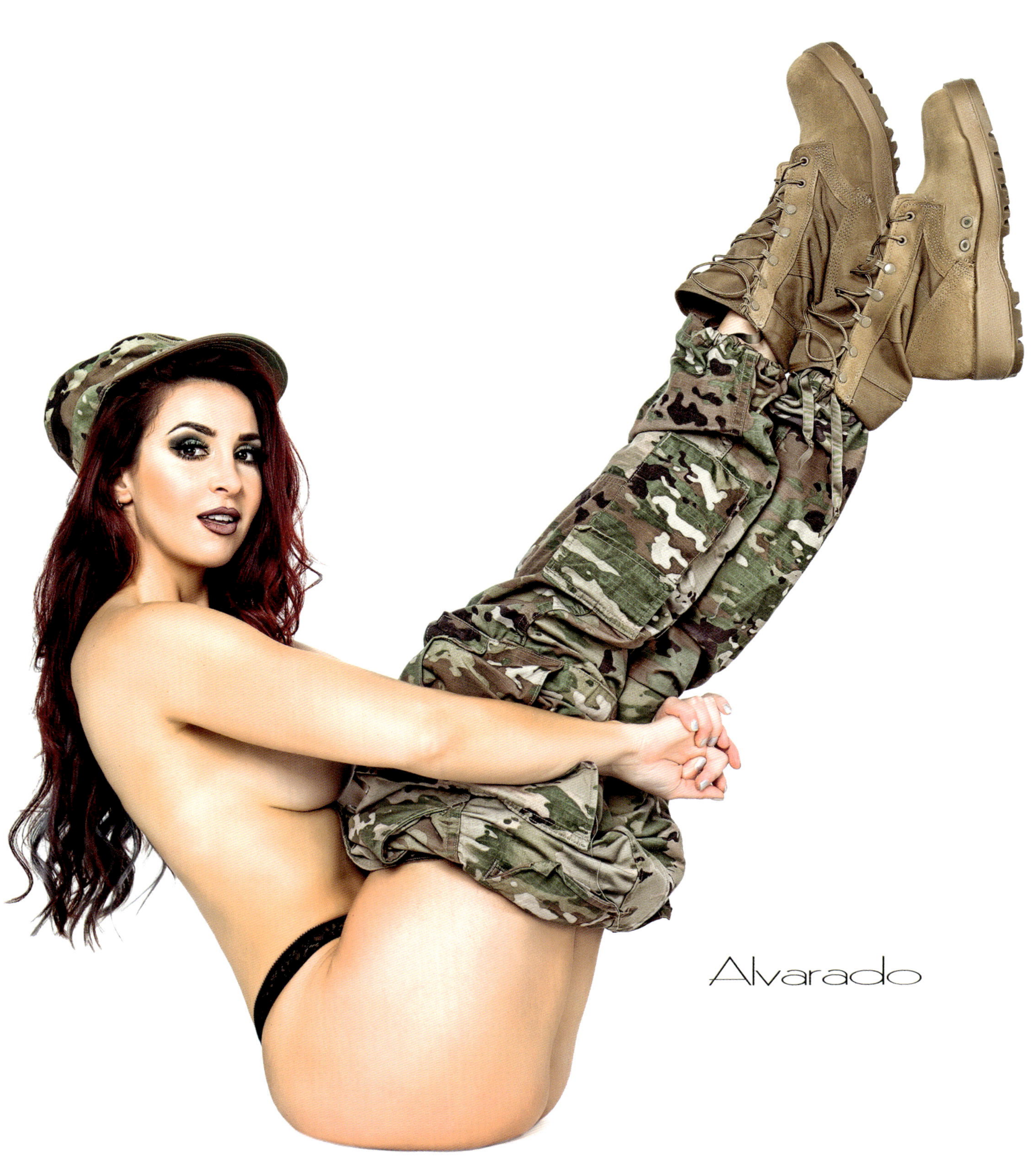

Alvarado

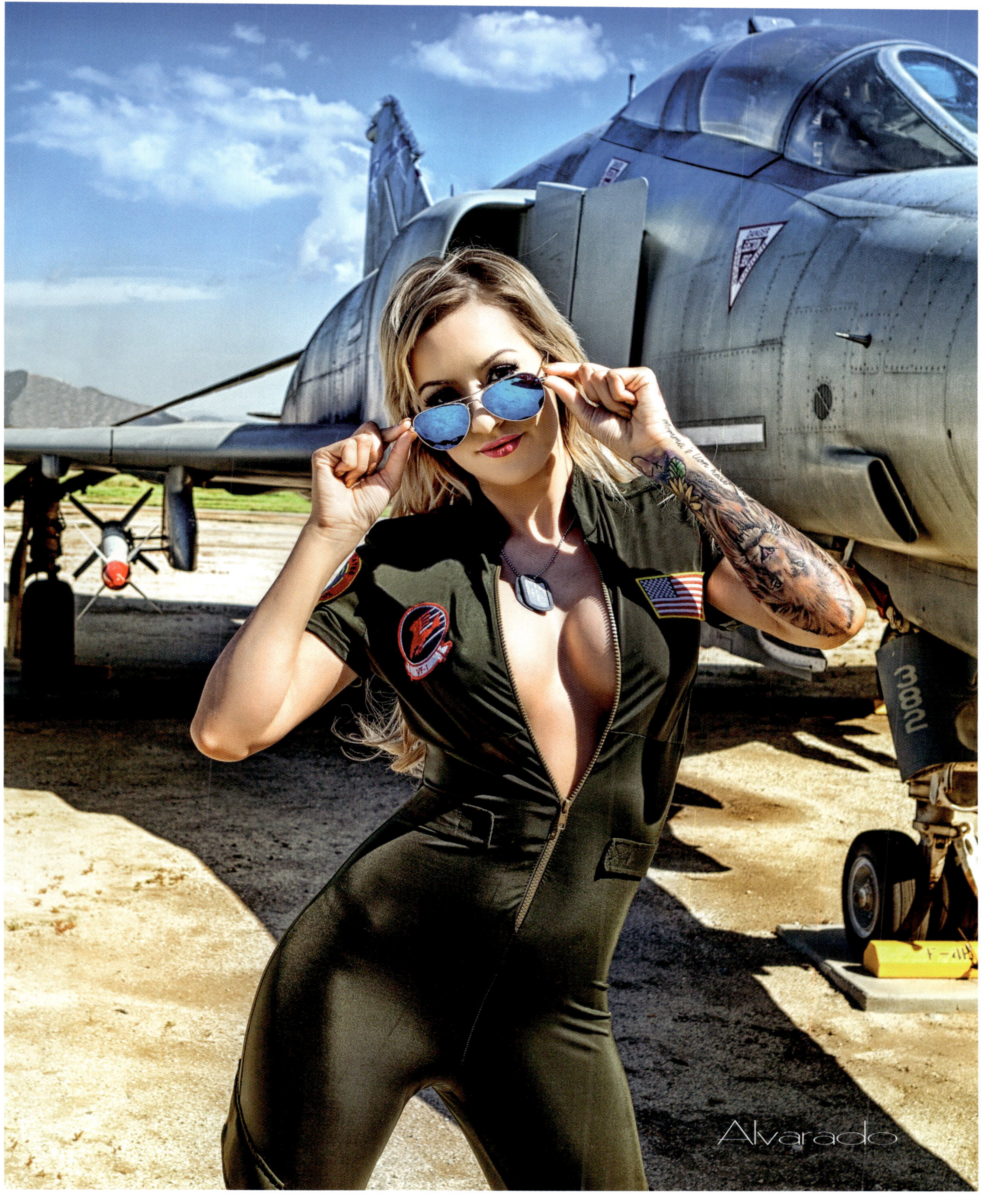
Alvarado

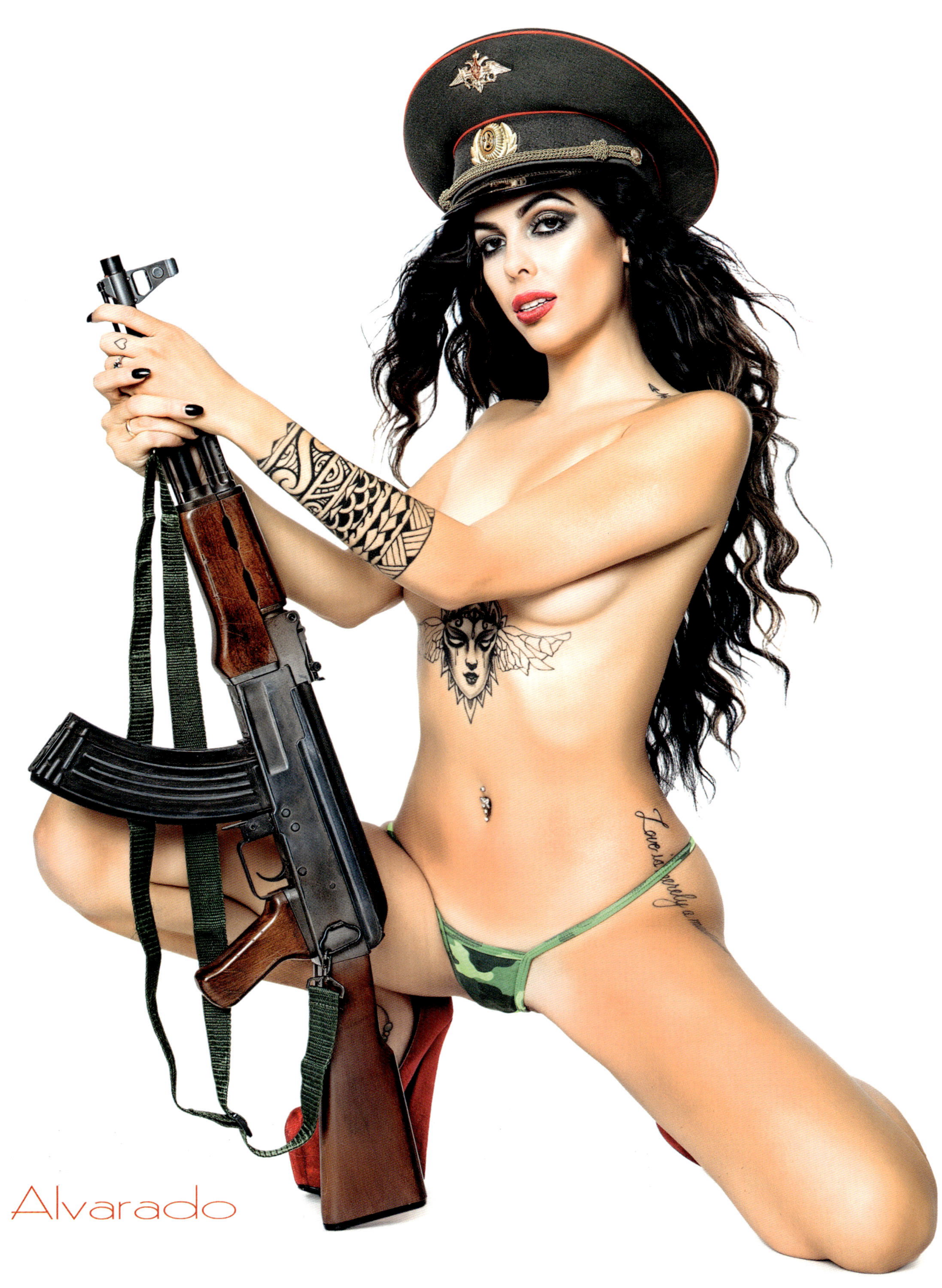

Alvarado

Alvarado

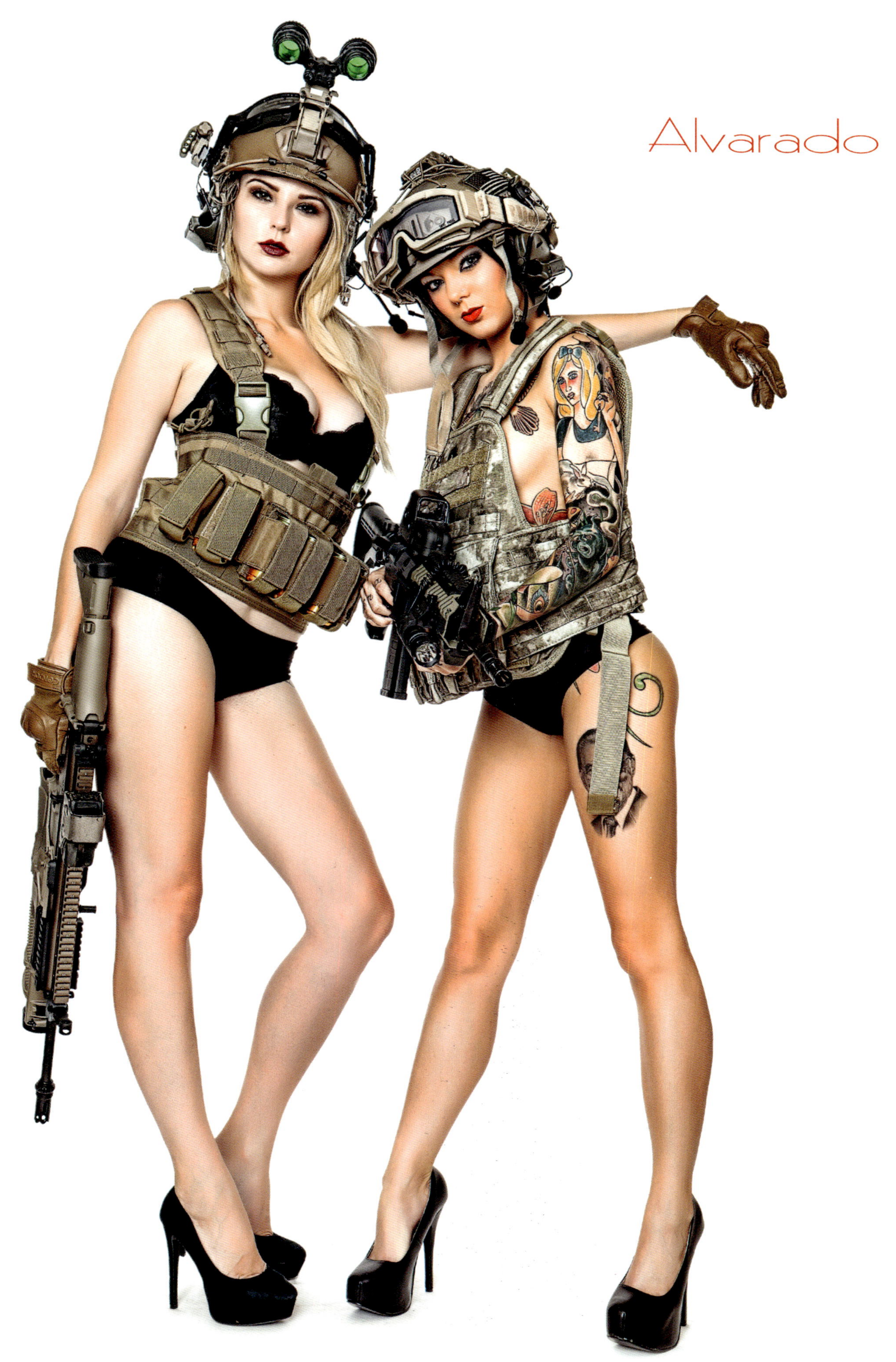

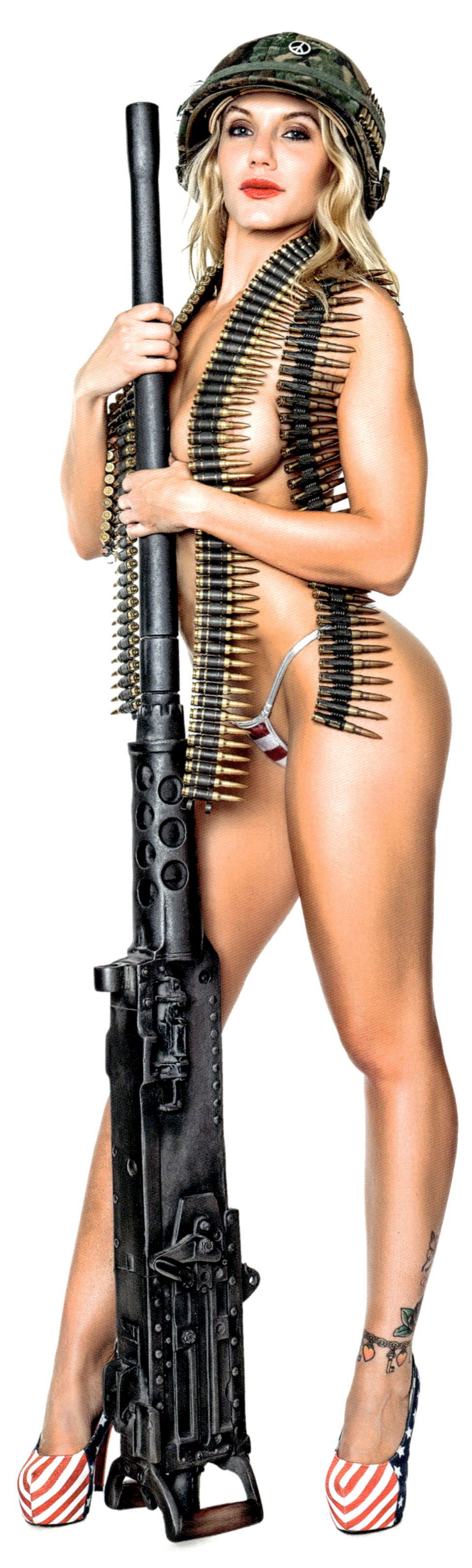

Alvarado

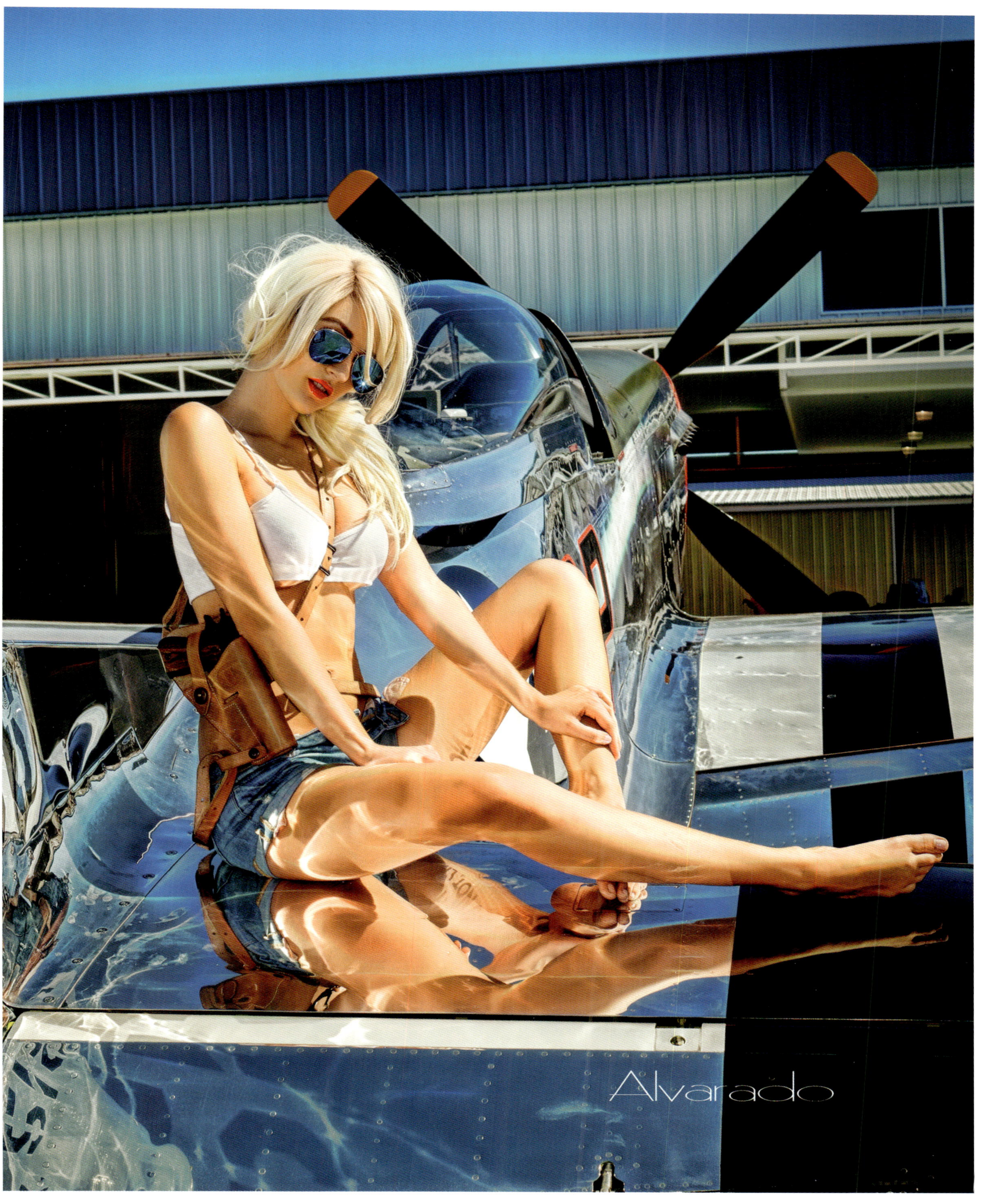
Alvarado

Alvarado

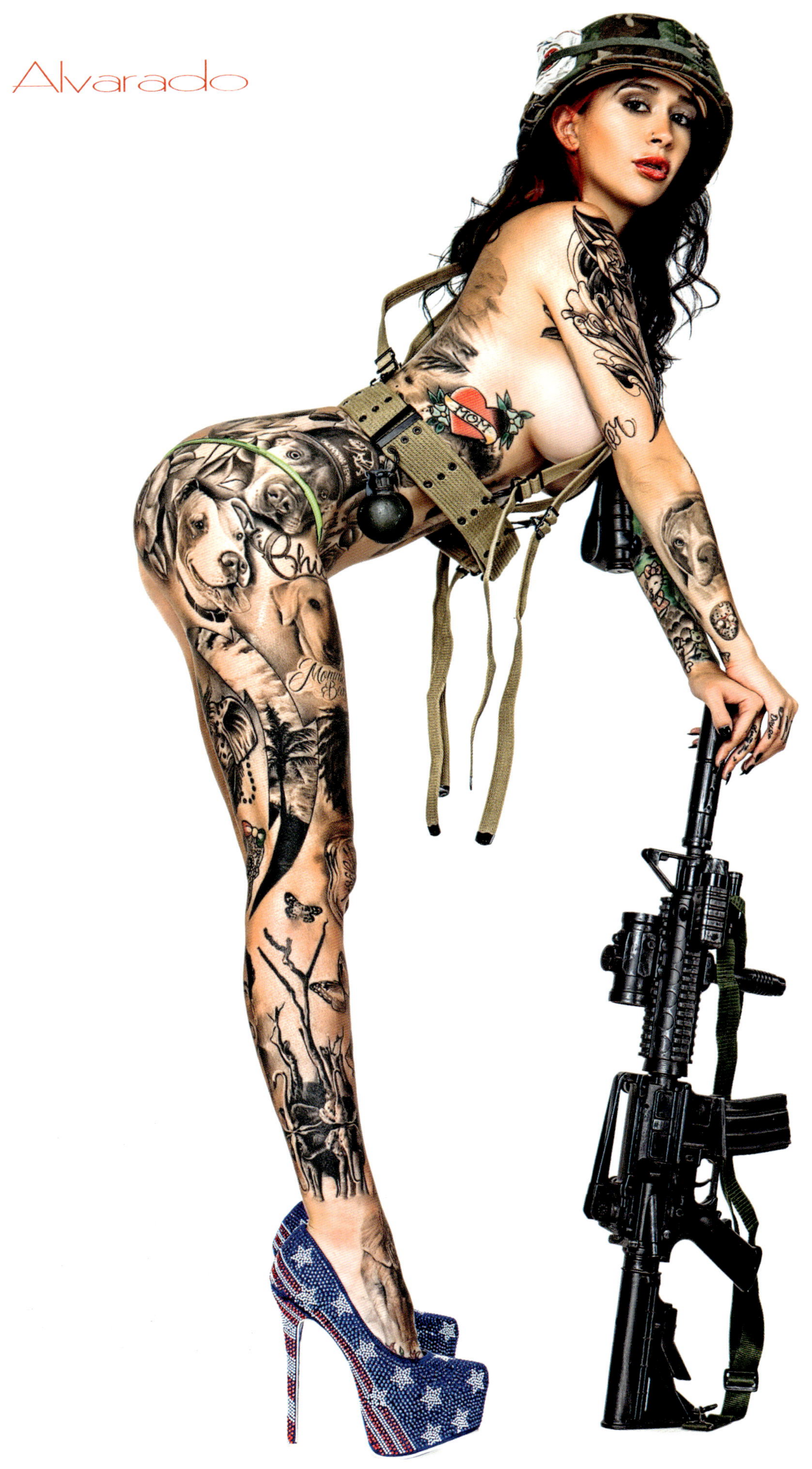

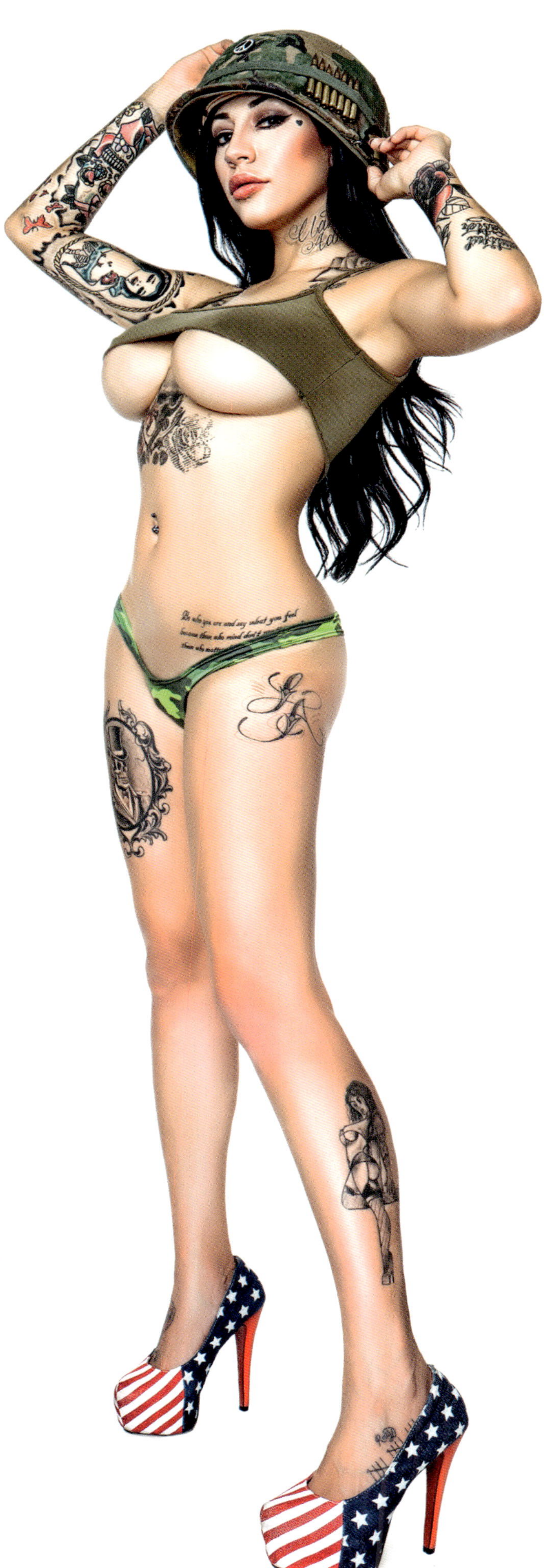

Alvarado

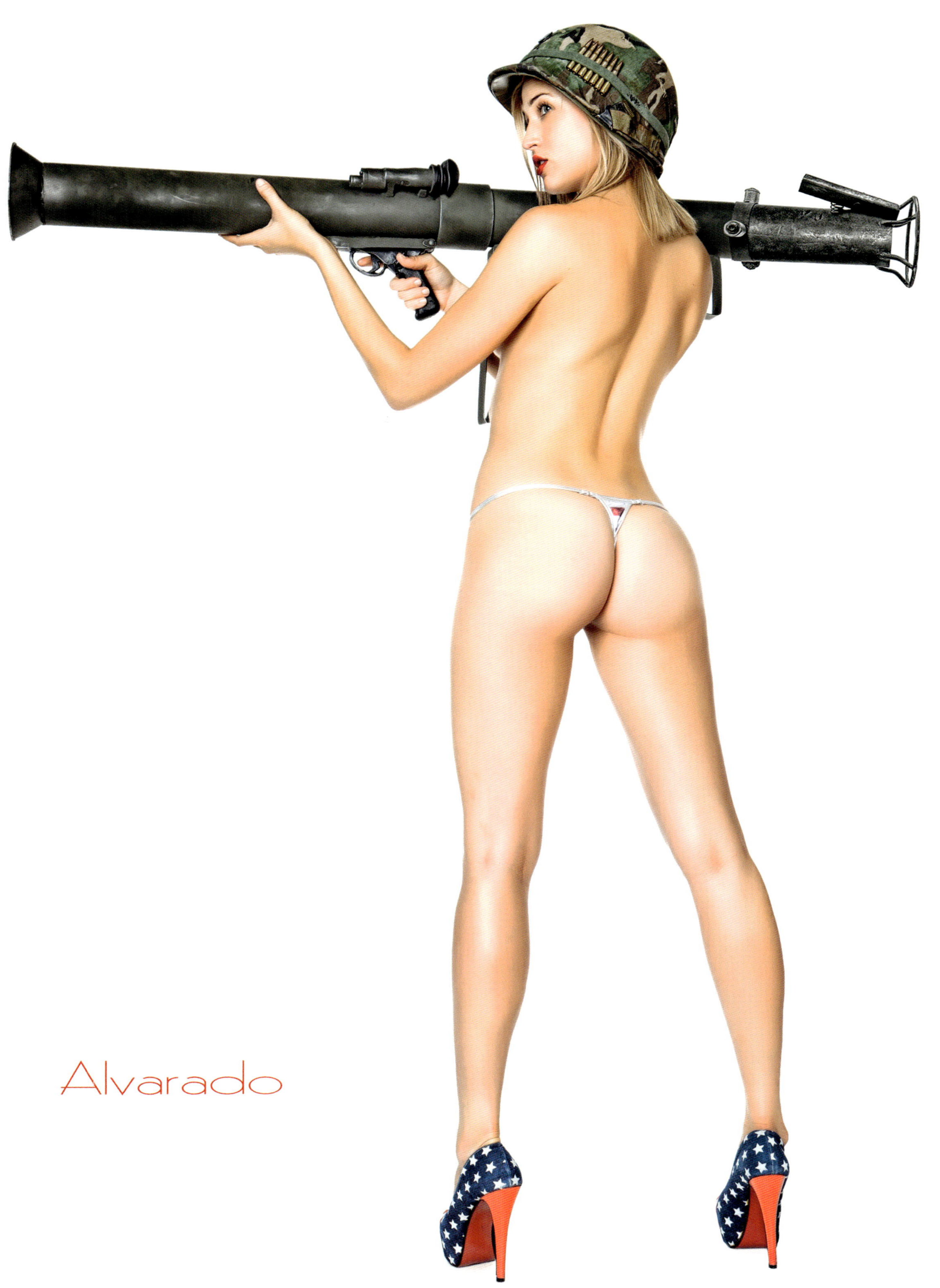

Alvarado

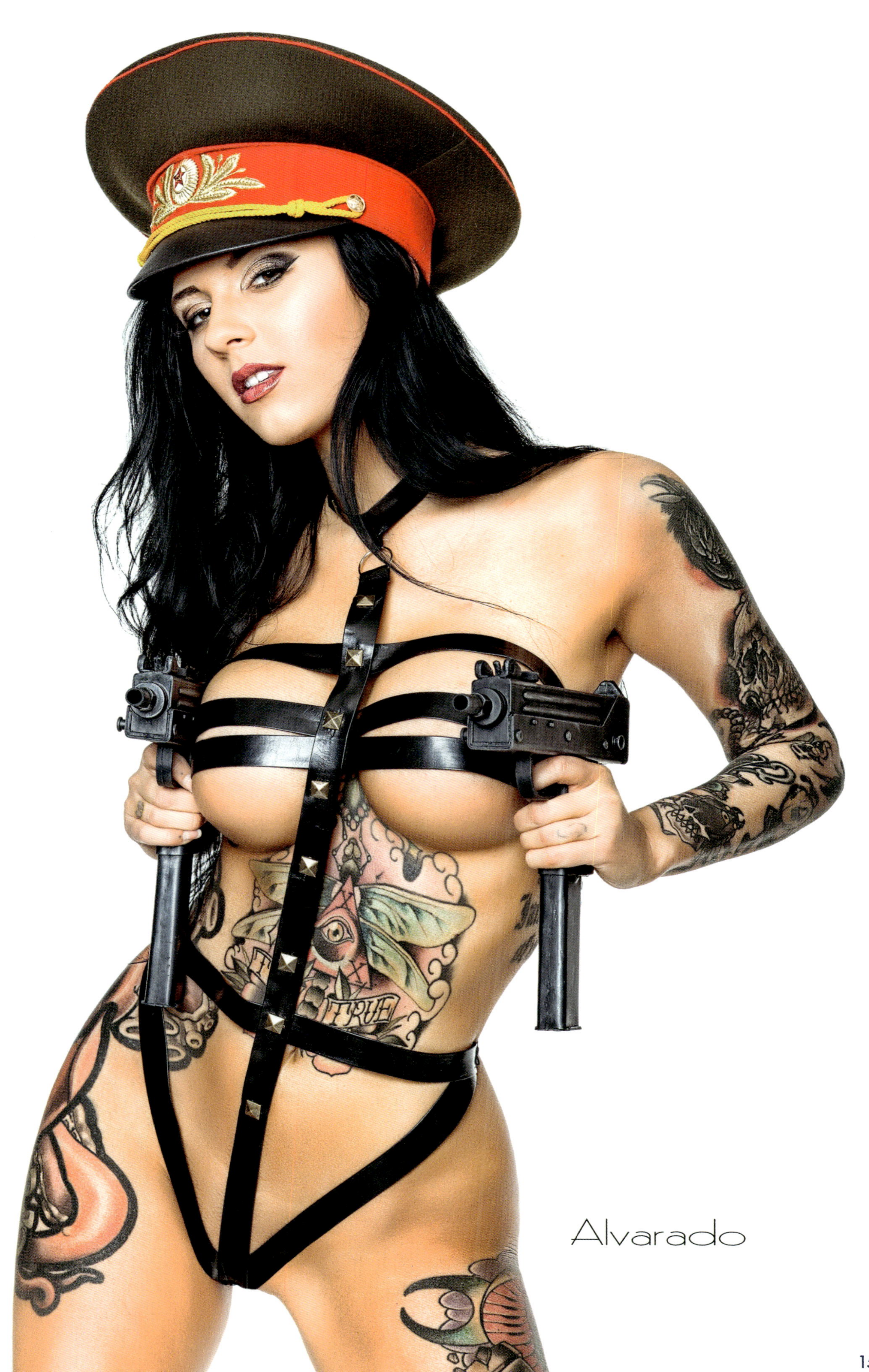

Alvarado

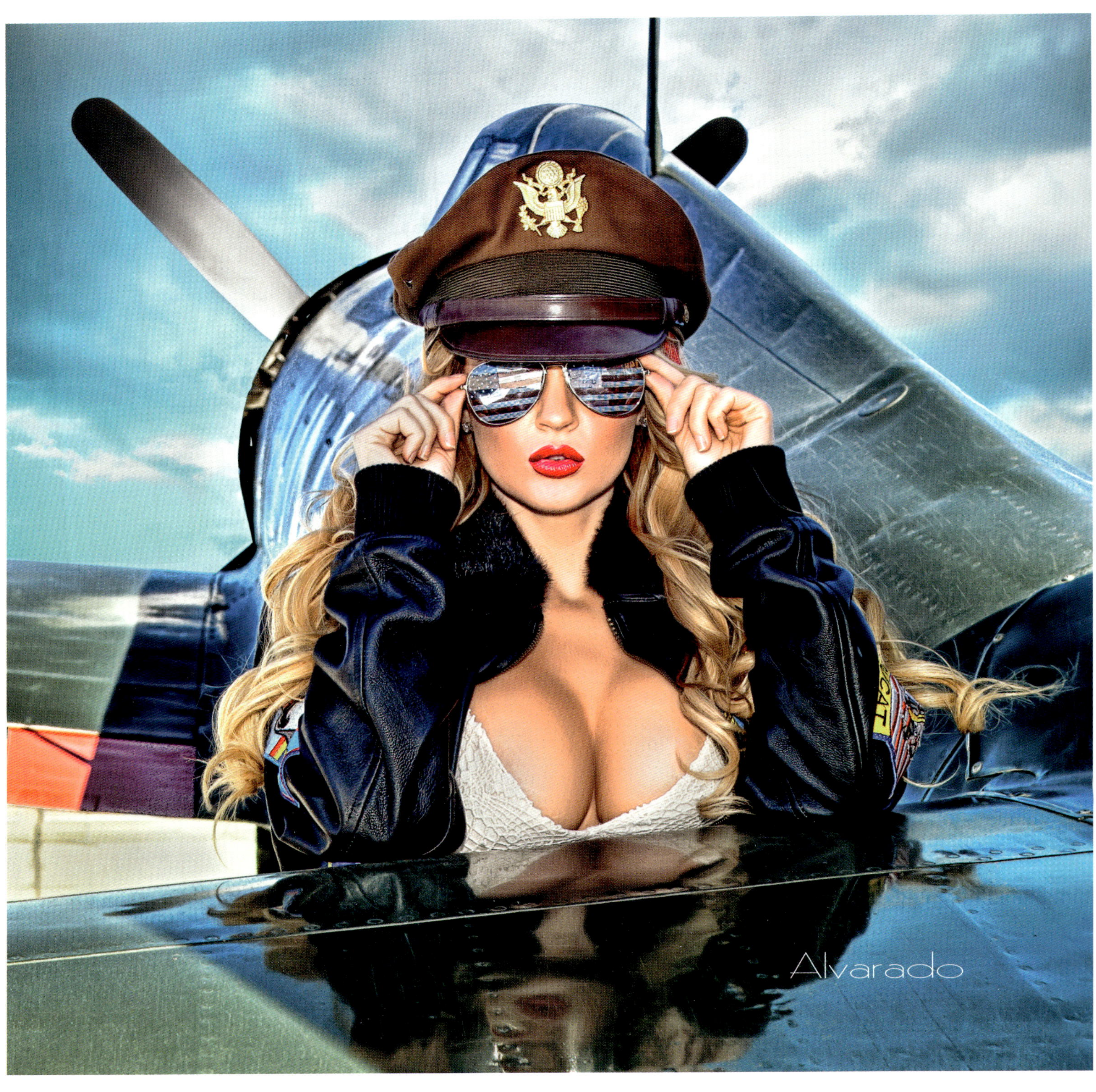
Alvarado

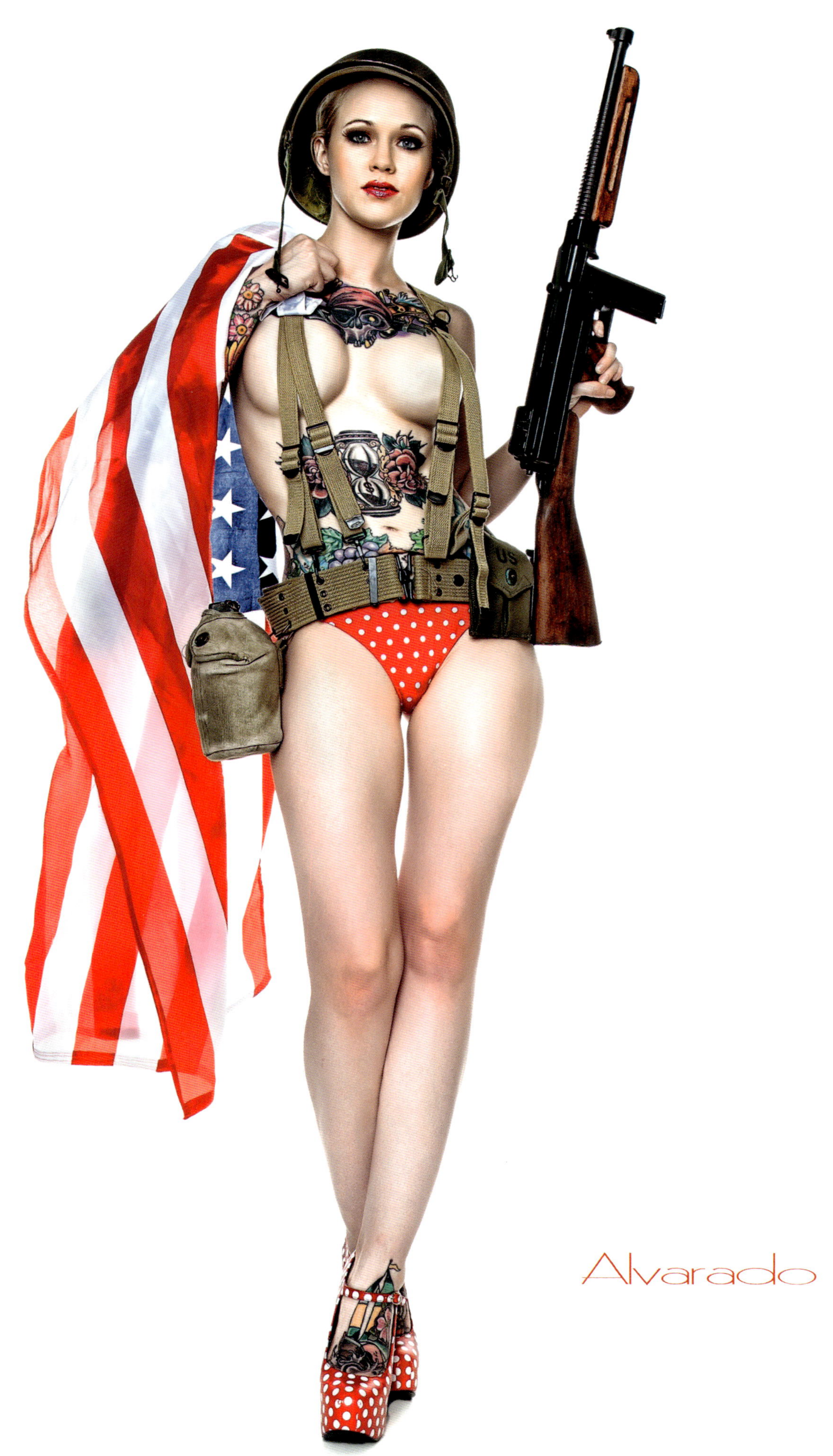

Alvarado

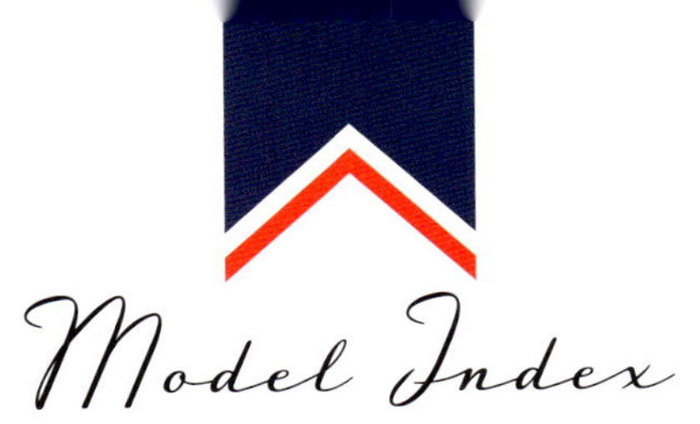

Model Index

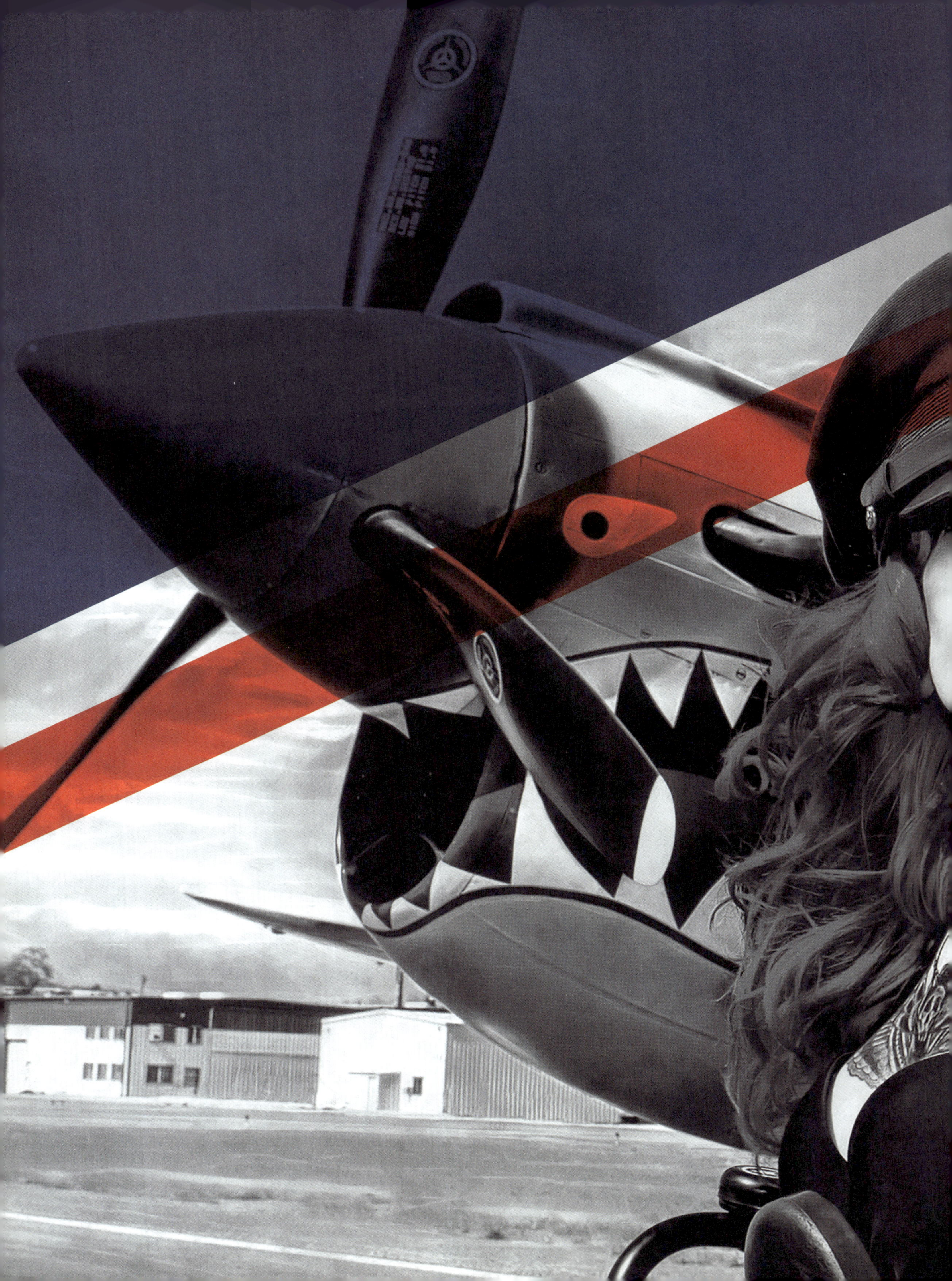